PLANT DISEASES

PLANT DISEASES

Editor

ASLAM KHAN

KALPAZ PUBLICATIONS

DELHI-110052

PLANT DISEASES

(Botany)

ISBN: 81-7835-052-1

Published in 2001 in India by
Kalpaz Publications
C-30, Satyawati Nagar
Ashok Vihar Phase-III
Delhi-110052
E-Mail: kaipaz@hotmail.com

Laser Typesetting at : A.S. Printers
Printed at : Mehra Offset Printers, New Delhi

Preface

Plant pathogens, unfavourable weather, weeds, and insect pests are the most common causes of reduction or destruction of plant growth and production. Plants suffer from diseases whose causes are similar to those affecting animals and humans. The detailed research on plant diseases includes the study of the living entities and the environmental conditions that cause disease in plants; the mechanisms by which these factors produce disease in plants; the interactions between the disease-causing agents and the diseased plant; and the methods of preventing or controlling disease and alleviating the damage it causes.

Plant Diseases is an ambitious title for the book because it suggests broad coverage of plant pathology. The book is written for introductory biological courses having an emphasis on plant pathology and plant diseases. Plant pathologists study diseases caused by fungi, bacteria, mycoplasmas, parasitic higher plants, viruses, viroids, nematodes, and protozoa and plant disorders caused by the excess, imbalance, or lack of such physical or chemical factors as moisture, temperature, and nutrients. Plant pathology profits from advances in any of these sciences, and many advances in other sciences have been made in an attempt to solve plant pathological problems. It also a science with a more practical goal to develop controls for all plant diseases in order to save the produce that today is destroyed by plant diseases and to make it available to the hungry and ill-clothed millions of our increasingly overpopulated world.

The book provides a comprehensive account on plant diseases. It has been intended primarily for the use of students engaged in advanced undergraduate and postgraduate courses in plant diseases. It will be also an asset to students studying food science, agriculture, environmental science and health administration. The book discusses on the role of plant pathogens play in food production, ecology and the emerging technologies of our time. It deals with different types of diseases affecting plants, and describes the control methods also.

Editor

Contents

Chapter 1

Fungal Diseases of Plants

Most fungi have a plantlike vegetative body consisting of more or less elongated, continuous, branched, microscopic filaments, which have definite cell walls. The body of the fungus is called mycelium, and the individual branches or filaments of the mycelium are called hyphae. Each hypha or mycelium is generally uniform in thickness. Hyphae of some fungi are only 0.5 μm in diameter, while in others they may be more than 100 μm thick. The length of the mycelium may be only a few micrometers in some fungi, but in others it may produce mycelial strands several meters long. In some fungi the mycelium consists of many cells containing one or two nuclei per cell. In others the mycelium is coenocytic, that is, it contains many nuclei and either the entire mycelium is one continuous, tubular, branched or unbranched multinucleate cell or it is partitioned by several cross walls, each segment being a multinucleate hypha. Growth of the mycelium occurs at the tips of the hyphae.

Fungi reproduce chiefly by means of spores. Spores are specialized propagative or reproductive bodies consisting of one or a few cells. Spores may be formed asexually or as the result of a sexual process. In the lower fungi, asexual spores are produced inside a sac called a sporangium and are released through an opening of the sporangium or upon its rupture. Some of these spores are motile by means of flagella and are, therefore, called zoospores.

Other fungi produce asexual spores called conidia by the cutting off of terminal or lateral cells from special hyphae called conidiophores. In some fungi terminal or intercalary cells of a hypha enlarge, round up, form a thick wall, and separate to form chlamydospores. In still other fungi, asexual spores are produced inside thick-walled structures called pyenidia.

Sexual reproduction, or processes resembling it, occur in most groups of fungi. In some, two cells (gametes) of similar size and appearance unite and produce a zygote, called a zygospore. In others, the gametes are of unequal size and the zygote they form is called an oospore. In some fungi no definite gametes are produced, but instead one mycelium may unite with another compatible mycelium. In one group of fungi (Ascomycetes) the sexual spores, usually eight in number, are produced within the zygote cell, the ascus, and the spores are called ascospores. In another group of fungi (Basidiomycetes), sexual spores are produced on the outside of the zygote cell called the basidium, and the spores are called basidiospores. For a large group of fungi no sexual reproduction is known either because they do not have one or because it has not yet been discovered. Apparently these fungi reproduce only asexually.

The union of the sexual nuclei in the zygote produces a diploid (2/V) nucleus. Usually the first divisions of this nucleus are meiotic so that throughout its life the fungus contains haploid (1*N*) nuclei. In some groups of fungi, however, especially in the Basidiomycetes, the cells of the entire mycelium contain two haploid nuclei that remain separate inside the cell. Such mycelium is called dikaryotic but behaves very much as though it were a diploid mycelium (in which the two nuclei are united). In most fungi both male and female gametes are produced on the same mycelium (hermaphroditic fungi). When the male gametes can fertilize the female ones of the same mycelium, the fungus is called homothallic. In many cases, however, the male gametes can fertilize only the female I gametes of another, sexually compatible mycelium, and the fungus then is called heterothallic.

Almost all plant pathogenic fungi spend part of their lives on their host plants and part in the soil or on plant debris on the soil. Some fungi pass all of their lives on the host, and only the spores may land on the soil, where they remain inactive until they are again carried to a host on which they grow and multiply.

Other fungi (such as *Venturia*) must pass part of their lives on the host as parasites and part on dead tissues on the ground as saprophytes in order to complete their life cycle in nature.

The latter group of fungi, however, remain continually associated with host tissues, whether living or dead, and in nature do not grow on any other kind of organic matter.

A third group of fungi grow parasitically on their hosts, but they continue to live, grow, and multiply on the dead tissues of the host after its death and may further move out of the host debris into the soil or other decaying plant material on which they grow and multiply as strict saprophytes.

The dead plant material that they colonize need not be related at all to the host they can parasitize. These fungi are usually soil pathogens, have a wide host range, and can survive in the soil for many years in the absence of their hosts. They, too, however, may need to infect a host from time to time in order to increase their populations, since protracted and continuous growth of these fungi as saprophytes in the soil results in more or less rapid reduction in their numbers.

During their parasitic phase fungi assume various positions in relation to the plant cells and tissues. Some fungi (such as powdery mildews) grow outside the plant surface but send their feeding organs (haustoria) into the epidermal cells of the plant. Some (such as Venturia) grow only between the cuticle and the epidermal cells. Others grow between the cells in the intercellular spaces and may or may not send haustoria into the cells. Still others grow between and through the cells indiscriminately. Obligate parasites (biotrophs) can grow only in association with living cells, being unable to feed on dead cells. On the other hand, the mycelium of some nonobligate parasites never comes in contact with living plant cells, because their enzymes macerate and kill the plant cells ahead of the mycelium. In most cases, however, regardless of the position of the mycelium in the host, the reproductive bodies (spores) of the fungus are produced at or very near the surface of the host tissues to ensure their prompt and efficient dissemination. The survival and performance of most plant pathogenic fungi depend greatly on the prevailing conditions of temperature and moisture or the presence of water in their environment. Free mycelium survives only within a certain range of temperatures (-5 to +45°C) and in contact with moist surfaces, inside or outside the host. Most kinds of spores, however, can withstand broader ranges of both temperature and moisture and carry the fungus through the low winter temperatures and the dry summer periods. Spores, however, also require favorable temperatures and moisture in order to germinate. Furthermore, lower fungi producing zoospores require free water for the production, movement, and germination of the zoospores.

Zoospores are the only fungus structures that can move by themselves. Zoospores, however, can move for only very short distances. Besides, only myxomycetes, chytridiomycetes, and oomycetes produce zoospores. The great majority of plant pathogenic fungi depend for their spread from plant to plant and to different parts of the same plant on chance distribution by such agents as wind, water, birds, insects, other animals, and humans. Spore dissemination in almost all fungi is passive, although their initial discharge in some fungi is forcible. The distance to which spores may be disseminated varies with the agent of dissemination. Wind is probably the most important disseminating agent of spores of most fungi and may carry spores over great distances. For specific fungi, other agents such as water or insects may play a much more important role than wind in the dissemination of their spores.

The fungi that cause diseases on plants are a diverse group. Because of their large numbers and diversity, only a sketchy classification of some of the most important phytopathogenic genera will be presented here. Fungi belong to the kingdom Mycetae (fungi).

The lower fungi

Division 1: MYXOMYCOTA—Produce a plasmodium or plasmodiumlike structure.

Class 1: MYXOMYCETES (The slime molds)—Lack mycelium. Their body is a naked, amorphous plasmodium. They produce zoospores.

Order: Physarales-Saprophytic plasmodium that gives rise to crusty fructifications containing spores. They produce zoospores that have two flagella.

Genus: *Fuligo, Mucilago*, and *Physarum* cause slime molds on low-lying plants.

Class 2: PLASMODIOPHOROMYCETES

Order: Plasmodiophorales-Plasmodia produced within cells of roots and stems of plants. They produce zoospores that have two flagella.

Genus: *Plasmodiophora, P. brassicae* causing clubroot of crucifers. *Polymyxa, P. graminis* parasitic in wheat and other cereals.

Spongospora, S. subterranea causing powdery scab of potato tubers.

Division If: EUMYCOTA (eumycetes)—Produced mycelium, not plasmodium.

Subdivision 1: MASTIGOMYCOTINA—Produce zoospores,

Class 1: CHYTRIDIOMYCETES—Have round or elongated mycelium that lacks cross walls.

Order: Chytridiales- Have cell wall but lack true mycelium, at most a rhizomycelium. Zoospores have a single flagellum.

Genus: *Olipidium, O. brassicae* being parasitic in roots of cabbage and other plants.

Physoderma, P. maydis causing brown spot of corn.

Synchytrium, S. endobioticum causing potato wart.

Urophlyctis, U. alfalfae causing crown wart of alfalfa,

Class 2: OOMYCETES (The water molds, white rusts, and downy mildews)

Have elongated mycelium. Produce zoospores in zoosporangia. Zoospores have two flagella. Sexual resting spores (oospores) produced by the union of morphologically different gametes.

Order: Saprolegniales—Have well-developed mycelium. Zoospores produced in long, cylindrical zoosporangia attached to mycelium. Oospores.

Genus: *Aphanomyces*, causing root rot of many vegetables.

Order: Peronosporales-Sporangia, usually zoosporangia produced along somatic hyphae or at tips of hyphae and set free. Oospores.

Family: Pythiaceae. Sporangia on somatic hyphae or on sporangiophores of indeterminate growth. Facultative parasites.

Genus: *Pythium*, causing damping off of seedlings, seed decay, root rots, and cottony blight of turf grasses.

Phytophthora, P. infestans causing late blight of potato, others causing mostly root rots.

Family: Albuginaceae (The white rusts). Sporangia borne in chains. Obligate parasites.

Genus: *Albugo, A. candida* causing white rust of crucifers.

Family: Peronosporaceae (The downy mildews) - Sporangia borne on sporangiophores of determinate growth. Sporangia wind-borne. Obligate parasites.

Genus: *Plasmopara, P. viticola* causing downy mildew of grape.

Peronospora, P. nicolianae causing downy mildew (blue mold) of tobacco.

Bremia, B. lactucae causing downy mildew of lettuce.

Sclerospora, S. graminicola causing downy mildew of grasses.

Pseudoperonospora, P. cubensis causing downy mildew of cucurbits.

Subdivision 2: ZYGOMYCOTINA

Class: ZYGOMYCETES (The bread molds)—Terrestrial fungi. Produce nonmotile asexual spores in sporangia. No zoospores. Their resting spore is a zygospore, produced by the fusion of two morphologically similar gametes.

Order: Mucorales-Nonmotile asexual spores formed in terminal sporangia.

Genus: *Rhizopus*, causing soft rot of fruits and vegetables.

Choanephora, C cricurbilarum causing soft rot of squash.

Order: Endogonales—Mycorrhizal fungi. Produce spores singly in soil, or in sporocarps containing zygospores, chlamydospores, or sporangia.

Genus: *Endogone*, and others.

The higher fungi

Subdivision 3: ASCOMYCOTINA (ascomycetes, the sac fungi)-Produce sexual spores, called ascospores, generally in groups of eight within an ascus.

Class 1: HEMIASCOMYCETES-Asci naked, no ascocarps produced.

Order: Endomycetales (the yeasts).

Genus: *Saccharomyces, S. cerevisiae*, the bread yeast.

Order: Taphrinales-Asci arising from binucleate ascogenous cells.

Genus: *Taphrina*- causing peach leaf curl, plum pocket, oak leaf blister, etc.

Class 2: PYRENOMYCETES (The perithecial fungi)-Asci in

fruiting bodies completely closed (cleistothecia) or in fruiting bodies with an opening (perithecia).

Order: Erysiphales (The powdery mildews)—Mycelium and cleistothecia on surface of host plant.

Genus: *Erysiphe*, causing powdery mildew of grasses, cucurbits, etc.

Microsphaera, one species causing powdery mildew of lilac.

Podosphaera, *P. leucotricha* causing powdery mildew of apple.

Spaerotheca, *S. pannosa* causing powdery mildew of roses and peach.

Uncinula, *U. necator* causing powdery mildew of grape.

Order: Sphaeriales-Perthecia with dark-colored, usually firm walls.

Genus: *Botryosphaeria (Physalospora) B. obtusa*, causing black rot and frogeye leafspot of apple.

Ceratocystis, causing vascular wilts and sapwood stains of trees.

Diaporthe, causing bean pod blight, soybean stem canker, citrus melanose, and fruit rot of eggplant.

Endothia, *E. parasitica* causing chestnut blight.

Eutypa armeniacae, causing dieback in grape and apricot.

Glomerella, *G. cingulata* causing many anthracnose diseases, and bitter rot of apple.

Gnomonia, causing anthracnose or leaf spot diseases.

Hypoxylon, *H. mammatum* causing a severe canker of poplars.

Rosellinia, causing root diseases of fruit trees and vines.

Valsa, causing canker diseases of peach and other trees.

Xylaria, causing tree cankers and wood decay.

Order: Hypocreales-Perithecia light-colored, or red or blue.

Genus: *Claviceps, C purpurea* causing ergot of rye.

Gibberella, causing foot or stalk rot of corn and small grains.

Nectria, causing twig and stem cankers of trees.

Class 3: LOCULOASCOMYCETES (The ascostromatic fungi)—Produce pseudothecia, i.e., peritheciumlike stromata with asci in separate or single large cavities.

Order: Myriangiales -Cavities arranged at various levels and containing single asci.

Genus: *Elsinoe*, causing anthracnose of grape and raspberry, and scab of citrus.

Order: Dothideales- Cavities arranged in a basal layer and containing many asci. Pseudothecia lack pseudoparaphyses.

Genus: *Capnodium*, one of many epiphytic genera causing the sooty molds.

Didymella (Mycosphaerella), causing leaf spots of many plants.

Guignardia, G. bidwellii causing black rot of grapes.

Microcyclus (Dothidella), M. ulei causing the leaf spot of rubber trees.

Plowrightia (Dibolryon), P. morbosum causing black knot

of cherries and plums.

Order: Pleosporales -Cavities arranged in a basal layer and containing many asci. Pseudothecia have pseudoparaphyses.

Genus: *Cochliobolus, C. sativus* causing leaf spots and root rots on grain crops.

Gaeumannomyces (Ophiobolus), G. graminis causing the take-all disease of wheat.

Pyrenophora causing leaf spots of cereals and grasses.

Venturia, V. inaequalis causing apple scab.

Class 4: DISCOMYCETES (The cup fungi)-Asci produced at the surface of fleshy cup- or saucer-shaped apothecia.

Order: Phacidiales - Apothecia develop within a stroma.

Genus: *Rhytisma, R. acerinum* causing tar spot of maple leaves.

Order: Helotiales - Apothecia not in a stroma but sometimes developing from a stroma or sclerotium. Asci release spores through an apical, circular perforation.

Genus: *Diplocarpon, D. rosae* causing black spot of roses.

Higginsia (Coccomyces), H. hiemalis causing cherry leaf spot.

Lophodermium causing pine needle blight.

Monilinia, M. fructicola causing brown rot of stone fruits.

Pseudopeziza, P. trffiolii (medicaginis) causing alfalfa leaf spot.

Sclerotinia, S. sclerotiorum causing watery soft rot of vegetables.

Subdivision 4: DEUTEROMYCOTINA -The imperfect fungi. Asexual fungi -Sexual reproduction and structures lacking or unknown.

Class I: COELOMYCETES - Conidia borne in pycnidia or acervuli.

Order.- Sphaeropsidales- Asexual spores produced in pycnidia.

Genus: *Ascochyta,* A. *pisi* causing pea blight.

Coniothyrium causing cane blight on raspberry.

Cytospora causing canker diseases on peach and other trees (its sexual stage is Valsa).

Diplodia, D. maydis causing stalk and ear rot of corn.

Phoma, P. lingam causing black leg of crucifers.

Phomopsis, causing blights and stem cankers of trees.

Phyllosticta, causing leaf spots of many plants,

·*Septoria, S. apii* causing late blight of celery.

Order: Melanconiales- Asexual spores produced in acervulus.

Genus: *Colletotrichum,* causing anthracnose on many field crops.

Coryneum (Stigmina), C beijerincki (S. carpophilum) causing blight on stone fruits.

Cylindrosporium, causing leaf spots on many kinds of plants.

Gloeosporium, similar if not identical to *Colletotrichum,* causing anthracnose on many plants.

Marssonina, causing leaf and twig blight of poplar, strawberry leaf scorch, and anthracnose of walnuts.

Melanconium, M. fuligenum causing bitter rot of grape.

Sphaceloma, causing anthracnose of grape, raspberry, and scab of citrus and avocado.

Class 2: HYPHOMYCETES.

Order: Hyphales (Moniliales) -Asexual spores produced on or within hyphae freely exposed to the air.

Genus: *Alternaria*, causing leaf spots and blights on many plants. *Asperigillus*, causing rots of stored seeds.

Bipolaris, Drechslerea, Exserohilum (Helminthosporium), causing leaf spots, root rots, and blights of cereals and turf grasses.

Botrytis, B. cinerea causing gray mold and blights on many plants.

Cercospora, one species causing early blight of celery.

Fulvia (Cladosporium), F. fulva causing leaf-mold of tomato.

Fusarium, causing wilt and root rot diseases of many annual plants and cankers of forest trees.

Geotrichum, G. candidum causing sour rot of fruits and vegetables.

Graphium, G. ulmi causing Dutch elm disease (its sexual stage is *Ceratocystis*).

Penicillium, causing blue mold rot of fruits and other fleshy organs.

Phymatotrichum, P. omnivorum causing root rot of cotton and other plants.

Pyricularia, causing rice blast and gray leaf-spot of turf grasses.

Spilocaea (Fusicladium), causing apple scab (its sexual stage is *Venturia*).

Strumella, causing cankers on oak.

Thielaviopsis, T. basicola causing black root rot of tobacco.

Trichoderma, antagonsitic to many plant pathogenic fungi.

Verticillium, causing wilt of many annuals and perennials.

Class 3: AGONOMYCETES (Mycelia Sterilia).

Order: Agonomycetales (Myceliales)-No sexual or asexual spore forms common or known.

Genus: *Rhizoctonia,* causing root rots and crown rots of annuals and brown-patch of turf grasses (sexual stage *Thanatephorus*).

Sclerotium causing root and stem rots of many plants (sexual stage *Aethalia*).

Subdivision 5: BASIDIOMYCOTINA (Basidiomycetes, the club fungi) - Sexual spores, called basidiospores or sporidia, are produced externally on a one- or four-celled spore-producing structure called a basidium.

Class 1: HEMIBASIDIOMYCETES (TELIOMYCETIDAE) (The rust and smut fungi) - Basidium with cross walls or being the promycelium of a teliospore. Teliospores single or united into crusts or columns, remaining in host tissue or bursting through the epidermis.

Order: Ustilaginales- Fertilization by means of union of compatible spores, hyphae, etc. Only teliospores and basidiospores (sporidia) are produced.

Genus: *Sphacelotheca,* several species causing loose

smut of sorghum.

Tilletia, several species causing bunt, or stinking smut, of wheat.

Urocystis, U. cepulae causing smut of onion.

Ustilago, causing smut of corn, wheat, barley, etc.

Order: Uredinales- Sperm cells called spermatia fertilize special receptive hyphae in spermogonia. Produce aeciospores, uredospores (repeating spores), teliospores, and basidiospores.

Genus: *Cronartium*, several species causing stem rusts of pines.

Gymnosporangium, G. juniperi-virginianae causing cedar apple rust.

Melampsora, M. fini causing rust of flax.

Phragmidium, one species causing rust of roses.

Puccinia, several species causing rust of cereals and of other plants.

Uromyces, U. appendiculatus causing rust of beans.

Class 2: HYMENOMYCETES (The wood decay and root rot fungi) Basidium without cross walls. Basidiocarp lacking or present. Include the mushrooms, shelf fungi, puff balls. Basidia produced in definite layers (hymenia) and becoming exposed to the air before the spores are shot off from the sterigmata.

Order: Exobasidiales - Basidiocarp lacking: basidia produced on surface of parasitized tissue.

Genus: *Exobasidium*, causing leaf, flower, and stem galls on ornamentals

Order: Aphyllochorales (Polyporales)-Hymenium lining the surfaces of small pores or tubes.

Genus: *Aethalia (Sclerotium),* causing root and stem rots of many plants.

Corticium, one species causing the red thread disease of turf grasses.

Heterobasidium (Fomes), causing heart rot of many trees.

Lenzites, causing brown rot of conifers and decay of wood products.

Peniophora, causing decay of conifer logs and pulpwood.

Polyporus, causing root and stem rot of many trees.

Poria, causing wood and root rots of forest trees.

Schizophyllum, causing white rot in deciduous forest trees.

Stereum, causing wood decay and silver leaf disease of trees.

Order: Tulasnellales-Saprobic, mycorrhizal, or parasitic. Basidiocarps weblike, inconspicuous, often waxy in appearance.

Genus: *Thanatephorus (Rhizoctonia),* causing root and stem rots of many annual plants and brown patch of turf grasses.

Typhula, one species causing snowmold or blight of turf grasses.

Order: Agaricales-Hymenium on radiating gills or lamellae. Many are mycorrhizal fungi.

Genus: *Armillaria, A. mellea* causing root rots of forest and fruit trees.

Marasmius, causing the fairy ring disease of turf grasses.

Pholiota, causing brown wood rot in deciduous forest trees.

Pleurotus, causing white rot on many deciduous forest trees.

Identification

Because each fungal disease of plants is usually caused by only one fungus, and because there are more than 100,000 different species of fungi, the identification of the fungus species on a diseased plant specimen or culture of a fungus means that all but one of all the known fungus species must be eliminated as being the fungus in question. The most significant fungus characteristics used for identification are spores and fructifications, or spore-beating structures, and to some extent the characteristics of the fungus body (plasmodium or mycelium). These items are examined under the compound microscope directly after removal from the specimen.

The specimen is often kept moist for a few days to promote fructification development, or the fungus may be isolated and grown on artificial media, and identification is made on the basis of the fructifications produced on the media. For some fungi, special nutrient media have been developed that allow selective growth only of the particular fungus, allowing quick identification of the fungus. The shape, size, color, and manner of arrangement of spores on the sporophores or the fruiting bodies, as well as the shape and color of the sporophores or fruiting bodies, are sufficient characteristics to suggest, to one somewhat experienced in the taxonomy of fungi, the class, order, family, and genus to which the particular fungus belongs.

In any case, these characteristics can be utilized to trace the fungus through published analytical keys of the fungi to the genus and, finally, to the species to which it belongs. Once the genus of the fungus has been determined, specific descriptions of the species are found in monographs of genera or in specific publications in research journals. Since there are usually lists of the pathogens affecting a particular host plant, one may use such host indexes as short cuts in quickly finding names of fungus species that might apply to the fungus at hand. Host indexes, however, merely offer suggestions in determining identities, which must ultimately be determined by reference to monographs and other more specific publications.

Symptoms caused by fungi on plants

Fungi cause local or general symptoms on their hosts, and such symptoms may occur separately on different hosts, concurrently on the same host, or follow one another on the same host. In general fungi cause local or general necrosis or killing of plant tissues, hypotrophy and hypoplasla (stunting) of plant organs or entire plants, and hyperplasia (excessive growth) of plant parts or whole plants.

The most common necrotic symptoms are:

Leaf spots -Localized lesions on host leaves consisting of dead and collapsed cells. Blight-General and extremely rapid browning of leaves, branches, twigs, and floral organs resulting in their death.

Canker-A localized wound or necrotic lesion, often sunken beneath the surface of the stem of a woody plant.

Dieback- Extensive necrosis of twigs beginning at their tips and advancing toward their bases.

Root rot- Disintegration or decay of part or all of the root system of a plant.

Damping off-The rapid death and collapse of very young seedlings in the seed bed or field.

Basal stem rot- Disintegration of the lower part of the stem.

Soft rots and dry rots-Maceration and disintegration of fruits, roots, bulbs, tubers, and fleshy leaves.

Anthracnose-A necrotic and sunken ulcerlike lesion on the stem, leaf, fruit, or flower of the host plant.

Scab-Localized lesions on host fruit, leaves, tubers, etc., usually slightly raised or sunken and cracked, giving a scabby appearance.

Decline-Plants growing poorly; leaves small, brittle, yellowish, or red; some defoliation and dieback present.

Almost all of the above symptoms may also cause pronounced stunting of the infected plants. In addition, certain other symptoms such as leaf rust, mildews, wilts, and even certain diseases causing hyperplasia of some plant organs, such as clubroot, may cause stunting of the plant as a whole.

Symptoms associated with hypertrophy or hyperplasia and distortion of plant parts include:

Clubroot- Enlarged roots appearing like spindles or clubs.

Galls-Enlarged portions of plants usually filled with fungus mycelium.

Warts-Wartlike protuberances on tubers and stems.

Witches'-brooms -Profuse, upward branching of twigs.

Leaf curls- Distortion, thickening, and curling of leaves,

In addition to the above, three goups of symptoms may be added:

Wilt-Usually a generalized secondary symptom in which leaves or shoots lose their turgidity and droop because of a disturbance in the vascular system of the root or of the stein.

Rust-Many, small lesions on leaves or stems, usually of a rusty color.

Mildew- Chlorotic or necrotic areas on leaves, stems, and fruit, usually covered with mycelium and the fructifications of the fungus.

In many diseases, the pathogen grows or produces various structures on the surface of the host. These structures, which include mycelium, sclerotia, sporophores, fruiting bodies, and spores, are called signs and are distinct from symptoms, which refer only to the appearance of infected plants or plant tissues. Thus, in the mildews, for example, one sees mostly the signs consisting of a whitish, downy growth of fungus mycelium and spores on the plant leaves, fruit, or stem, while the symptoms consist of chlorotic or necrotic lesions on leaves, fruit, and stem, reduced growth of the plant, and so on,

Isolation of fungi

Most plant diseases can be diagnosed by observation with the naked eye or with the microscope, and for these, isolation of the pathogen is not necessary, There are many fungal and bacterial diseases, though, in which the pathogen cannot be identified because it is mixed with one or more contaminants, because it has not yet produced its characteristic fruiting structures and spores, because the same disease could be caused by more than one similar-looking pathogen and perhaps by some environmental factor, or because the disease is caused by a new, previously unknown pathogen that must be isolated and studied. Just as often, pathogens of even known diseases must be isolated from diseased plant tissues whenever a study of the characteristics and habits of these pathogens is to be undertaken.

Preparing for Isolation

Even before attempting to isolate the fungus or bacterium pathogen from a diseased plant tissue, one must perform several preliminary operations, including the following.

Sterilize glassware, such as Petri dishes, test tubes, and pipettes, by dry heat (150-150°C for 1 hour or more) or autoclaving or by dipping for 1 minute or more in a potassium dichromate -sulfuric acid solution, or in 5 percent formalin or 95 percent ethyl alcohol. All chemically treated glassware should be rinsed through at least three changes of sterile (boiled or autoclaved) water.

Prepare solutions for treating the surface of the infected or infested tissue to eliminate or markedly reduce surface contaminants that could interfere with the isolation of the pathogen. These solutions can be used either as a surface wipe or as a dip. The most commonly used surface sterilants are: 0.525 percent sodium hypochlorite (I part Clorox to 9 parts water) solution, used both for wiping infected tissues or dipping sections of such tissues in it and for wiping down table or bench surfaces before making isolations; and 95 percent ethyl alcohol, which is mild and is used for leaf dips for 3 seconds or more. The tissues must be blotted dry with a sterile paper towel.

Prepare culture media on which the isolated fungal or bacterial pathogens will grow. An almost infinite number of culture media can be used to grow plant pathogenic fungi and bacteria. Some of them are entirely synthetic-made up of known amounts of certain chemical compounds-and are usually quite specific for certain pathogens. Some are liquid or semiliquid and are used primarily for growth of bacteria but also of fungi in certain cases. Most media contain an extract of a natural source of carbohydrates and other nutrients, such as potato, corn meal, lima bean, or malt extract, to which variable amounts of agar are added to solidify the medium and form a gel on or in which the pathogen can grow and be observed.

The most commonly used media are potato dextrose agar (PDA), which is good for most, but not all fungi, water agar or glucose agar 0 -3 percent glucose in water agar) for separating some fungi (*Pythium* and *Fusarium*) from bacteria, and nutrient agar, which contains beef extract and peptone and is good for isolating bacterial plant pathogens. Fungi can also be separated in culture from bacteria by adding 1 or 2 drops of a 25 percent solution of lactic acid, which inhibits growth of bacteria, to io ml of the medium before pouring it in the plate. Solutions of culture media are prepared in flasks, which are then plugged and placed in an autoclave at 120°C and 15 pounds pressure for 20 minutes.

The sterilized media are then allowed to cool somewhat and are subsequently poured from the flask into sterilized Petri dishes, test tubes, or other appropriate containers. If agar was added to the medium, the latter will soon solidify and is then ready to be used for growth of the fungus or bacterium. The pouring of the culture medium into Petri dishes, tubes, and so on is carried out as aseptically as possible either in a separate culture room or in a clean room free from drafts and dust. In either case, the work table should be wiped with a io percent Clorox solution, hands should be clean, and tools such as scalpels, forceps, and needles should be dipped in alcohol and flamed to prevent introduction of contaminating microorganisms. Although most fungi and most bacteria can be cultured on nutrient media with ease, some of them have specific and exacting requirements and will not grow on most commonly used nutrient media.

Some groups of fungi, namely the Erysiphales, the causes of the powdery mildew diseases, and the Peronosporales, which cause the downy mildews, are considered strictly obligate parasites and cannot be grown on culture media. Another group of fungi, the Uredinales, which cause the rust diseases of plants, were, until recently, also thought to be strictly obligate parasites. In the last several years, however, it has become possible to grow in culture some stages of some rust fungi by adding certain components to the media, and so the rust fungi are no longer considered to be obligate parasites, although they are, of course, obligate parasites in nature. The fastidious phloem- and xylem-limited bacteria also are either so far impossible to grow in culture or are grown on special complex nutrient media. Of the other pathogens, only some spiroplasmas have been grown in culture. None of the other 100 or so mycoplasmalike organisms and none of the viruses, nematodes, or protozoa has been grown on nutrient culture media, so far, although it is expected that media for culturing mycoplasmalike organisms will soon be discovered.

Life cycles of fungi

Although the life cycles of the fungi of the different groups vary greatly, the great majority of them go through a series of steps that are quite similar. Thus almost all fungi have a spore stage with a simple, haploid (possessing one set of chromosomes or 1*N*) nucleus. The spore germinates into a hypha, which also contains haploid nuclei.

The hypha may either produce simple, haploid spores again (as is always the case in the Imperfect Fungi) or it may fuse with another hypha to produce a fertilized hypha in which the nuclei unite to form one diploid nucleus, called a zygote (containing two sets of chromosomes, or 2*N*). In the Oomycetes the zygote will divide to produce simple, haploid spores, which close the cycle.

In a brief phase of most Ascomycetes, and generally

in the Basidiomycetes, the two nuclei of the fertilized hypha do not unite but remain separate within the cell in pairs (dikaryotic or $N + N$) and divide simultaneously to produce more hyphal cells with pairs of nuclei. In the Ascomycetes, the dikaryotic hyphae are found only inside the fruiting body, in which they become the ascogenous hyphae, since the two nuclei of one cell of each hypha unite into a zygote ($2N$), which divides meiotically to produce ascospores that contain haploid nuclei. In the Basidiomycetes haploid spores produce only short haploid hyphae. Upon fertilization, dikaryotic ($N + N$) mycelium is produced, and this develops into the main body of the fungus. Such dikaryotic hyphae may produce, asexually, dikaryotic spores that will grow again into a dikaryotic mycelium. Finally, however, the paired nuclei of the cells unite and form zygotes.

The zygotes divide meiotically and produce basidiospores that contain haploid nuclei. In the Imperfect Fungi, of course, only the asexual cycle (haploid spore → haploid mycelium → haploid spore) is found. Even in the other fungi, however, a similar asexual cycle is the most common one by far, since it can be replaced many times during each growth season. The sexual cycle usually occurs only once a year.

Control of fungal diseases of plants

The endless variety and the complexity of the many fungus diseases of plants have led to the development of a correspondingly large number of approaches for their control. The particular characteristics in the life cycle of each fungus, its habitat preferences, and its performance under certain environmental conditions are some of the most important points to be considered in attempting to control a plant disease caused by a fungus.

Although some diseases can be controlled completely by just one type of control measure, a combination of measures is usually necessary for satisfactory control of most diseases. The most common control measures include: The use of pathogen-free seed or propagating stock; destruction of plant parts or refuse harboring the pathogen; destruction of volunteer plants or alternate hosts of the pathogen; use of clean tools and containers; proper drainage of fields and aeration of plants; crop rotation; and the use of resistant plant varieties. The most effective method, however, and sometimes the only one available for controlling most of the fungus diseases of plants, is the application of chemical sprays or dusts on the plants, their seeds, or into the soil where the plants are to be grown. Soil-inhabiting fungi may be controlled by steam or electric heat and by volatile liquids.

In some diseases the fungus is carried in the seed, and control can be obtained only through treatment of the seed with systemic fungicides or hot water. In others, control of the insect vectors may be the only available possibility. In general, great advances have been made toward controlling fungus diseases of plants, especially through resistant varieties and through chemicals, and as a result, these diseases are probably much easier to control than any other group of plant diseases, although the losses caused by fungus diseases of plants are still very great.

Diseases by myxomycetes

Myxomycetes are fungi whose vegetative body is a plasmodium, that is, an amoeboid mass of protoplasm that has many nuclei and no definite cell wall. In the true Myxomycetes, also called slime molds, the plasmodium does not invade plant cells, and at a certain point of its life cycle, it is used up to form superficial fructifications that contain resting spore. The slime molds produce zoospores that have two flagella. Only one group of Myxomycetes causes diseases in plants by simply growing externally on the surface of leaves, stems, and fruits without parasitizing the plant.

The order Physarales includes the true slime mold genera *Fuligo, Mucilago,* and *Physarum,* which cause slime molds on plants growing low on the ground, such as turf grasses, strawberries, vegetables, and small ornamentals. They are most common in warm weather after heavy rains or watering. All aboveground parts of plants in some areas, and even the soil between plants, may be covered by a creamy white or colored slimy growth, which later changes to distinct, crusty, ash-gray, or colored fruiting structures. The latter give the affected plants a dull gray appearance. Slime molds are saprophytic members of the true slime molds (Myxomycetes). Their plasmodium creeps like an amoeba and feeds on decaying organic matter and microorganisms such as bacteria, which it simply engulfs and digests. There are many species of slime mold fungi, the most common of which are *Physarum, Fuligo,* and *Mucilago.*

The plasmodium grows mostly in the upper layer of the soil and in the thatch, but during or after warm wet weather it comes to the soil surface and creeps over low-lying vegetation. On the plant surface, which these fungi use merely as a means of support, the plasmodium produces the crusty fruiting structures, which vary in size, shape, and color depending on the species of slime mold. The fruiting structures are sporangia, that is, containers filled with dark masses of powdery spores, and are easily rubbed off the plant.

The spores are spread by wind, water, mowers, or other equipment and can survive unfavorable weather. In cool, humid weather, the spores absorb water, their cell wall cracks open, and a single, naked, motile swarm spore emerges from each. The swarm spores feed like the plasmodium while they undergo several divisions and various changes. Finally they unite in pairs to form amoeboid zygotes, which enlarge, become multinucleate, and become the plasmodium. No control is usually considered necessary against slime molds. When they become too numerous and unsightly, breaking up of the spore masses by raking, brushing, or hosing down with water in dry weather, and removal of affected leaves or mowing of grass corrects the problem.

Slime mold fungi are generally quite sensitive to many fungicides, so if the problem becomes serious, spraying with any fungicide, such as captan or thiram, used to control other diseases of the particular plant should also control the slime molds.

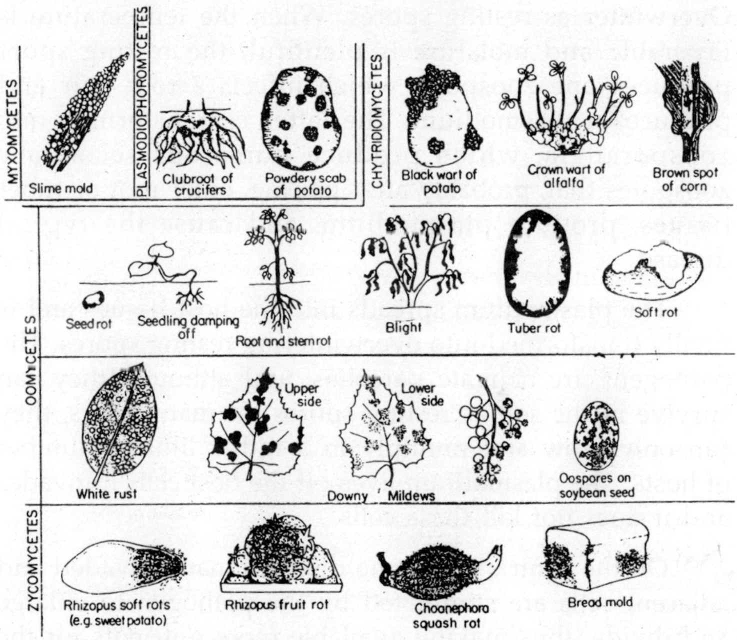

Diseases by plasmodiophoromycetes

Three common and often severe diseases of plants are caused by plasmodiophoromycetes. The following fungi are involved:

Plasmodiophora, causing clubroot of crucifers

Polymyxa, causing a root disease of cereals and grasses

Spongospora, causing the powdery scab of potato

These fungi are widespread in soils in which they Overwinter as resting spores. When the temperature is favorable and moisture is plentiful, the resting spore produces one zoospore, which infects a root hair and produces a plasmodium. The latter is transformed into zoosporangia, which produce numerous secondary zoospores that, probably after pairing, enter root or tuber tissues, produce plasmodium, and cause the typical disease.

The plasmodium spreads into the host tissues and is finally transformed into overwintering resting spores. The pathogens are obligate parasites, and although they can survive in the soil as resting spores for many years, they can only grow and multiply in a rather limited number of hosts. The plasmodium lives off the host cells it invades and it does not kill these cells.

On the contrary, in some diseases many invaded and adjacent cells are stimulated by the pathogen to enlarge and divide, thus making available more nutrients for the pathogen. These pathogens spread from plant to plant by means of zoospores and by anything that moves soil or water containing spores by infected transplants and so on.

Control of these pathogens is difficult and depends mostly on avoiding contamination of pathogen-free soils, use of healthy transplants, tubers, and crop rotation with nonhost plants, and adjustment of soil pH. *Polymyxa* and *Spongospora,* in addition to the diseases they cause, can also transmit destructive plant viruses. *Polymyxa graminis* is a vector of several viruses, including soilborne wheat mosaic virus, barley yellow mosaic, oat mosaic, wheat spindle streak, and peanut clump viruses, while *P. betae* is a vector of beet necrotic yellow vein virus. Spongospora is a vector of the potato mop-top virus.

Clubroot of crucifers

The clubroot disease of cruciferous plants, such as cabbage and cauliflower, is widely distributed all over the world, found wherever plants of the mustard family grow. It has been observed most frequently in Europe and North America. Clubroot causes serious losses when susceptible varieties of any cruciferous species are grown in infested -fields. Fields once infested with the clubroot pathogen remain so indefinitely and become unfit for cultivation of crucifers.

Symptoms. Infected plants may have pale green to yellowish leaves, which may show flagging and wilting in the middle of hot, sunny days but may recover during the night. Affected plants show almost normal vigor at first, but then gradually become stunted. Young plants may be killed by the disease within a short time after infection, while older plants may remain alive but fail to produce marketable heads. The most characteristic symptoms of the disease appear on the roots and sometimes the underground part of the stem.

The symptoms consist of small or large spindlelike, spherical, knobby, or club-shaped swellings on the roots and rootlets. These malformations may be isolated and cover only part of some roots or they may coalesce and cover the entire root system of the plant. The older and usually the larger clubbed roots disintegrate before the end of the season due to invasion by bacteria and other weakly parasitic soil microorganisms.

The Pathogen: Plasmodiophora brassicae. Plasmodiophora brassicae's body is a plasmodium. The plasmodium gives rise to zoosporangia or to resting spores. Upon germination, they produce zoospores. The single zoospore from resting spores penetrates host root hairs and there develops into a plasmodium. After a few days, the plasmodium cleaves into multinucleate portions surrounded by separate membranes; each portion develops into a zoosporangium. Each zoosporangium contains four to eight secondary zoospores which are discharged outside the host through pores dissolved in the host cell wall.

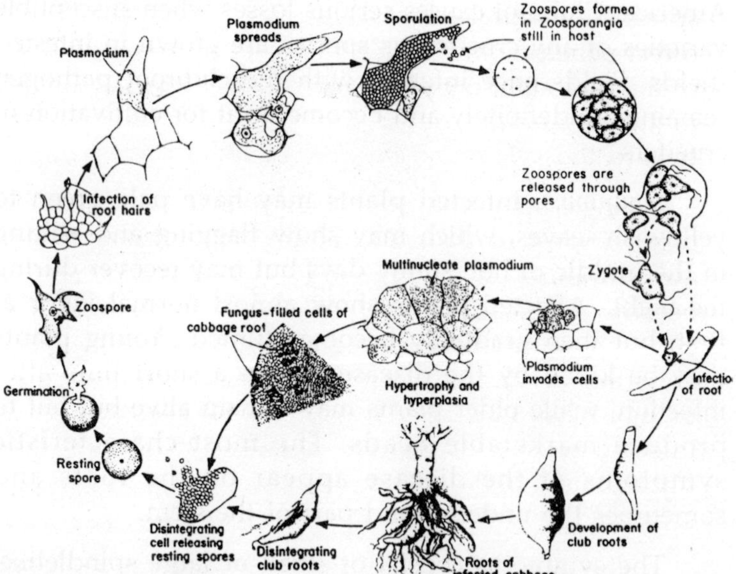

Fig. 2. Disease cycle of clubroot of crucifers caused by Plasmodiophora brassicae.

Some of these zoospores fuse in pairs to produce probably dikaryotic zygotes, which can cause new infections and produce new plasmodium containing many, paired "dikaryotic" nuclei. These nuclei undergo fusion (karyogamy) followed by meiosis. The plasmodium finally turns into resting spores, which are released into the soil upon disintegration of the host cell walls by secondary microorganisms.

Development of disease. The plasmodium resulting from the germination of the secondary zoospores penetrates young root tissues directly; it can also penetrate secondarily thickened roots and underground stems through wounds. From these points of primary infection the plasmodium spreads to cortical cells and reaches the cambium through direct penetration of host cell. From the point of infection of the cambium, the plasmodium spreads in all directions in the cambium, outward into the cortex and inward toward the xylem and into the medullary rays.

Single-point infections result in spindle-shaped clubs, being widest at the point of invasion and tapering off away from it. As the plasmodia pass through cells, they become established in some of them and stimulate these cells to abnormal enlargement (hypertrophy) and abnormal division (hyperplasia). Infected cells may be five or more times as large as adjacent uninfected ones. The infected cells of a club are distributed in small groups throughout the diseased tissue, and the groups are usually separated by uninfected cells.

The stimulus that is responsible for the abnormal growth of the cells appears to diffuse in advance of the pathogen and acts on the noninvaded cells of diseased tissues as well as on the infected ones. Actively growing and dividing cells, that is, cambial cells, are more easily invaded by the pathogen and are more responsive to the stimulus than other cells. In most cases many cells of infected clubs remain free from plasmodia, but in rare instances almost all the cells of a club may be infected. When few cells are infected the plasmodia become large, whereas when many cells are infected, they remain relatively small. Thus, there seems to be a fairly constant ratio between the volume occupied by the plasmodium and that of the diseased tissue, the former being approximately 30 percent of the latter. The plasmodium-infected clubs not only utilize much of the food required for the normal growth of the plant, but they also interfere with the absorption and translocation of mineral nutrients and water through the root system, resulting, in gradual stunting and wilting of the aboveground parts of the plant.

Furthermore, the rapid growing and greatly enlarged cells of the club tissues are unable to form a cork layer at the surface and are easily ruptured and invaded by secondary, weakly parasitic microorganisms. The invasion of clubs by bacteria and the subsequent disintegration by them lead to formation of substances toxic to the plant that are partly responsible for the wilting of the tops.

Control. Growing cruciferous crops in fields known to be infested with the clubroot pathogen should be avoided. If that is not possible, cabbage and the other susceptible cruciferous crops should be planted in well-drained fields with a pH slightly above neutral (usually about 7.2) or in fields in which the pH is adjusted to 7.2 by the addition of the proper amount of hydrated lime. The use of soil liming in the control of clubroot is based on the fact that spores of the clubroot organism germinate poorly or not at all in alkaline media. Although soil fumigants capable of disinfecting fields from the clubroot organism are available, the cost of materials and application is as yet prohibitive.

However, seedbed areas can be kept free of clubroot by treating the soil with chloropicrin, methyl bromide, dazomet, sodium-metam, or Vorlex approximately 2 weeks before planting. The clean, clubroot-free seedlings should, upon transplanting, be watered with a solution of PCNB (pentachloronitrobenzene). The search for varieties of cruciferous hosts resistant to clubroot has been only partially successful. Such resistance has been most highly developed ill varieties of rutabaga and turnip, but the extensive use of resistant varieties in infested soil has resulted in the appearance of highly virulent new races of the pathogen, sometimes within three years of the time of the release of the resistant varieties.

Although some varieties of the most popular cruciferous hosts are resistant to certain races of the clubroot organism and can be grown in areas infested with these races, no varieties of cabbage, cauliflower, Brussels sprouts, or broccoli resistant to all the races of *P. brassicae* are currently available.

Diseases by zoosporic true fungi

The zoosporic true fungi (Mastigomycotina) contain two classes of plant pathogenic fungi, Chytridiomycetes and Oomycetes, whose body consists of a round or oval thallus or an elongated mycelium that lacks cross walls and produces zoospores.

The plant-pathogenic Chytridiomycetes, the Chytridiales, usually known as chytrids, lack true mycelium, having mostly a round or irregularly shaped thallus that lives entirely within the host cells. Upon maturity, the vegetative body is transformed into one or many thick-walled resting spores or sporangia. The plant-pathogenic Oomycetes, which include the orders Saprolegniales and Peronosporales, have a well-developed, elongated mycelium, and produce zoospores in zoosporangia. Their resting spores are oospores, produced by the union of two morphologically different gametes. Chytridiomycetes and most Oomycetes are water- or soil-inhabiting fungi.

Since they produce zoospores, all require or are favored by free water or a film of water in the soil or on the plant surface. The Peronosporales that attack mostly aboveground parts of plants also require a film of water on the plant surface or very humid atmosphere for infection and further development.

Diseases by chytridiomycetes

The class Chytridiomycetes contains four plant pathogenic genera: *Olpidium, Physoderma, Synchytrium,* and *Urophlyctis*. Three diseases of moderate importance are caused by Chytridiomycetes that attack roots, tubers, or stems at or below the soil line. The fungi and the diseases they cause are listed below:

Olpidium, infecting the roots of many kinds of plants

Synchytrium, causing black wart of potato

Urophlyctis, causing crown wart of alfalfa

These fungi survive in the soil as resting spores or in host plants as a spherical or irregularly shaped thallus. The resting spores germinate to produce one or many zoospores. These infect plant cells and either produce thallus directly and cause the typical infection, or they first produce zoosporangia.

The zoosporangia produce secondary zoospores, which then cause the typical infection. Abundant moisture favors the local spread of the pathogens. Over long distances the pathogens are spread in infected plant parts or on contaminated plants and soil. Infected plant cells are not usually killed. Instead, in the diseases caused by *Synchytrium* and *Urophlyctis,* infected tissues are stimulated to divide and enlarge excessively.

Olpidium can also transmit viruses from the hosts in which it is produced to those it infects next. *Olpidium* is a vector of at least six plant viruses, including tobacco necrosis virus and lettuce big vein virus.

Physoderma maydis is the only Chytridiomycete that causes a disease of some importance in aboveground parts of plants. It causes the brown spot disease of corn.

Diseases by oomycetes

The most important plant pathogenic Oomycetes, that is, fungi that have elongated mycelium without cross walls and produce oospores, as their resting spores and zoospores or zoosporangia as their asexual spores, belong to two orders: Saprolegniales and Peronosporales. Of the Saprolegniales, only the genus *Aphanomyces* is important as a plant pathogen, causing root rot diseases of many annual plants, particularly of pea and sugar beet. The Peronosporales include some of the most important plant pathogens known.

Pythium, one of the causes of seed rot, seedling damping off, and root rot of all types of plants, and also of soft rots of fleshy fruits in contact with the soil.

Phytophthora, the cause of late blight of potato and of root rots and blights of many other plants.

Bremia, Peronospora, Plasmopara, Pseudoperonospora, and *Sclerospora*, causing the very destructive diseases known as downy mildews.

Albugo, causing the common but usually not serious white rust diseases of cruciferous plants.

The plant diseases caused by Oomycetes are basically of two types (1) Those that affect plant parts present in the soil or in contact with the soil, for example, roots, lower stems, tubers, seeds, and fleshy fruits lying on the soil. Such diseases are caused by all the species of Aphanomyces and Pythium and by some species of Phytophthora. (2) Those that affect only or primarily aboveground plant parts, particularly the leaves, young stems, and fruits. Diseases of this type are caused by some species of Phytophthora and by all the species of the downy mildew fungi (Bremia, Peronospora, Plasmopara, Pseudoperonospora, and Sclerospora), and by all the species of Albugo.

Pythium seed rot, damping off, root rot, and soft rot

Damping-off disease of seedlings is widely distributed all over the world. It occurs in valleys and forest soils, in tropical and temperate climates, and in every greenhouse. The disease affects seeds, seedlings, and older plants of almost all kinds of vegetables, flowers, cereals, and fruit and forest trees. In all cases, however, the greatest damage is done to the seed and seedling roots during germination either before or after emergence. Losses from this disease vary considerably with soil moisture, temperature, and other factors.

Quite frequently, however, seedlings in seedbeds are completely destroyed by damping off, or they die soon after they are transplanted. In many instances, poor germination of seeds or poor emergence of seedlings is the result of damping-off infections in the preemergence stage. Older plants are seldom killed when infected with the damping-off pathogen, but they develop root and stem lesions or root rots, their growth may be retarded considerably, and their yields may be reduced drastically. Some species of the damping-off fungus also attack the fleshy organs of plants, which rot in the field or in storage.

Symptoms. The symptoms caused by the damping-off fungi vary with the age and stage of development of the plant affected. When seeds of susceptible plants are planted in infested soils and are attacked by the damping-off fungi, they fail to germinate, become soft and mushy, then turn brown, shrink, and finally disintegrate. Seed infections taking place in the soil cannot be observed, and the only manifestations of the disease are poor stands.

Poor stands, however, are also the result of infections of the seedlings by the damping-off fungus after the seed has germinated but before the seedling has emerged above the soil line. Tissues of such young seedlings can be attacked at any point. The initial infection appears as a slightly darkened, water-soaked spot.

The infected area enlarges rapidly, the invaded cells collapse, and the seedling is overrun by the fungus and dies shortly after the beginning of infection. In both cases infection takes place before the seedlings emerge, and this phase of the disease is called preemergence damping off. Seedlings that have already emerged are usually attacked at the roots and sometimes at or below the soil line.

The succulent tissues of the seedling are easily penetrated by the fungus, which invades and kills the cells very rapidly. The invaded areas become water soaked and discolored, and the cells soon collapse. At this stage of infection the basal part of the seedling stem is much thinner and softer than the above, yet uninvaded, parts; owing to loss of firmness and supporting power, the invaded portion of the stem cannot support the part of the seedling above it, whereupon the seedling falls over on the soil.

The fungus continues to invade the seedling after it has fallen to the ground, and the seedling quickly withers and dies. This phase of the disease is called postemergence damping off. When older plants are attacked by the damping-off fungus they usually show only small lesions on the stem; these, however, if sufficiently large or numerous, can girdle the plant and cause stunting or death. More commonly, infections on older plants are limited to rootlets, which are damaged and frequently killed by the fungus; this results in stunting, wilting, and death of the aboveground part of the plant.

Soft fleshy organs of some vegetables, such as cucurbit fruits, green beans, potatoes, and cabbage heads, are sometimes infected by the damping-off fungi during extended wet periods in the field, in storage, and in transit. Such infections result in a cottony fungus growth on the surface of the fleshy organ, while the interior turns into a soft, watery, rotten mass, called "leak".

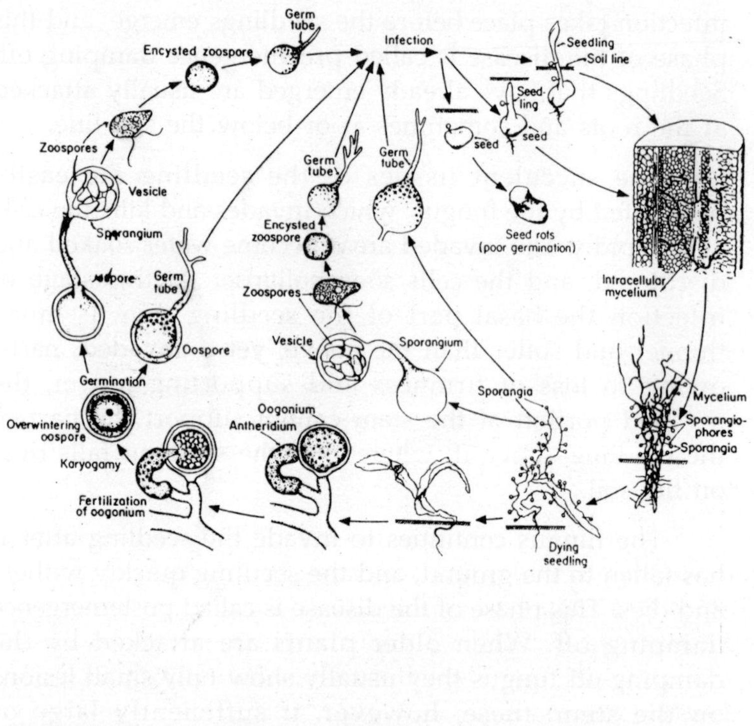

Fig. 3. Disease cycle of damping off and seed decay caused by Pythium sp.

The Pathogen: Pythium Sp. Pythium is the most important cause of the pre and postemergence phases of damping off. Several species of *Pythium* are involved, namely *P.*

aphanidermatum, P. debaryanum,. P. irregulare, and *P. ultimum*. The effect of each one of them on its hosts, however, is usually similar to that of the others. It should be noted, however, that several different fungi, such as *Phytophthora*, Rhizoctonia, and Fusarium, can and often do cause symptoms quite similar to one or the other phase of those described above. Several other fungi, such as *Cercospora, Septoria, Mycosphaerella, Glomerella, Colletotrichum, Helminthosporium, Alternaria*, and *Botrytis*, and even some bacteria, such as *Pseudomonas* and *Xanthomonas*, when they are carried in or on the seed, also cause damping off and kill seedlings.

Pythium produces a white, slender, profusely branching, and rapidly growing mycelium. The mycelium gives rise to terminal, or intercalary sporangia, which may be spherical, filamentous, or variously shaped. Sporangia germinate directly by producing one to several germ tubes, or by producing a short hypha at the end of which a vesicle is formed. The protoplasm passes from the sporangium into the vesicle, and there it forms more than 100 zoospores. When the zoospores are released they swarm about in the water for a few minutes, come to rest, encyst by rounding off, and germinate by producing a germ tube.

The germ tube usually penetrates the host tissue and starts new infection, but sometimes it produces another vesicle in which several secondary zoospores are formed, and this may be repeated. The mycelium also gives rise to spherical oogonia and club-shaped antheridia at the ends of short hyphae. The hypha bearing the antheridium may originate from the hypha bearing the oogonium or from another hypha of the mycelium. Upon contact with the oogonium the antheridium produces a fertilization tube, which enters the oogonium. Through this tube the male nuclei of the antheridium move toward the female nuclei of the oogonium, unite with them, and form the zygote. A thickening of the wall of the fertilized oogonium takes place, and the thick-walled structure containing the zygote is called an oospore. Oospores are resistant to high or low temperatures and other adverse factors and serve as the overwintering stage of the fungus. Since oospores require a resting period before they germinate, they are also called resting spores. Oospores, too, germinate either by producing germ tubes that develop into mycelium or by producing vesicles in which zoospores are formed in a way similar to that described for sporangia.

The type of germination of both sporangia and oospores is determined primarily by the temperature of the medium, temperatures above 18°C favoring germination by germ tubes, while temperatures between io and 18°C induce germination by means of zoospores. *Pythium* species are widely distributed in waters and soils throughout the world. They live on dead plant and animal substrata as saprophytes or as low-grade parasites attacking the fibrous roots of plants. When a wet soil is heavily infested with Pythium, any seeds, or young plants emerging from seeds, in such a soil may be attacked by the fungus.

Development of disease. Spore germ tubes or saprophytic mycelium of Pythium come in contact with seeds or seedling tissues of host plants either by chance or because the exudates of these plants serve as nutrients and chemotropic stimulants to its zoospores and mycelium that move or grow toward the plants.

The fungus enters the seeds by direct penetration of the moistened, swollen seed coats or through cracks and further penetrates the embryo or emerging seedling tissues through mechanical pressure and dissolution by means of enzymes. Pectinolytic enzymes secreted by the fungus dissolve the middle lamella, which holds the cells together, resulting in maceration of the tissues. Further invasion and breakdown of tissues occurs as a result of growth of the fungus between and through the cells. At the points where the hyphae pass through the cell walls they are constricted to approximately half their normal diameter. Proteolytic enzymes break down the protoplasts of invaded cells, while physical forces and, in some cases, fungal cellulolytic enzymes bring about complete collapse and disintegration of the cell walls.

The fungus consumes many of the plant cell substances and the products of their breakdown and uses them as building blocks for its own body or as an energy source for its own metabolic activities. Thus, infected seeds are killed and turn into a rotten mass consisting primarily of fungus and substances such as suberin and lignin, which this fungus cannot break down. The infection of roots and stems of young, tender seedlings progresses in essentially the manner described above. The initial infection usually occurs at or slightly below the surface of the soil, depending on moisture level and depth of planting.

The mycelium penetrates the epidermal and cortical cells of the stem directly, consumes part or all of their contents, and breaks down their cell walls, bringing about the collapse of cells and tissues. In this area vascular tissues may also be invaded, in which case they become discolored even beyond the extent of the cortical lesion. Seedlings so invaded die quickly. When the invasion of the fungus is limited to the cortex of the belowground stem of the seedling, the latter may continue to live and grow for a short time until the lesion extends above the soil line.

Then, the invaded, collapsed tissues cannot support the seedling, which falls over and dies. If the initial infection occurs when the seedling is already well developed and has well-thickened and lignified cell walls and active cambium, the advance of the fungus is checked at or near the point of infection, and only relatively small lesions develop. Well-developed, mature tissues present considerable resistance to the mechanical pressure and to the enzymatic activity of the fungus by means of their increased thickness and modified chemical and physical structure of their cell walls.

Rootlets of most plants can be attacked by *Pythium* at almost any stage of plant growth. The fungus enters root tips and proliferates in the young cells, causing a rapid collapse and death of the rootlet. Further advance of the fungus into older roots is usually limited to the cortex of the root Fleshy or relatively young roots are invaded to a much greater extent, the lesions extending to several centimeters in length and through the thickness of the cortex in depth. Infections by *Pythium* of fleshy vegetable fruits and other organs can take place in the field, in storage, in transit, and in the market. Field infections begin at the point of contact of the fruit with wet soil heavily infested with the fungus.

Enzymes secreted by the fungus macerate the tissue, which becomes soft and watery. An entire cucumber fruit may be invaded by the fungus within 3 days of inoculation. As the mycelium advances through the fleshy tissue it also bursts through the confining epidermis and forms, at first, small patches of aerial mycelium; these soon enlarge, coalesce, and form a continuous, luxuriant, cottony mycelial weft encasing most or all of the fruit. In storage, the aerial mycelium of an infected fruit grows out between adjacent fruits, invests them partially or completely, and soon penetrates, infects, and destroys these fruits.

During the development of infection, only mycelium

can be found in the infected tissues. As the infection progresses, however, sporangia begin to appear, followed by the production of oospores. Sporangia and oospores can be produced inside or outside the host tissues or both, depending on the particular fungus species involved. The severity of the diseases and amount of losses caused by *Phythium* infections are greater when the soil is kept wet (when its water content is at least 50 percent of its water-holding capacity) for prolonged periods; when the temperature is unfavorable for the host plant (too low for plants requiring high temperatures for optimum growth or too high for plants requiring relatively low temperatures for best growth); when there is an excess of nitrogen in the soil; and when the same crop is planted in the same field for several consecutive years.

Control. Pythium diseases in the greenhouse can be controlled through the use of soil sterilized by steam or dry heat or with volatile chemicals, such as methyl bromide with or without chloropicrin, and through the use of chemically treated seed. Greenhouse benches and containers must also be sterilized, however, or they must be treated with a i percent copper sulfate solution. Even so, recontamination often and easily occurs from infested soil on the greenhouse floor, tools, water hoses, and other items. Few crops are known in which varieties showing any resistance to *Pythium* have been found, and so far no commercial varieties resistant to this pathogen are available.

In recent years, however, control of *Pythium* seed rot and damping off has been obtained by treating the seeds with conidia of the antagonistic fungus *Trichoderma*, sp., *Penicillium oxalicum*, or *Gliocladium virens*, or by incorporating conidia of *Trichoderma* or *Streptomyces* sp. into commercial soilless mixes used in greenhouses and by nursery owners, or by incorporating into naturally infected soils organic matter carrying the antagonistic fungus *Laetisaria arvalis* (*Corticium* sp.). Certain cultural practices are sometimes helpful in reducing the amount of infection. Good soil drainage is the most important of all. Improvement of heavy soils and improvement of air circulation among plants are advisable; planting should be done when temperatures are favorable for fast plant growth; application of excessive amounts of nitrate forms of nitrogen fertilizers should be avoided. No one crop should be planted in the same field for more than two consecutive years since that would increase the fungus population in the soil unless the soil is sterilized periodically.

For container-grown nursery crops and ornamentals, including composted tree bark as a replacement for most of the peat markedly reduced the root rots caused by *Phythium* and several other root pathogens. In the field, where soil sterilization is difficult and expensive, seed treatment with one or more of a number of chemicals is the most important disease preventive measure.

The most commonly used materials for seed or bulb treatment are chloranil, thiram, captan, dichlone, ferbam, and diazoben. The systemic fungicide metalaxyl gives excellent control of damping off, seedling blights, and root rots caused by *Pythium* and *Phytophthora*. It can be applied as soil or seed treatment. Although more than one of these chemicals may be used on any crop with good results, there are usually some chemical-crop combinations that are much more effective than the rest, while some other combinations may be phytotoxic or ineffective under certain conditions. Seed treatment is sometimes followed by spraying of seedlings with metalaxyl, ziram, chloranil, captan, or soluble coppers. This is especially important when the soil is heavily infested with Pythium or when the soil stays wet for prolonged periods during the early stages of plant growth.

Phytophthora diseases

Species of *Phytophthora* cause a variety of diseases on many different types of plants ranging from seedlings of annual vegetables or ornamentals to fully developed fruit and forest trees. Most species cause root rots, damping off of seedlings, and rots of lower stems, tubers, and corms similar to those caused by Pythium sp. Others cause rots of buds or fruits, and some cause foliar blights that attack the foliage, young twigs, and fruit.

Some species are host specific, that is, they attack only one or two species of host plants, but others have a wide host range and may cause similar or different symptoms on many different kinds of host plants. The best-known species is *Phytophthora infestans*, the cause of late blight of potatoes and tomatoes, but several other species cause extremely destructive diseases on their hosts.

Phytophthora root rots

Several species of *Phytophthora*, particularly *P. cinnamomi*, *P. cryptogea*, *P. fragariae*, and *P. megasperma*, causes root rots on numerous species of plants that include fruit, forest, and ornamental trees and shrubs, annual vegetables and ornamentals, and strawberries. The most common Phytophthora root rots are littleleaf disease of pine, root rot of avocado and pineaple, root rots of alfalfa, azalea, calla lily, crucifers, tomato, carrot, red stele of strawberries, and many others. The losses caused by Phytophthora root rots are great, especially on trees and shrubs, but the pathogen often goes undetected or unidentified. Plants suffering from such root rots often begin by showing symptoms of drought and starvation, and become weakened and susceptible to attack by other pathogens or various other causes that are then mistakenly taken as the causes of the death of the plants.

Phytophthora root rots cause damage in their hosts in nearly every part of the world where the soil becomes too wet for good growth of susceptible plants and the temperature remains fairly low, that is, between 15 and 23°C. Young seedlings of trees and annual plants may be killed by the disease within a few days, weeks, or months, while in older plants the killing of roots may be slow or rapid, depending on the amount of fungus present in the soil and the prevailing environmental conditions. As a result, older trees show sparse foliage, shorter, cupped, and yellow leaves, and dieback of twigs and branches. Such trees increase very little in height and diameter and usually die within 3 to 10 years after infection.

Fewer and smaller fruit and seeds are produced each succeeding year. On all hosts affected by *Phytophthora* root rot, many of the small roots are dead, and necrotic brown lesions are often present on the larger roots. On young plants, or on older succulent plants, the whole root system may decay, followed by a more or less rapid death of the plant. In strawberries, as in the other plants, most of the small rootlets rot away, while the larger ones show progressive stages of browning beginning at the tips. In addition, in late spring and before or through harvest, affected larger strawberry roots show a red-colored core- or stele, a symptom diagnostic of the strawberry red stele root rot caused by *Phytophthora fragariae*.

The behavior of the various Phytophthora species that cause root rots is generally similar. The fungus overwinters as oospores, chlamydospores, or mycelium in infected roots, and these spores may also overwinter in the soil. In the spring, the oospores and chlamydospores germinate by means of zoospores, while the mycelium grows further and produces zoosporangia that release zoospores.

The zoospores swim around in the soil water and infect roots of susceptible hosts with which they come in contact. More mycelium and zoospores are produced during wet, cool weather and spread the disease to more plants. In dry, hot, or too cold weather the fungus survives as oospores, chlamydospores, or mycelium that can start infections again when the soil is wet and the temperature favorable. Control of *Pytophthora* root rots depends on planting susceptible crops in soils free of the pathogen or in soils that are light and drain well and quickly.

All planting stock should be free of infection and, when available, only resistant varieties should be planted. For plants in pots, greenhouses, or seedbeds, the soil and containers should be sterilized with steam before planting. In recent years, excellent control of Phytophthora root and lower stem rots has been obtained through the use of several systemic fungicides such as metalaxyl, fosetyl Al, ethazol, and propamocarb, which are applied as seed treatments, soil treatments, transplant dips, and as sprays, or with overhead irrigation water. For some crops, such as strawberries, Phytophthora root rot has also been effectively controlled through soil fumigation with a mixture of methyl bromide and chloropicrin. In some cases, *Phytophthora* root rots have been controlled by planting seedlings in suppressive soil that contains either microorganisms antagonistic to Phytophthora or inorganic substances toxic to the fungus.

Several fungi and bacteria have been shown to parasitize Phytophthora oospores or to be antagonistic to *Phytophthora*, but none of them has been used to effectively control Phytophthora so far. In the last several years, however, composted tree bark mixed with soil or soilless mixes used in production of container-grown plants or in greenhouse beds has significantly reduced plant infections by Phytophthora.

Phytophthora foot, crown, collar, stem, or trunk rots

Most species of *Phytophthora* listed in the general part cause diseases primarily of the lower stem that are described by one or another of the terms listed here. The most common and most serious of such diseases include the trunk canker or collar rot of apple trees, foot rot of citrus trees, root and crown rot of cherry trees black shank of tobacco, foot rot of lily and stock, stem rot and wilt of snapdragon and soybeans, pink rot of potato, soft rot of sugarcane cuttings, stem rot of dieffenbachia and peperomia, and others.

In many of these diseases the fungus also attacks the roots, it may attack and kill seedlings before or after emergence above the soil line, thus causing damping-off symptoms, and in some cases the fungus also attacks and causes partial or complete rot of the fruit, as for example, in tomato, pepper, cucurbits, citrus, and cacao. The general characteristics of *Phytophthora* rots of the lower stem of plants, considering the wide variety of host plants and fungus species involved, appear quite similar. Like the other *Phytophthora* diseases, these are also favored by rather low temperatures and by high soil moisture and atmospheric humidity, and are therefore more common and most severe in low-lying, poorly drained areas.

In some host-fungus combinations, the fungus attacks the stem below the soil line or it may first attack the main root and thus cause droughtlike symptoms and general decline of the aboveground parts of the plant before any direct lesions or cankers appear above the soil line. In most cases, however, the fungus attacks the plant at or near the soil line where it causes a water soaking of the bark that appears as a dark area on the trunk. The dark area enlarges in all directions and, if the plant is small and succulent, the darkening may soon encircle the entire stem, after which the lower leaves drop and eventually the whole plant wilts.

On larger plants and on trees, the darkening may be on one side of the stem and soon becomes a depressed canker below the level of healthy bark. In early stages, the diseased bark is firm and intact while the inner bark is slimy and may produce moist, gummy exudate. Later, the affected area becomes shrunken and cracked. The collar rot canker may spread through the tissue up into the trunk and sometimes the branches or down into the root system.

Invasion of the root usually begins at the crown area or at ground level. As the cankers spread and enlarge, they may girdle the trunk, limbs, or roots, at first causing the plant or tree to grow poorly, produce fewer and smaller fruit, show sparse foliage and dieback of twigs, and finally killing the plant parts beyond the infected area.

The *Phytophthora* species that cause these diseases live and reproduce primarily in the soil and usually attack susceptible plants at or below the soil line. Sometimes, however, spores of the fungus may be splashed into injured aboveground bark or low-lying fruit and may cause infections at these points. Fleshy fruits, such as cucurbits, lying on wet soil infested with the fungus are also attacked directly. The fungus overwinters in infected tissues as mycelium, oospores, or chlamydospores.

Control of *Phytophthora* diseases of the lower stem requires all precautions described for *Phytophthora* root rots. In addition, they can be controlled by applying metalaxyl, fosetyl Al, propamocarb, or ethazol to the soil, seeds, or transplants, and by injections of fosetyl Al into the trunks of trees. Also, on dormant, susceptible plants, primarily trees, and in the soil around them, application of a solution of copper oxychloride or Bordeaux mixture seems to greatly inhibit the growth and activity of the fungus. Resistant varieties should always be preferred, especially for heavy, poorly drained soils. With fruit trees, resistant rootstocks and sometimes interstocks offer the most effective means of controlling foot rot or collar rot.

Late blight of potatoes

The late blight disease of potatoes is found in nearly all

areas of the world where potatoes are grown. It is most destructive, however, in the eastern half of North America and in northwestern Europe, where potatoes are grown in large acreage and where cool, moist weather favors both potato production and the late blight disease. Late blight is also very destructive to tomatoes and to several other species in the family Solanaceae. Late blight may kill the foliage and stems of potato and tomato plants at any time during the growing season, It also attacks potato tubers and tomato fruits in the field, which rot either in the field or while in storage, in transit, and at market.

Late blight may cause total destruction of all plants in a field within a week or two when weather conditions are favorable and when no control measures are applied. Losses, however, vary from one area to another and from year to year, depending on the prevailing temperature and moisture at certain periods of the growing season and on the control measures practiced. Even when losses in the field are small, potatoes may become infected during harvest and may rot in storage.

Symptoms. Symptoms appear at first as circular or irregular water-soaked spots, usually at the tips or edges of the lower leaves. In moist weather the spots enlarge rapidly and form brown, blighted areas with indefinite borders. A zone of white, downy fungus growth 3-5 mm wide appears at the border of the lesions on the undersides of the leaves. Soon the entire leaflet and then all the leaflets on a leaf are infected, die, and become limp. Under continuously wet conditions all tender, aboveground parts of the plants blight and quickly rot away, giving off a characteristic odor. In dry weather the activities of the fungus are checked.

Existing lesions stop enlarging, turn black, curl, and wither, and no fungus appears on the underside of the leaves. When the weather becomes moist again the fungus resumes its activities and the disease once again develops rapidly. Affected tubers at first show more or less irregular, purplish-black or brownish blotches. When cut open, the affected tissue appears water-soaked, dark, somewhat reddish brown, and extends 5- 15 mm into the flesh of the tuber. Later the affected areas become firm and dry and somewhat sunken. Such lesions may be small or may involve almost the entire surface of the tuber without spreading deeper into the tuber.

The rot, however, continues to develop after the tubers are harvested, or infected tubers may be subsequently invaded by secondary fungi and bacteria, causing soft rots and giving the rotting potatoes a putrid, offensive odor. Tomato fruit is attacked and may rot rapidly in the field or in storage.

The Pathogen: Phytophthora Infestans. The mycelium produces branched sporangiophores of unrestricted growth. Lemon-shaped, papillate sporangia are produced at the tips of the sporangiophore branches, but as the tips of the branches continue to grow the sporangia are pushed aside and later fall off. At the places where sporangia are produced, the sporangiophores form swellings that are characteristic for this fungus.

Sporangia germinate almost entirely by means of zoospores at temperatures up to 12 or 15°C, while above 15°C sporangia may germinate directly by producing a germ tube. Each sporangium produces 3 - 8, sometimes more, zoospores, which are liberated by the bursting of the sporangial wall at the papilla. This fungus requires two mating types for sexual reproduction, and because only one of them is present in most countries, the sexual stage of the fungus has rarely been found. In Mexico and other areas of Central and South America, however, both mating types are widely distributed, and oospores are common.

When the two mating types grow adjacently, the female hypha grows through the young antheridium and develops into globose oogonium above the antheridium. The antheridium then fertilizes the oogonium, which develops into a thick-walled and hardy oospore. Oospores germinate by means of a germ tube, which produces a sporangium, although at times the germ tube grows directly into mycelium.

Development of disease. The pathogen overwinters as mycelium in infected potato tubers. The mycelium spreads in the tissues of the potato tubers and it finally reaches a few of the shoots produced from infected tubers used as seed, volunteer plants that develop from diseased tubers left in the field, or sprouts produced by infected potatoes in cull piles or dumps.

The mycelium spreads up the stem most rapidly in the cortical region causing discoloration and collapse of the cells. Later, the mycelium grows between the pith cells of the stem, but it is seldom found in the vascular system. The mycelium grows through the stem and travels up to the surface of the soil. When the mycelium reaches the aerial parts of plants, it produces sporangiophores, which emerge through the stomata of the stems and leaves and project into the air.

The sporangia produced on the sporangiophores become detached and drift off when ripe, or are dispersed by rain. When the sporangia land on wet potato leaves or stems, they germinate and cause new infections. The germ tube penetrates the leaf cuticle or enters through a stoma and produces mycelium, which grows profusely between the cells and sends long, curled haustoria into the cells. The cells on which the mycelium feeds are killed, and as they begin to decay, the mycelium spreads peripherally into fresh tissue. A few days after infection, new sporangiophores emerge from the stomata of the leaves and produce numerous sporangia, which are spread by the wind and infect new plants. In favorable weather the period from infection to sporangia formation may be as short as 4 days and, therefore, a large number of asexual generations and new infections may be produced in one growing season. With the advance of the disease the established lesions increase in area and new ones develop resulting in premature killing of the foliage and proportional reduction in potato tuber yields. The second phase of the disease, the infection of tubers, begins in the field when, during wet weather, sporangia are washed down from the leaves and are carried into the soil.

The tubers near the surface of the soil are attacked, by the emerging zoospores, which germinate and penetrate the tubers through lenticels or through wounds. In the tuber the mycelium grows mostly between the cells and sends its long, sicklelike haustoria into the cells. Tubers are rarely infected by mycelium growing down the stem of a diseased mother plant. If, however, at harvest, the tubers are contaminated with living sporangia still present on the soil or if the tubers are exposed while the fungus is still sporulating on partially diseased foliage, further infection will occur, which may not be apparent at the time, but it will develop in storage.

Most of the blighted tubers rot in the ground or during storage. The development of late blight epidemics depends greatly on the effect of humidity and temperature on the different stages of the life cycle of the fungus. The fungus sporulates most abundantly at relative humidity near 100 percent and at temperatures between 16 and 22°C. Sporangia lose their viability in 3 - 6 hours at relative humidities below 80 percent. Germination of sporangia takes place only when free water or dew is present on the leaves and, at 10-15°C, it may be completed within 0.5 - 2 hours. After germination a period of 2 - 2.5 hours at 15 -

25°C is required for penetration of the germ tubes into the host tissue. After penetration, the mycelium develops most rapidly at 17-21°C, which is also Optimal for sporulation. Temperatures above 30°C check the growth of the fungus in the field but do not kill it, and the fungus can start to sporulate again when the temperature becomes favorable, provided of course that the relative humidity is sufficiently high.

Control. Late blight of potatoes can be successfully controlled by a combination of sanitary measures, resistant varieties, and well-timed chemical sprays. Only disease-free potatoes should be used for seed. Potato dumps or cull piles should be burned before planting time in the spring or sprayed with strong herbicides to kill all sprouts or green growth. All volunteer potato plants in the area, whether in the potato or other fields should be destroyed, since any volunteer potato, plant can be a source of late blight infection.

The blight fungus comprises a number of races, which differ from each other in the potato varieties that they can attack. Several potato varieties resist one or more races of the late blight fungus. Some of them are resistant to vine infection but not to tuber infection. New varieties, derived from crosses with *Solanum demissum*, have one or more of the R genes for resistance to late blight and have withstood attack by all known races of the fungus for a short while but were attacked by other races not previously distinguished or perhaps not previously existent. Many varieties possess so-called "field resistance," which is only a partial horizontal resistance of varying degrees but which is effective against all races of the blight fungus.

However, it is not sufficient to rely on varietal resistance to control late blight, since in favorable weather, blight can severely infect these varieties unless they are sprayed with a good protective fungicide. Even resistant varieties should be regularly sprayed with fungicides to eliminate, as much as possible, the possibility of becoming suddenly attacked by races of the fungus to which they are not resistant or by entirely new races.

On the other hand, it is always advisable to use resistant varieties, even when sprays with fungicides are considered the main control strategy, since resistant varieties delay the onset of the disease or reduce its rate of development, so that fewer sprays on a resistant variety may be needed to obtain a satisfactory level of control of the disease. Chemical sprays with fungicides, if applied properly, generally will keep late blight under control. Spraying should start when potato plants are 15 - 30 cm high or at least io days before the date late blight usually appears in the area. Sprays should be applied once every 5 - 10 days when the weather is damp, misty, or rainy and when the nights are cool and should continue until the foliage dies naturally or is killed artificially by "vine-killers." Proper timing and thorough coverage of old and new foliage are essential if plants are to be protected from the disease. Once late blight becomes established, it is extremely difficult to control unless the weather turns hot (35°C and above) and dry.

During the last several years, several computerized (Blitecast is an example) and noncomputerized programs have been developed for forecasting periods of occurrence of late blight and for scheduling timely applications of appropriate fungicides. All these programs depend on the fact that late blight is favored by moderate temperatures and abundant moisture. An abundant supply of fungal inoculum is assumed. By frequent (weekly or daily) field scouting for the initial appearance of disease symptoms in each location, a relationship between temperature, moisture, and infection is established. By recording daily occurrence and duration of temperature, relative humidity, and rainfall, and by analyzing all the data through the computer, it is possible to predict the first and subsequent infection periods and, therefore, to schedule timely application of appropriate fungicides to prevent or reduce infection.

Some forecasting schemes are even programmed to take into account the degree of resistance of the variety to the fungus and the effectiveness (protectant, eradicant, systemic) of the fungicide in formulating the recommendation for fungicide application. Materials used for late blight control include mancozeb, metalaxyl, a combination of metalaxyl and mancozeb, captafol, chlorothalonil, polyram, fentin hydroxide, and several copper materials, such as Kocide, copper oxychloride, and Bordeaux mixture.

Protective spraying of foliage usually effects a considerable reduction in tuber infection. When, however, partially blighted leaves and stems are surviving at harvest time, it is necessary to remove the aboveground parts of potato plants or destroy them by chemical sprays or mechanical means. Herbicides used for this purpose include dinoseb, diquat, paraquat, endothall, ametryn, several inorganic compounds such as copper sulfate, sodium and potassium arsenites, sulfuric acid, and certain dinitro compounds.

Downy mildews

The downy mildews are primarily foliage blights that attack and spread rapidly in young, tender green tissues including leaves, twigs, and fruit. Their development and severity, in areas where susceptible hosts and the respective downy mildew fungus are present, depend greatly on the presence of a film of water on the plant tissues and on high relative humidity in the air during cool or warm, but not hot, periods.

The reproduction and spread of the downy mildew fungi are rapid and their diseases can cause heavy losses in short periods of time. Although even the late blight of potato and tomato looks like and is often called a downy mildew, the true downy mildews are caused by a group of oomycetous fungi that belong to the family Peronosporaceae. All species of this family are obligate parasites of higher plants and cause downy mildew diseases on a large number of plants including most of the cultivated grain crops and vegetables, and many field crops, ornamentals, shrubs, and vines.

The downy mildews of several crops have caused spectacular and catastrophic epidemics in the past, and some of them continue to the present to cause epidemics and severe losses. In recent years, the downy mildew of sorghum has appeared and spread in the United States and has raised fears of future introduction of other, even more serious, downy mildews of gramineous crops now present in Asia and Africa.

A devastating epidemic of downy mildew (blue mold) of tobacco spread rapidly from Florida up the eastern states to New England and into Canada and destroyed much of the tobacco in its path, causing losses to growers of more than 250 million dollars. Similar epidemics also began in the following three years but were kept in check with heavy uses of fungicides, although not before they spread over several states. The downy mildew fungi produce sporangia on sporanglophores that are distinct from the mycelium in their way of branching.

The sporangia arc located at the tips of the branches. Each genus of downy mildew fungi has its own distinctive type of branching of its sporangiophores, and this is used for their identification. The sporanglophores are usually long, white at first, emerging in groups from the plant tissues through the stomata. Later on the~ appear grayish or light brown and form a visible mat of fungus growth on the lower or both sides of leaves and on other affected tissues. Each sporangiophore grows until it reaches maturity and then produces its crop of sporangia, all at about the same time. In most downy mildews, the sporangia germinate generally by producing zoospores or, at higher temperatures, by producing germ tubes. In the genus *Bremia*, however, the sporangia germinate most commonly by means of a germ tube, and in the genera *Peronospora* and *Peronosclerospora* the sporangia germinate only by means of a germ tube. Whenever sporangia germinate by producing a germ tube, they are considered spores in themselves rather than sporangia, and in that case they are often called conidia, which always germinate by germ tubes.

The oospores of the downy mildews usually germinate by germ tubes, but in a few cases they may produce a sporangium that releases zoospores. In most downy mildews, for example, of alfalfa, corn, lettuce, onion, sorghum, spinach, sugarcane, sunflower, and tobacco, the pathogen routinely causes systemic shoot infection of its host when it is carried in the seed or bulb or when infection take place at the seedling or young plant stage, When organs of older plants are attacked they may develop localized, although not necessarily small, infected areas, or they may allow the fungus to spread into young tissues and become locally systemic. In some downy mildews, for example, of grape, soybean, and some grasses, infections usually result in small or large lesions on the leaves and stem, but even in these the fungus often becomes systemic when it infects young shoots and fruit stalks.

The downy mildews can and often do cause rap ' id and severe losses of crop plants while still in the seedbed or later on in the field. They often destroy from 40 to go percent of the young plants or young shoots in the field, causing heavy or total losses of crop yields. The amount of losses depends somewhat on the initial amount of inoculum but, most importantly, on the prolonged presence of wet, cool weather during which the downy mildew fungi sporulate profusely, cause numerous new infections, and spread into and rapidly kill young succulent tissues. The spread and destructiveness of downy mildews in cool, wet weather used to be uncontrollable. For some field crops, and in many less developed countries, downy mildews are still uncontrollable, checked only when the weather turns hot and dry.

Downy mildew of grape

Downy mildew of grape occurs in most parts of the world where grapes are grown under humid conditions. The fungus that causes downy mildew of grape is native to North America, and although it attacks the native American grape vines it does not affect them very seriously. When the fungus, however, was introduced inadvertently into Europe at the European grape, *Vitis vinifera*, which had evolved in the absence of the downy mildew fungus, was extremely susceptible to it, and the fungus began to spread among vineyards throughout France and throughout most of Europe, destroying the crop and the vineyards in its path. Even today, although other grapes may be attacked by downy mildew, it is the popular Vinifera grapes that are affected by far the most severely.

Downy mildew is still most destructive in Europe and in the eastern half of the United States, where it may cause severe epiphytotics year after year, but it is also known to have caused serious losses in some years in northern Africa, in South Africa, in parts of Asia, Australia, and South America. Dry areas are usually free of the disease.

Downy mildew affects the leaves, fruit, and vines of grape plants and causes losses through killing of leaf tissues and defoliation, through production of low quality, unsightly, or entirely destroyed grapes, and through weakening, dwarfing, and killing of young shoots. When weather is favorable and no protection against the disease is provided, downy mildew can easily destroy 50 - 75 percent of the crop in one season.

Symptoms. Downy mildew is usually first observed as small, pale yellow spots with indefinite borders on the upper surface of the leaves, while on the under surface of the leaves, and directly under the spots, a downy growth of the sporophores of the fungus appears. Later, the infected leaf areas are killed and turn brown, while the sporophores of the fungus on the under surface of the leaves become dark gray. The necrotic lesions are irregular in outline, and as they enlarge they may coalesce to form large dead areas on the leaf, frequently resulting in defoliation. During blossom or early fruiting stages, entire clusters or parts of them may be attacked, are quickly covered with the downy growth, and die. If infection takes place after the berries are half-grown, the fungus grows mostly internally, the berries become leathery and somewhat wrinkled and develop a reddish-marbling to brown coloration.

Infection of green young shoots, tendrils, leaf stems, and fruit stalks results in stunting, distortion, and thickening (hypertrophy) of the tissues. Entire shoots may be covered with the downy growth of the fungus. Later the fungus growth breaks down and disappears, and the infected tissues turn brown and die. In late or localized infections the shoots may not be killed, but they show various degrees of distortion.

The Pathogen: Plasmopara viticola. The mycelium diameter varies from i to 60 µm because the hyphae take up the shape of the intercellular spaces of the infected tissues. The mycelium grows between the cells but sends numerous, globose haustoria into the cells. In humid weather the mycelium produces sporangiophores, which emerge on the underside of the leaves and on the stems through the stomata or rarely by pushing directly through the epidermis. In the young fruit, sporangiophores emerge through lenticels. Usually 4-6 sporangiophores arise through a single stoma, but sometimes there may be as many as 20. Each produces 4-6 branches at nearly right angles to the main stem of the sporangiophore, and each branch produces 2, sometimes 3, secondary branches in a similar manner. At the tips of the secondary branches, single, lemon-shaped sporangia (conidia) are produced. The sporangia are blown by the wind or are transported by water, and in the presence of free moisture they germinate.

Sporangia generally germinate by means of zoospores, which emerge from the sporangia, swim about for a few minutes, encyst, and then produce a germ tube by which they can infect the plant. In rare instances sporangia may germinate by directly producing a germ tube. The fungus also produces oospores that germinate by producing a germ tube, which terminates in a sporangium. The sporangium then germinates by means of zoospores, as described above.

Development of disease. The pathogen overwinters as oospores embedded in the dead leaves, and occasionally, in dead berries and shoots. In certain areas, the fungus may also overwinter as mycelium in infected, but not killed, twigs. The dead leaves containing the oospores disintegrate during the winter and liberate the oospores. During rainy periods in the spring the oospores germinate either on the ground or on parts of grape plants to which they are carried by wind or splashing rain drops.

The produced sporangium or its zoospores are transported by wind or water to the - wet leaves near the ground, which they infect. Penetration takes place through stomata of the lower surface of the leaves. The mycelium then spreads into the intercellular spaces of the leaf, obtaining food through globose haustoria, which it sends into the cells.

The mycelium continues to spread into the tissues, and when it reaches the substomatal cavity it forms a cushion of mycelium from which the sporanglophores arise and emerge through the stoma. On these primary lesions, great numbers of sporangia are produced, which may be carried by wind or rain to nearby healthy plants, germinate quickly, and produce many zoospores. The zoospores then cause secondary infections through stomata or lenticels and thus rapidly spread the disease. The period from infection to new sporangia formation varies from 5 to 18 days, depending on temperature, humidity, and varietal susceptibility.

In the stems the fungus invades the cortex, ray parenchyma, and pith. The distortion and hypertrophy of infected stems is caused by the enlargement of the affected cells and the large volume of mycelium present in the intercellular spaces. Finally, the affected stem cells are killed and collapse, producing brown sunken areas in the stem. In the young berries, infection is also intercellular, the chlorophyll breaks down and disappears the cells collapse and turn brown. At the end of the growing season the fungus forms oospores in the infected old leaves, and sometimes in the shoots and berries.

Control. Several American grape varieties show considerable resistance to downy mildew, but most European (*vinifera*) varieties are quite susceptible: even the relatively resistant varieties, however, require protection through chemicals.

The most effective fungicides for control of downy mildew have been Bordeaux mixture, ferbam, zineb, mancozeb, folpet, and captan. The applications begin before bloom and are continued at 7- to 10-day intervals, although the time and number of applications vary with the local conditions, particularly the frequency and duration of rainfall during the growing season.

Disease prediction systems, based on duration of leaf wetness, relative humidity, and temperature are used in Europe and elsewhere to identify infection periods and time fungicide applications. In recent years, soil applications or sprays of the systemic fungicides metalaxyl, fosetyl Al, cyprofuram, and others, alone or in combination with copper oxychloride or mancozeb, have given excellent control of grape down mildew.

Diseases by zygomycetes

The Zygomycetes have well-developed mycelium, also without cross wall, produce nonmotile spores in sporangia, and their resting spore is a thick-walled zygospore produced by the union of two morphologically similar gametes. The Zygomycetes are strictly terrestrial fungi, their spores often floating around in the air, and are either saprophytes or weak parasites of plants and plant products on which they cause soft rots or molds. Some, for example, *Rhizopus*, are opportunistic pathogens of humans.

Two genera of Zygomycetes are known to cause disease in living plants or living plant tissue. These are: (i) *Choanephora*, which attacks the withering floral parts of many plants after fertilization and from them invades the fruit and causes a soft rot of squash, pumpkin, pepper, and okra, but most severely of summer squash; and (2) *Rhizopus*, the common bread mold fungus, which in addition causes soft rot of many fleshy fruits, vegetables, flowers, bulbs, corms, and seeds. Another genus, *Mucor*, also causes molding of bread and other processed plant products, and rarely, a rot of sweet potatoes stored at low temperatures. Other genera, for example, *Glomus* and *Gigaspora*, are fungi that become associated with roots of plants and form endomycorrhizae that are beneficial to the plant.

The plant-pathogenic Zygomycetes ' are weak parasites. They grow mostly as saprophytes on dead or processed plant products, and even when they infect living plant tissues, they first attack injured or dead plant tissues. In the latter, the fungi build up large masses of mycelium. This secretes enzymes that diffuse into the living tissue and disrupt and kill the cells. The mycelium then grows into the "living" tissue.

The Zygomycetes have typical elongated mycelium without cross walls. Their asexual spores are produced within sporangia, are nonmotile, and are called sporangiospores, or conidia. They are generally spread by air currents. Their sexual spores are produced through the fusion of two more or less similar-looking sex cells, they are called zygospores. The zygospores are thick walled and can overwinter or withstand other adverse conditions. Under favorable moisture and temperature conditions the zygospores germinate by producing a sporangium containing sporangiospores.

Rhizopus soft rot of fruits and vegetables

Rhizopus soft rot of fruits and vegetables occurs throughout the world on harvested fleshy organs of vegetable, fruit, and flower crops and is important only during storage, transit, and marketing of these products. Among the crops affected most by this disease are sweet potatoes, strawberries, all cucurbits, peaches, cherries, peanuts, and several other fruits and vegetables. Corn and some other cereals are affected under fairly high conditions of moisture. Bulbs, corms, and rhizomes of flower crops, for example, gladiolus and tulips, are also susceptible to this disease.

When conditions are favorable, the disease spreads rapidly throughout the containers, and losses can be great in a short period of time.

Symptoms. Infected areas of fleshy organs appear water soaked at first, and they are very soft. If the skin of the infected tissues remains intact, the softened fleshy organ gradually loses moisture until it shrivels into a mummy. More frequently, however, the softened skin ruptures during handling or under pressure, for example, from surrounding fruits, and a whitish-yellow liquid drops out. Soon fungus hyphae grow outward through the wounds and cover the affected portions by producing tufts of whiskerlike gray sporangiospores bearing black sporangia at their tips.

The bushy growth of the fungus extends to the surface of the healthy portions of affected fruit when they become wet with the exticling liquid and even to the surface of the containers. Affected tissues at first give off a mildly pleasant smell, but soon yeasts and bacteria move in and a sour odor develops. When loss of moisture is rapid, infected organs finally dry up an mummify; otherwise they break down and disintegrate in a watery rot.

The pathogen: Rhizopus sp. Rhizopus is found almost everywhere in nature. It lives usually as a saprophyte and sometimes as a weak parasite on stored organs of plants. The mycelium of the fungus has no cross walls and produces long, aerial sporangiophores at the tips of which black spherical sporangia develop. These consist of a thin membrane containing thousands of small spherical sporangiospores. When the membrane of the sporangium is ruptured, the liberated sporangiospores are released and float about in the air or drop to the surface. If they fall on a moist surface or wound of a susceptible plant organ, the sporangiospores germinate and produce mycelium again. When the mycelium grows on a surface, it produces stolons, that is, hyphae that arch over the surface and at the next point of contact with the surface produce both rootlike hyphae, called rhizoids, which grow toward the surface, and more aerial sporangiophores bearing sporangia. From each point of contact more stolons are produced in all directions.

Adjacent hyphae produce short branches called progametangia, which grow toward each other. When they come in contact, the tip of each hyphae is separated from the progametangium by a cross wall. The terminal cells are the gametangia. These fuse, their protoplasts mix, and their nuclei pair. The cell formed by the fusion enlarges and develops a thick, black, and warty cell wall. This sexually produced spore is called a zygospore and is the overwintering or resting stage of the fungus. When it germinates it produces a sporangiophore bearing a sporangium full of sporangiospores.

Development of disease. Throughout the year, sporangiospores float about and if they land on wounds of fleshy fruits, roots, corms, or bulbs they germinate. The hyphae thus produced secrete pectinolytic enzymes, which break down and dissolve the pectic substances of the middle lamella, that is, the substances that hold the cells in place in the tissues. This results in loss of cohesion among the cells, since they are now surrounded by liquefied substance, and upon pressure they move freely among each other, resulting in "soft rot."

The pectinolytic enzymes secreted by the fungus advance ahead of the mycelium and separate the cells before the mycelium gets there. Cells in the macerated tissues are then attacked by the cellulolytic enzymes of the fungus, which break down the cellulose of the cell wall, and the cells disintegrate. The mycelium grows intercellularly and does not seem to invade cells until after they are killed and have begun to disintegrate. Thus the mycelium seems never to be in contact with living host cells but is instead surrounded by dead cells, and nonliving organic substances, living more like a saprophyte than a parasite. The epidermis of infected organs is not usually broken down by the fungus, which continues to grow inside the tissues.

The epidermis, however, is softened greatly and breaks easily with the slightest pressure during handling of the product or by the weight of the fruits above it. The fungus then emerges through wounds already existing on the fruit or through subsequent ruptures of the epidermis and produces aerial sporangiophores, sporangia, stolons, and rhizoids, the latter capable of piercing the softened epidermis. In extremely fleshy fruits, such as peaches and strawberries, the mycelium arising from an infected fruit or from a sporangiospore can penetrate healthy fruit in contact with the infected fruit in the absence of visible wounds. In some cases the epidermis of such fruits has already been softened by the fungal enzymes present in the liquid exuding from the infected fruit, but this is not always necessary. Sporangiospores are produced on infected tissue within a few days and can cause new infections immediately after they are released.

Zygospores, however, are produced later, when the food supply in the infected tissues begins to diminish and, with heterothallic species, only when a compatible strain is also present. Since zygospores germinate after a rest period, most infections in storage are caused by asexual sporangiospores, and within a package of fruit, most infections occur from the hyphae growing from the surface of the previously rotted fruit rather than from spores.

The initiation of infection and the invasion of the tissues by the fungus are influenced greatly by temperature and humidity and by the stage of ripeness of the tissue. Unfavorable combinations of temperature and humidity or insufficient maturity of the fruit slow down the growth and activity of the fungus, and they may allow the host to form layers of cork cells and other histological barriers that retard or completely inhibit further infections by the fungus.

Control. Since the spores of the fungus are present everywhere, wounds of any size can be points of infection. Wounding of fleshy fruits, roots, tubers, and bulbs should, therefore, be avoided as much as possible during harvest, handling, and transportation of these products. Wounded organs should be discarded or packed and stored separately from healthy ones. Storage containers and warehouses should be cleaned before use and should be disinfected with a copper sulfate solution, formaldehyde, sulfur fumes or chloropicrin.

Temperature control of storage rooms and shipping cars is important. With very succulent fruits, such as strawberries, picking fruit in the morning when it is cool and keeping it at temperatures below 10°C reduces losses considerably. Sweet potatoes and some other not so succulent organs may be protected from the disease by keeping them at 25-30°C and go percent humidity for 10-14 days, during which the cut surfaces cork over and do not allow subsequent penetration by the fungus. After this period is over, temperature is lowered again to about 12°C. Quite effective control of the disease can be obtained by wrapping susceptible fruit in paper impregnated with various fungicidal substances such as dichloran.

Chapter 2

Protection of Plants

The most common means of direct protection of plants from pathogens include some biological controls (fungal and bacterial antagonists) but primarily the chemical 'control measures, that is, the use of chemicals for foliar sprays and dusts, seed treatments, treatment of tree wounds, and control of postharvest diseases of produce. Biological control practices for direct protection of plants from pathogens involve the deployment of antagonistic microorganisms at the infection court before or after infection takes place. Biocontrol of chestnut blight with hypovirulent strains of the pathogen Chestnut blight, caused by the fungus Endothia parasitica, is controlled naturally in Italy, and artificially in France through inoculation of cankers, caused by the normal pathogenic strains of the fungus, with hypovirulent strains of the same fungus. The hypovirulent strains carry viruslike double-stranded (ds) RNAs that apparently limit their pathogenicity. The ds RNAs apparently pass through mycelial anastomoses from the hypovirulent to the virulent strains, the latter are rendered hypovirulent, and the development of the canker slows down or stops. Hypovirulent strains are being tested in the United States also, but so far control of chestnut blight has been limited to experimental trees.

Biological cntrol of fusarium wilt with a nonpathogenic strain fusarium wilt of sweet potato, caused by Fusarium oxysporum f, sp. batatas, was recently reported to be successfully controlled by inoculating sweet potato cuttings with a nonpathogenic strain of the same fungus. This strain had been isolated from the vascular tissue of a sweet potato plant that remained healthy among other plants that had been killed by the wilt-inducing strains of the fungus.

Biological control of diseases of aerial plant parts with fungi Many filamentous fungi and yeasts have been shown to be effective antagonists of fungi infecting the aerial parts of plants. For example, inoculation of postbloom, dead, tomato flowers with conidia of Cladosporium herbarum or Penicillium sp. almost completely suppressed subsequent infection of developing fruits by Botrytis cinerea. Similarly, spraying spores of common bark saprophytes, such as Cladosporium sp. and Epicoccum sp., and of the soil fungus Trichoderma on pruning cuts of fruit trees has prevented infection by canker-causing pathogens such as Nectria galligena and Cytospora sp. Sprays with Trichoderma in the field also reduced Botrytis rot of strawberries and of grapes at the time of harvest and in storage. Several foliar diseases have also been reduced significantly (by more than 50 percent) when the leaves were sprayed with spores of common phylloplane fungi, for example, Alternaria, Cochliobolus, Septoria, Colletotrichum, and Phoma, or with spores of hyperparasites, for example, the cucumber powdery mildew fungus Sphaerotheca fuliginea with spores of Ampelomyces quisqualis, of the wheat leaf rust fungus Puccinia recondita with spores of Darluca filum, and of the carnation rust fungus with *Verticillium lecanii*. None of the above, and of numerous other known cases of fungal antagonism by fungi, is used as yet for practical control of any disease of aerial plant parts.

Biological control of postharvest diseases Postharvest rots of several fruits could be reduced considerably by spraying with spores of antagonistic fungi at different stages of fruit development or by dipping the harvested fruit in the inoculum. For example, significant reduction of citrus green mold (caused by Penicillium digitatum) was obtained by treating the fruit with the antagonist Trichodernia viride, while preharvest and postharvest Botrytis rot of strawberries was reduced by several sprays of Trichoderma spores on strawberry blossoms and young fruit. Similarly, Penicilliurn rot of pineapple was reduced considerably by spraying the fruit with nonpathogenic strains of the pathogen.

Biocontrol of root pathogens by mycorrhizae Roots of most plants form a symbiotic relationship with certain kinds of zygomycete, ascomycete, and basidiomycete fungi (mycorrhizae). Mycorrhizae colonize roots intercellularly (ectomycorrhizae) or intracellularly (endomycorrhizae). Although mycorrhizae obtain organic nutrients from the plant, they benefit the plant by promoting nutrient uptake and enhancing water transport by the plant, thus increasing growth and yield, and sometimes by providing the plant with considerable protection against several soil-borne pathogens. Mycorrhizae have been shown to provide considerable protection to pine seedlings from Phytophthora cinnamomi, to tomato and douglas fir seedlings from Fusarium oxysporum, to cotton from Verticillium wilt and the root knot nematode, and to soybean from Phytophthora megasperma and Fusarium solani. Commercial preparations of certain mycorrhizal fungi are available against some of these pathogens, but problems of production, specificity, and application of mycorrhizae to plants remain.

Biocontrol of crown gaff with agrobacterium radiobacter strain K84 Crown gall of pome, stone, and several small fruits (grapes, raspberries) and ornamentals (rose and euvonymous) is caused by the bacterium Agrobacterium tumefaciens. For several years now, crown gall has been controlled commercially by treating the seeds, seedlings, and cuttings with a suspension of strain K84 of the related but nonpathogenic bacterium Agrobacterium radiobacter.

Control is based on production by strain 84 of a bacteriocin, that is, an antibiotic specific against related bacteria and called agrocin 84. The bacteriocin selectively inhibits most pathogenic agrobacteria that arrive at surfaces occupied by strain 84. Strains of A. tumefaciens insensitive to agrocin 84 have been reported in several countries. Seed bacterization Treatment of seeds such as cereals, sweet corn, and carrots with water suspensions, slurries, or powders containing the bacteria Bacillus subtilis strain A' 3 or Streptomyces sp. has protected the plants against root pathogens and has resulted in better growth and yield of these crops. *Pseudomonas* rhizobacteria, primarily of the P. fluorescens and P. putida groups, applied to seeds, seed pieces, and roots of plants have resulted in less soft rot and in consistent increases in growth and yield in several crops. For example, in some experiments, treated potato seed tubers produced from 5 to 33 percent greater yield; treated sugarbeet seeds produced 4-6 more tons of sugarbeets per hectare, corresponding to an increase of from 955 to 1227 kilograms of sugar per acre; treated radish seeds produced from 60 to 144 percent more root weight than untreated ones, and treated wheat seed planted in Gaeumannomyces graminis tritici (take-all of wheat)-infected soil, produced 27 percent more yield than untreated seed, The mechanism or mechanisms by which these plant growth-promoting rhizobacteria increase yield is not clear. It appears, however, that inhibition of harmful, toxic microorganism & and of soil-borne pathogens by antibiotics or by competition for iron, are at least some of the determinants of their effectiveness.

Biocontrol of postharvest diseases

When several kinds of stone fruits, that is, peaches, nectarines, apricots, and plums, were treated after harvest with suspensions of the antagonistic bacterium Bacillus subtilis, they remained free of brown rot, caused by the fungus Monilinia fructicola, for at least nine days.

Biocontrol with bacteria of bacteria-mediated frost injury

Frost-sensitive plants are injured when temperatures drop below 0°C because ice forms within their tissues. Small volumes of pure water can be supercooled to -10°C or below without ice formation, provided no catalyst centers or nuclei are present to influence ice formation. It has been shown recently, however, that certain strains of at least three species of epiphytic bacteria (Pseudomonas syringae, P. fluorescens, and Erwinia herbicola), which are present on many plants, serve as ice-nucleaction-active catalysts for ice formation at as high temperatures as -1°C. Such bacteria usually make up a small proportion (0.1- 10 percent) of the bacteria found on leaf surfaces. By isolating, culturing, mass producing, and applying on the plant surfaces non-ice-nucleation active bacteria antagonistic to the ice-nucleation-active bacteria, it has been possible to reduce and replace numbers of ice-nucleation-active bacteria on treated plant surfaces with non-ice-nucleation active bacteria. This treatment protects frost-sensitive plants from injury at temperatures at which untreated plants may be severely injured.

Biological control of diseases of aerial plant parts with bacteria

Numerous bacteria, most of them saprophytic Gram-negative bacteria of the genera Erwinia, Pseudomonas, and Xanthomonas, and fewer of the Gram-positive genera Bacillus, Lactobacillus, and Corynebacterium, are found on aerial plant surfaces, particularly early in the growing season. Some pathogenic bacteria, such as

Pseudomonas syringae pv. syringae, Ps. pv. morsprunorum, R's. pv glycinea, Erwinia amylovora, and E. carotovora also live epiphytically (on the surface) on leaves, buds, and so on before they infect and cause disease. In several cases, spraying leaf surfaces with preparations of saprophytic bacteria, or with avirulent strains of pathogenic bacteria, has reduced considerably the number of infections caused by bacteria] -and fungal pathogens.

For example, fire blight of apple blossoms, caused by Erwinia amylovora, was partially controlled with sprays of Erwinia herbicola; bacteria leaf streak of rice, caused by Xanthomonas translucens ssp. oryzicola, was reduced with sprays of isolates of Erwinia and of Pseudomonas. Similarly, sprays with non-ice-nucleating strains of Pseudomonas syringae and Erwinia herbicola reduced the numbers and protected from frost plants carrying the normal complement of ice-nucleating strains of the same species of bacteria.

Several cases of added epiphytic bacteria inhibiting plant infections by fungi are also known. For example, spraying grass plants with Pseudomonas fluorescens reduced infection by Drechslera (Helminthosporium) dictyoides, spraying with Bacillus subtilis reduced infection of apple leaf scars by Nectria galligena, and spraying of peanut or tobacco plants with Pseudomonas cepacia or Bacillus sp. reduced Cercospora and Alternaria leaf spot on these hosts, respectively. None of these biological controls is used in practice to control any disease of aerial plant parts as well.

All pathogens—fungi, bacteria, mycoplasmas, and nematodes—are attacked by viruses. So far, however, only for bacterial pathogens have viruses been tested as possible biological controls. Bacteriophages or phage (bacteria-destroying viruses) are known to exist in nature for most plant pathogenic bacteria. Successful experimental control of several bacterial diseases was obtained when the bacteriophages were mixed with the inoculated bacteria, when the plants were first treated with bacteriophages and then inoculated with bacteria, and when the seed was treated with the phage. In practice, however, not one bacterial disease is controlled effectively by bacteriophage. Also, no plant disease caused by a bacterium has been cured yet by treatment with phage after the disease has developed.

The most commonly known means of controlling plant diseases in the field and in the greenhouse and, sometimes, in storage, is through the use of chemical compounds that are toxic to the pathogens. Such chemicals either inhibit germination, growth, and multiplication of the pathogen or are outright lethal to the pathogen. Depending on the kind of pathogens they affect, the chemicals are called fungicides, bactericides, nematicides, viricides, or for the parasitic higher plants, herbicides. Some chemicals are toxic to all or most kinds of pathogens, others affect only one kind of pathogen, and certain compound are toxic to only a few or a single specific pathogen. About 60 percent of all the chemicals (mostly fungicides) used to control plant diseases is applied to fruit and about 25 percent to vegetables. Most of the chemicals are used to control diseases of the foliage and of other aboveground parts of plants. Others are used to disinfects and protect from infection seeds, tubers, and bulbs. Some are used to disinfest the soil, others to disinfest warehouses, to treat wounds, or to protect stored fruit and vegetables from infection. Still others (insecticides) are used to control the insect vectors of some pathogens.

The great majority of older chemicals applied on plants or plant organs could only protect them from subsequent infection and could not stop or cure a disease after it had started. The great majority of these chemicals are effective only in the plant area to which they have been applied (iocal action) and are not absorbed or translocated by the plants. Many new chemicals, however, do have a therapeutic (eradicant) action, and several are absorbed and systemically translocated by the plant (systemic fungicides and antibiotics).

Faliage sprays and dusts

Chemicals applied as sprays or dusts on the foliage of plants are usually aimed at control of fungus diseases and to a lesser extent control of bacterial diseases. Most fungicides and bactericides are protectants and must be present on the surface of the plant in advance of the pathogen in order to prevent infection. Their presence usually does not allow fungus spores to germinate or they may kill spores upon germination. Contact of bacteria with bactericides may inhibit their multiplication or cause their death. Some newer fungicides also have a direct effect on pathogens that have already invaded the leaves, fruit, and stem, and in this case they act as eradicants, that is they kill the fungus inside the host, or they may suppress the sporulation of the fungus without killing it. Some fungicides, such as dodine, have a partial systemic action because they can be absorbed by a part of the leaf tissues and translocated internally into the whole leaf area. Several fungicides- benomyl, thiabendazole, carboxin, and metalaxyl-are clearly systemics and can be translocated internally throughout the host plant. Some bactericides, for example, streptomycin, are also systemics, as are most antibiotics. Some newer systemic fungicides, such as the sterol inhibitors triadimefon, fenarimol, and metalaxyl, are so effective in postinfection applications that they can be used as rescue treatments of crops; in other words, they can be applied effectively after an epidemic is well under way.

Fungicides and bactericides applied as sprays appear to be more efficient than when applied as dusts. Although it may appear that dusts are preferable to sprays if application is to be made during a rain because they adhere better to wet plant tissues, in reality, neither sticks well when applied during a rain.

Sometimes other compounds, for example, lime, may be added to the active chemical in order to reduce its phytotoxicity and make it safer for the plant. Compounds with a low surface tension, such as detergents, are often added to fungicides so that they spread better, thereby increasing the contact area between fungicide and the sprayed surface. Finally, some compounds, for example, starch and oils, are added to increase the adherence of the fungicide to the plant surface. In fields with sprinkler irrigation available, satisfactory control of many foliar diseases on a variety of crops has recently been obtained by applying protectant or systemic fungicides to the foliage, and somewhat to the roots, through the irrigation system (fungigation). Because many fungicides and bactericides are protectant in their action, it is important that they be at the plant surface before the pathogen arrives or at least before it has had time to germinate, enter, and establish itself in the host. Considering that many fungicides and bactericides are effective only upon contact with the pathogen, it is important that the whole surface of the plant be covered with the chemical in order to be protected. For this reason, young, expanding leaves, twigs, and fruits must be sprayed more often than mature tissues, since small, growing leaves may outgrow protection 3 to 5 days after spraying. The interval between sprays of mature tissue may vary from 7 to 14 days or longer, depending on the particular disease, the frequency and duration of rains, the persistence or residual life of the fungicide, and the season of the year.

The same factors also determine the optimal number of sprays per season, which may vary from 2 or 3 to 15 or more. Some types of equipment used for spraying and dusting plants and for injecting chemicals into plants or into the soil.

In the last several years, several systemic fungicides have become available, and their number, ease of application, duration of effectiveness, and even the number of diseases they control are increasing steadily. Systemic chemicals are gradually replacing many of the contact, preventive fungicides because of their effectiveness, long-lasting activity, and the limited number of applications required to protect a crop from one or many diseases.

The number and variety of chemicals used for foliar sprays and dusts is quite large. Some of these compounds are specific against certain diseases, others are effective against a wide spectrum of pathogens. Sprays with these materials usually contain 0.5-2 lb of the compound per hundred gallons of water, although some, for example, sulfur, are applied at 4-6 lb per 100 gallons of water. Some of the fungicides used for foliar sprays or dusts are also used for seed treatments.

Seeds, tubers, bulbs, and roots are usually treated with chemicals to prevent their decay after planting or damping off of young seedlings by controlling pathogens carried on them or existing in the soil where they will be planted. More recently, seeds have been treated with systemic fungicides in order to inactivate pathogens in infected seeds (for example, carboxin for control of loose smut), or in order to provide the foliage of the developing plant with systemic protection against the pathogen (for example, metalaxyl for control of downy mildews of oats and sorghum and triadimenol for control of leaf rust and Septoria leaf blotch of wheat and of Pyrenophora net blotch of barley). Chemicals can be applied on the seed as dusts or as thick water suspensions mixed with the seed. The seed can also be soaked in a water or solvent solution of the chemical and then allowed to dry.

Tubers, bulbs, corms, and roots can be treated in similar ways. In treating seeds or any other propagative organs with chemicals, precautions must be taken so that their viability is not lowered or destroyed.

At the same time, enough chemical must stick to the seed to protect it from attacks of pathogens and, when the seed is planted, to diffuse into, and disinfest a sphere of soil around the seed in which the new plant will grow without being attacked at this particularly vulnerable period of growth. Chemicals used to treat seeds, bulbs, corms, tubers, and roots include some inorganic copper and zinc compounds, but mostly organic protectant compounds such as captan, chloroneb, chloranil, dichlone, hexachlorobenzene, maneb, zineb, mancozeb, thiram, pentachloronitrobenzene (PCNB), and the systemic compounds carboxin, benomyl, thiabendazole, methalaxyl, triadimenol, and streptomycin. Some chemicals may control specific diseases of some plants while others are more general in their action and may control many diseases of a number of plants.

In addition to treating (fumigating) soil to be planted with vegetables, ornamentals, or trees with volatile chemicals (fumigants) for control of nematodes, fungi, and bacteria by reducing the inoculum, certain fungicides are applied to the soil as dusts, drenches, or granules to control damping off, seedling blights, crown and root rots, and other diseases. Such fungicides include captan, diazoben, PCNB, and chloroneb, metalaxyl, fosetyl-Al, triadimefon, ethazol, and propamocarb. Many of the systemic fungicides, for example, matalaxyl, fosetyl-Al, are so effective even in small amounts that a single preplant broadcast soil spray followed by disking can provide a full season's protection to the crop from several of the pathogens it normally controls. In many cases, foliar diseases (such as downy mildews and rusts) can be controlled by impregnating the fungicide (for example, metalaxyl, triadimenol) into the fertilizer and applying them together before planting. In recent years, protective and systemic fungicides have been applied to the soil (and to the foliage) through the irrigation water (fungigation) for control of soil-borne diseases.

Large pruning cuts and wounds made on the bark of branches and trunks accidentally or in the process of removing infections of fungi and bacteria need to be protected from drying and from becoming ports of entry for new pathogens. Drying of the margins of large tree wounds is usually prevented by painting them with shellac or any commercial wound dressing. The exposed wood is then sterilized by swabbing it with a solution of either 0.5-1.0 per cent sodium hypochlorite (10-20 per cent Clorox), or with 70 percent ethyl alcohol. Finally, the entire wound is painted with a permanent, tree wound dressing, such as a 10: 2: 2 mixture of lanolin, rosin, and gum, or Cerano, or Bordeaux paint, or an asphalt-varnish tree paint. Some wound dressings, such as Cerano and Bordeaux paint, are themselves disinfectants, while most others require the addition of a disinfectant, such as 0.25 percent phenyl mercuric nitrate or 6 percent phenol. It must be kept in mind, however, that many commercial wound dressings, especially those that are asphalt-based, are phytotoxic enough to prevent, rather than promote, wound healing.

The use of chemicals for the control of postharvest diseases of fruits and vegetables is complicated enormously by the fact that most compounds effective against storage diseases leave on the produce high concentrations of residues that are toxic to consumers.

Many chemicals also cause injury to the products under storage conditions and give off undesirable odors.

A number of fungitoxic chemicals, however, most of them used specifically for control of postharvest diseases, have been developed. Most of them are used as dilute solutions into which the fruits or vegetables are dipped before storage, or as solutions used for washing or hydrocooling of fruits and vegetables immediately after harvest.

Some chemicals, for example, elemental sulfur, are used as dusts or crystals that undergo sublimation in storage, and others, such as SO_2, as gases. Finally, some chemicals are impregnated in the boxes or wrappers containing the fruit.

Among the compounds used for commercial control of postharvest diseases of, primarily, citrus fruits but also of other fruits are borax, biphenyl, sodium o-phenylphenate, benomyl, thiabendazole, and imazalil.

Certain other chemicals, such as elemental sulfur, sulfur dioxide, dichloran, captan, and benzoic acid, have been used mostly for the control of storage rots of stone and pome fruits, bananas, grapes, strawberries, melons, and potatoes.

Many hundreds of chemicals have been advanced to date for crop protection as fumigants, soil treatments, sprays, dusts, paints, pastes, and systemics. The most important of these chemicals and some of their properties and uses are described below.

Copper compounds Bordeaux mixture, the product of reaction of copper sulfate and calcium hydroxide (lime), is the most widely used copper fungicide throughout the world. It controls many fungus and bacterial leaf spots, blights, anthracnoses, downy mildews, and cankers but causes burning of leaves or russeting of fruit such as apples when applied in cool, wet weather. The phytotoxicity of Bordeaux is reduced by increasing the ratio of lime to copper sulfate. Copper is the only ingredient in the Bordeaux mixture that is toxic to pathogens and, sometimes, to plants, while lime's role is primarily that of a "safener."

For dormant sprays, concentrated Bordeaux is made by mixing io pounds of copper sulfate, io pounds of lime, and 100 gallons of water; it has the formula 10: 10: 100. The most commonly used formula for Bordeaux is 8: 8: 100. For spraying young, actively growing plants, the amounts of copper sulfate and lime are reduced, and the formulas used may be 2:2:100, 2:6: 100, and so on. For plants known to be sensitive to Bordeaux, a much greater concentration of lime may be used, as in the formula 8:24:100. In the "fixed" or "insoluble" copper compounds the copper ion is only slightly soluble, and these compounds are, therefore, less phytotoxic than Bordeaux, but also less effective as fungicides.

Kocide is a copper formulation fungicide and bactericide that contains copper hydroxide. The latter is formulated so that it exhibits a large surface area, which probably accounts for the increased availability of the soluble cupric ion at the plant surface. It controls the same diseases as the other copper compounds, but because it is more soluble and it is used in smaller amounts, it does not clog spray nozzles as often.

The element sulfur as a dust, wettable powder, paste, or liquid is used primarily to control powdery mildews on many plants, but it is also effective against certain rusts, leaf blights, and fruit rots. Sulfur, in its different forms, is available under a variety of trade names. Most sulfur formulations are applied at the rate of i to 6 lb per 100 gallons of water and may cause injury in hot (temperatures above 30°C), dry weather, especially to sulfur-sensitive plants such as tomato, melons, and grape. By boiling lime and sulfur together lime-sulfur, self-boiled lime-sulfur, and dry lime-sulfur are produced, which are used as sprays for dormant fruit trees to control blight or anthracnose, powdery mildew, apple scab, brown rot of stone fruits, and peach leaf curl and are sometimes used for summer control of the same diseases.

Chapter 3

Diseases by Ascomycetes and Imperfect Fungi

Ascomycetes and imperfect fungi (Deuteromycetes) are two groups of fungi that closely resemble each other in the structure of the mycelium, the production of asexual spores, and in the kinds of diseases they cause in plants, as well as in the way they induce these diseases. Thus, both produce a haploid mycelium that has cross walls, both produce conidia in identical types of conidiophores or fruiting bodies, and both cause plant diseases that may appear as leaf spots, blights, cankers, fruit spots, fruit rots, anthracnoses, stem rots, root rots, vascular wilts, or soft rots.

The only difference between Ascomycetes and Imperfect Fungi is that the former also produce, regularly or rarely, sexual spores, known as ascospores. In many Ascomycetes, however, ascospores are seldom found in nature and seem to play little or no role in the survival of the fungus and in its ability to cause disease in plants. Thus, such Ascomycetes reproduce, spread, cause disease, and overwinter as mycelium or conidia, or both, so that they actually behave as, and for all practical purposes could be considered, Imperfect Fungi.

On the other hand, for many fungi that were earlier classified as Imperfect Fungi, fruiting bodies containing sexual spores were later shown to be produced by them, and since the sexual spores were almost always ascospores, these Imperfect Fungi were then reclassified as Ascomycetes. It would appear, therefore, that Imperfect Fungi are really Ascomycetes that have lost the need for or the ability to produce their sexual stage. Actually, for many of the Ascomycetes, the asexual, imperfect stages are the most common or the only ones found on diseased plants during the growing season and even during the winter. Such Ascomycetes are usually referred to and are best known by the name of their asexual stage, which is generally completely different from the name of the sexual, ascigerous stage.

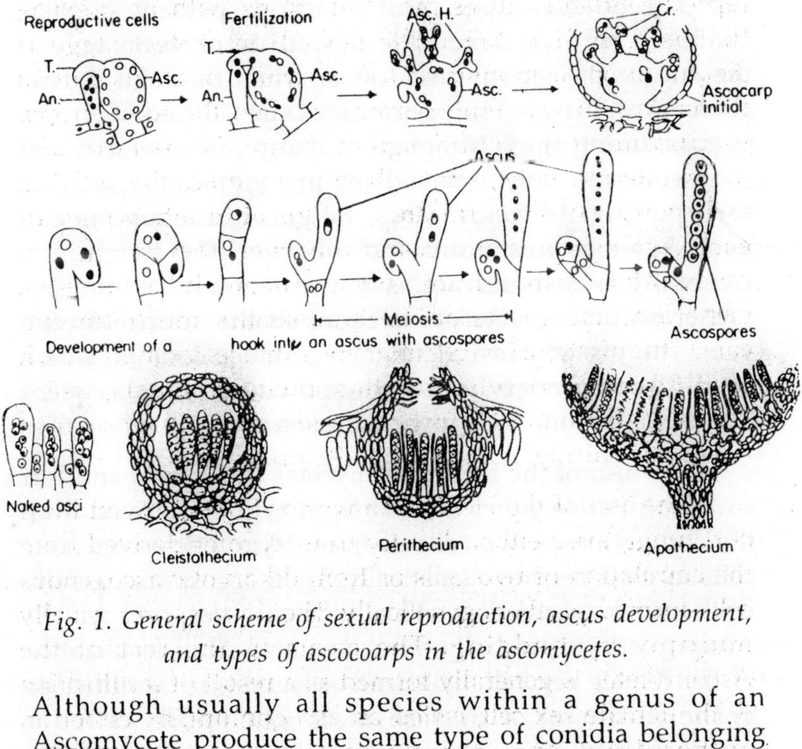

Fig. 1. General scheme of sexual reproduction, ascus development, and types of ascocoarps in the ascomycetes.

Although usually all species within a genus of an Ascomycete produce the same type of conidia belonging to one genus of an Imperfect Fungus, and various species within a genus of an Imperfect Fungus belong to one genus of an Ascomycete, this is not always so. In many instances, different species within a genus of an Ascomycete have asexual stages that belong to species in other genera of Imperfect Fungi, and vice versa. Ascomycetes (the sac fungi) produce mycelium that has cross walls, sexual spores - ascospores -within a sac-ascus- and asexual spores-conidia.

The ascus or sexual stage of Ascomycetes is often called the teleomorph or perfect stage, while the conidial or asexual stage is the anamorph or imperfect stage. In almost all plant pathogenic Ascomycetes during the growing season, the fungus exists as mycelium and reproduces and causes most infections with its asexual, that is, conidial stage. The sexual or perfect stage is produced on or in infected leaves, fruits, or stems only at the end of the growing season or when the food supply is diminishing. The perfect stage is usually the overwintering stage, although in many cases the asci and ascospores do not form and mature until late winter or early spring. In many cases, however, the fungus can overwinter as mycelium and, occasionally, as conidia. Generally, ascospores act as the primary inoculum and cause the first (primary) infections in the spring of each year. The primary infections then produce conidia, which act as the secondary inoculum and cause all subsequent infections during the growing season.

The asci of the Herniascomycetes (the yeasts and leaf curl fungi) arise either directly from zygotes derived from the copulation of two cells or from dikaryotic ascogenous cells formed parthenogenetically. Their ascospores usually multiply by budding. The ascus in the rest of the Ascomycetes is generally formed as a result of fertilization of the female sex cell, called an ascogonium, by either an antheridium or a minute male sex spore called a spermatium.

In either case, the fertilized ascogonium produces one to many ascogenous hyphae, the cells of which are dikaryotic, that is, they contain two haploid nuclei, one male and one female. By a rather complicated process, the cell at the tip of each ascogenous hypha develops into an ascus, in which the two nuclei fuse to produce a zygote which then undergoes meiosis to produce four haploid nuclei. The cell, in which these nuclei are, elongates and all four nuclei undergo mitosis and produce eight haploid nuclei. Each nucleus is then surrounded by a portion of the cytoplasm and is enveloped by a wall, thus becoming a spore inside an ascus, that is, an ascospore. There are usually eight ascospores per ascus.

The asci in some Ascomycetes, for, example, in the yeasts and leaf curl fungi, are naked-they are not produced inside fruiting bodies but in all other Ascomycetes the asci are produced, singly or in groups, in fruiting bodies called ascocarps. In some, such as the powdery mildews, of the Pyrenomycetes (Perithecial Ascomycetes), the ascocarp is a completely closed spherical container and is called a cleistothecium. In others, such as most of the Pyrenomycetes, the ascocarp is more or less closed, but at maturity it has an opening through which the ascospores escape and such ascocarp is called a perithecium. In the Loculoascomycetes (ascostromatic ascomycetes), the asci are formed directly in cavities within a stroma (matrix) of mycelium, and this ascocarp is called pseudothecium or an ascotroma.

Finally, in the Discomycetes (cup ascomycetes), the asci are produced in an open, cup or saucer-shaped ascocarp called an apothecium. Ascomycetes are characterizd and identified by the characteristics of their ascocarps, asci, and ascospores. However, during the growing season and most of the year, these structures are not produced and cannot be found on diseased plant tissue. What one finds on diseased plants during the growing season are mycelium and asexual spores, that is, conidia.

The conidia themselves often have distinct characteristics that may be sufficient to identify the fungus. In the Imperfect Fungi and in those of the Ascomycetes that exist primarily as their imperfect stage, the conidial characteristics plus the shape of the conidiophore, that is, the hypha that produces the conidium, the arrangement of the conidiophores and the way the conidia are borne on the conidiophore may have to be determined so that the fungus can be identified. In many cases, the conidia are borne singly or in chains at the tips of conidiophores arising from the mycelium, free from each other.

These fungi belong to the order Hyphales (Moniliales) of the class Hyphomycetes of the Imperfect Fungi. In the same order, Hyphales, belong the fungi whose conidiophores are produced on a cushion-shaped stroma of mycelium and the whole structure is called a sporodochium, or whose conidiophores are cemented together into an elongated spore-bearing structure called synnema. In many other cases, conidiophores may be organized into definite fruiting bodies. The most common fruiting body that contains conidiophores and conidia is the pycnidium, and fungi that produce pycnidium belong to the other Sphaeropsidales of the class Coelomycetes of the Imperfect Fungi.

Pycnidium is a hollow, more or less spherical or flask-shaped structure, its walls made of mycelial cells that give rise to the conidiophores. Pycnidia may be almost on the surface of the diseased plant or may be more or less embedded in the diseased tissues. Another type of asexual fruiting body, produced by fungi belonging to the order Melanconiales of the Imperfect Fungi, is the acervulus; this is formed by a mat of hyphae below the epidermis or cuticle of the diseased plant giving rise to short conidiophores packed closely together and producing conidia at their tips. As a rule, Ascomycetes overwinter as immature or mature ascocarps that in late winter or early spring produce ascospores in asci. In the spring the ascus releases the ascospores, which germinate by one or more germ tubes and cause the primary-the first infection-of the host plant.

The germ tubes grow into hyphae and mycelium that have cross walls. The mycelium soon forms conidiophores that produce conidia. The conidia, produced continually by the myceliurn as long as conditions are favorable, spread to other plants, germinate by one or more germ tubes and cause new, secondary infections, which will again produce identical mycelium, conidiophores, and conidia. Thus, a large number of asexual generations are produced during the growing season. When conditions become unfavorable, the same myceliurn produces the sexual cells that result in the overwintering structure and production of the ascus and ascospores the following spring.

Some Ascomycetes and all Imperfect Fungi overwinter as mycelium or conidia. These then, with or without the presence of ascospores, may start the primary infections.

Sooty molds

Sooty molds appear on the leaves or stems of plants as a superficial, black growth of mycelium forming a film or crust on these plant parts. Sooty molds may be found on all types of plants, including grasses, ornamentals, crop plants, shrubs, and trees. They are most common in warm, humid weather. Sooty molds are caused by several species of fungi of various types, but primarily dark-colored Ascomycetes of the order Dothideales.

These fungi for example, *Capnodium, Limacinia,* are not parasitic but live off the "honey dew," the sugary deposit forming on plant parts from the droppings of certain insects, particularly aphids and scale insects. The fungal growth is so abundant that it gives the leaf the black, sooty appearance and interferes with the amount of light that reaches the plant. This mycelium sometimes forms a black papery layer that can be peeled off from the underlying leaf.

The presence of the sooty mold fungi is usually of rather minor importance to the health of the plant, but it does indicate the presence of insects and may be a warning of a severe aphid or scale problem. Sooty molds can be diagnosed easily by the fact that the black sooty mycelial growth can be completely wiped off a leaf or stem with a moistened cloth, paper, or hand, leaving a clean, healthy-looking plant surface underneath. No control measures are applied against the sooty mold fungi. Since they grow on the excretions of the insects, control of the particular insect with the appropriate insecticide or other means also results in the elimination of the sooty mold fungi.

Leaf curt diseases by taphrina

Several species of *Taphrina* cause leaf, flower, and fruit deformation on several stone fruit and forest trees. Thus *T. deformans* causes leaf curl on peach and nectarine, *T. communis* and *T. pruni* cause plum pocket on American and European plums, respectively, *T. cerasi* causes leaf curl and witches'-broom on cherries, and *T. coerulescens* causes leaf blister of oak. Leaf blister of oak causes local swollen areas on leaves that sometimes result in moderate to heavy (50-85 percent) defoliation by midsummer and weakening of the trees. The most important losses, however, are those caused primarily on peach, nectarine, and sometimes plum.

The *Taphrina* diseases are best known in Europe and North America but probably occur all over the world.

Taphrina causes defoliation of peach trees, which may lead to small fruit or fruit drop. In plum, 50 percent or more of the fruit may be affected and lost in years when the disease is severe. In both peach and plum, buds and twigs may also be affected, thus devitalizing the tree.

Symptoms. In peach and nectarine parts of or entire infected leaves are thickened, swollen, distorted, and curled downward and inward. Affected leaves at first appear reddish or purplish but later turn reddish yellow or yellowish gray. At this stage the fungus produces its spores on the swollen areas, which appear powdery gray. The leaves later turn yellow to brown and drop. Blossoms, young fruit, and the current year's twigs may also be attacked. Infected blossoms and fruit generally fall early in the season. The infected twigs are always swollen and stunted and die during the summer.

In plum, the disease first appears as small white blisters on the fruit. The blisters enlarge rapidly as the fruit develops and soon involve the entire fruit. The fruit increases abnormally in size and is distorted, the flesh becoming spongy. The seed ceases to develop, turns brown, and withers, leaving a hollow cavity. The fruit appears reddish at first, but later becomes gray and covered with a grayish powder. Leaves and twigs may also be affected, as in peach.

The Pathogen: Taphrina sp. The mycelial cells of Taphrina contain two nuclei. These cells may develop into an ascus, usually containing eight uninucleate ascospores. The ascospores multiply by budding inside or outside the ascus producing blastospores (conidia).

The latter may bud again to produce more thin- or thick-walled conidia or may germinate to produce mycelium. Upon germination, the conidial nucleus divides and the two nuclei move into the germ tube. As the mycelium grows; both nuclei divide concurrently, producing the binucleate cells of the mycelium. Mycelial cells near the plant surface separate from each other and produce the asci.

Development of disease. The fungus apparently overwinters as ascospores or thick-walled conidia on the tree, perhaps on the bud scales. In the spring, these spores are washed, splashed, or blown onto young tissues, germinate, and penetrate the developing leaves and other organs directly through the cuticle or through stomata.

The binucleate mycelium then grows between cells and invades the tissues extensively, inducing excessive cell enlargement and cell division, which result in the enlargement and distortion of the plant organs. Later, numerous hyphae grow outward in the area between the cuticle and epidermis. There they break into their component cells, which produce the asci. The asci enlarge, exert pressure on the host cuticle from below, and eventually break through to form a compact, feltlike layer of naked asci.

The ascospores are released into the air, carried to new tissues, and bud to form conidia. Infection occurs mainly during a short period after the buds open. All organs become resistant to infection as they grow older. Infection is favored by low temperature and a high humidity from the time of bud swell until young shoots and leaves develop, that is, the period during which the new tissues are susceptible.

Control. Taphrina diseases are easily controlled by a single fungicide spray, preferably in late fall after the leaves have fallen or in early spring before leaf buds swell. The fungicides most commonly used are ferbam, elgetol, and Bordeaux mixture (8:8:100). Difolatan may also be used as one application only, before leaf drop is complete, while chlorothalonil controls the disease applied twice, in late fall and in early spring.

Powdery mildews

Powdery mildews are probably the most common, conspicuous, wide-spread, and easily recognizable plant diseases. They affect all kinds of plants: cereals and grasses, vegetables, ornamentals, weeds, shrubs, fruit trees, and broad-leaved shade and forest trees.

Powdery mildews are characterized by the appearance of spots or patches of a white to grayish, powdery, mildewy growth on young plant tissues, or of entire leaves and other organs being completely covered by the white powdery mildew.

Tiny, pinhead-sized, spherical fruiting bodies, at first white, later yellow-brown, and finally black cleistothecia may be present singly or in groups on the white to grayish mildew in the older areas of infection. Powdery mildew is most commonly observed on the upper side of the leaves, but it also affects the under side of leaves, young shoots and sterns, buds, flowers, and young fruit. The fungi causing powdery mildews are obligate parasites they cannot be cultured on artificial nutrient media. They produce mycelium that grows only on the surface of plant tissues, never invading the tissues themselves. They obtain nutrients from the plant by sending haustoria (feeding organs) into the epidermal cells of the plant organs.

The myceliurn produces short conidiophores on the plant surface. Each canidiophore produces chains of rectangular, ovoid, or round conidia that are carried by air currents. When environmental conditions or nutrition become unfavorable, the fungus may produce one or a few asci inside a closed ascocarp, the cleistothecium. The powdery mildew fungi, although they are common and cause serious diseases in coot or warm, humid areas, are even more common and severe in warm, dry climates.

This happens because their spores can be released, germinate, and cause infection even when the relative humidity in the air is fairly high but there is no film of water on the plant surface.

Once infection has begun, the myceliurn continues to spread on the plant surface regardless of the moisture conditions in the atmosphere. Powdery mildews are so common, widespread, and ever present among crop plants and ornamentals that the total losses, in plant growth and crop yield they cause each year on all crops, probably surpass the losses caused by any other single type of plant disease. Powdery mildews seldom kill their hosts but utilize their nutrients, reduce photosynthesis, increase respiration and transpiration, impair their growth, and reduce yields, sometimes by as much as 20-40 percent. Among the plants most severely affected by powdery mildew are the various cereals, such as wheat and barley, primarily because in these crops chemical control of plant diseases is difficult or impractical.

Other crops that suffer common and severe losses from powdery mildew are the cucurbits, especially cantaloupe, squash and cucumber, sugar beets, strawberries, and clovers, many ornamentals such as rose, begonia, delphinium, azalea and lilac, grape, and many trees, particularly apple, catalpa, and oak. The control of powdery mildews in cereals and several other annual crops has been primarily through the use of resistant varieties but, more recently, also with systemic fungicides such as ethirimol, triadimenol, and triforine used as seed treatments, or prochloraz, triadirmefon, tridemorph, and triforine, and others, used as foliar sprays.

The same chemicals are used for control of powdery mildews in the other crops and in ornamentals, although elemental sulfur and dinocap have been and still are used extensively and effectively. Powdery mildew on trees, such as apple, Is effectively controlled with sprays of any, of several sterol-inhibiting systemic fungicides such as triadimefon, etaconazole, bitertanol, and triforine. The powdery mildew diseases of the various crop or other plants are caused by many species of fungi of the family Erysiphaceae grouped into six main genera. These genera are distinguished from each other by the number (one versus several) of asci per cleistothecium and by the morphology of hyphal appendages growing out of the wall of the cleistothecium.

Powdery mildew of rose

Powdery mildew of roses occurs everywhere in the world where roses are grown. Powdery mildew is one of the most important diseases of roses, both in the garden and in the greenhouse. The disease appears on roses year after year and causes reduced flower production and weakening of the plants by attacking the buds, young leaves, and growing tips of the plants.

Symptoms. On the young leaves the disease appears at first as slightly raised blisterlike areas that soon become covered with a gravish white, powdery fungus growth, and as the leaves expand they become curled and distorted. On the older leaves, large white patches of fungus growth appear, but there is usually little distortion. Lesions on leaves may appear more or less discolored and may eventually become necrotic. White patches of fungus growth, similar to those on the leaves, usually appear on young, green shoots, and they may coalesce and cover the entire terminal portions of the growing shoots, which may become arched or curved at their tip.

Sometimes buds may be attacked and become covered with white mildew before they open. They then either fail to open or open improperly, the infection spreading to the flower parts, which become discolored, dwarfed, and eventually die.

The Pathogen: Sphaerotheca pannosa f. sp. *rosae*. The pathogen that causes powdery mildew on roses seems to be a distinct special form of *S. pannosa*, since it has been shown in some cases that *S. pannosa* fungus from roses does not attack peaches, and vice versa. The mycelium is white and grows on the surface of the plant tissues, sending globose haustoria into the epidermal cells of the plant.

The mycelium forms a weft of hyphae on the surface, some of which develop into short, erect, conidiophores. At the tip of each conidiophore egg-shaped conidia are produced that cling together in chains. With the coming of cool weather late in the season, conidia production ceases and cleistothecia may be formed. The young cleistothecia are globose and at first white, then brown, and finally black when mature. The mature cleistothecia also have several mycelioid appendages, which are flaccid, indefinite hyphae arising from cells of the cleistothecium. The cleistothecia are more or less buried in the mycelial wefts on the plant tissues.

The ascospores continue to develop during the fall, and in the spring they are mature and ready for dissemination. In the spring the cleistothecia absorb water and crack open. The single ascus in each cleistothecium protrudes its tip, bursts open, and discharges its eight mature ascospores, which the wind carries away. The ascospores are about the size of conidia and behave exactly like conidia with respect to germination, infection, and formation of subsequent structures.

Development of disease. On outdoor roses the powdery mildew of rose fungus apparently overwinters mostly as mycelium in the buds, although cleistothecia form occasionally on leaves, petals, and stems, -especially around the thorns, toward the end of the season. On greenhouse roses the pathogen perpetuates itself almost exclusively as mycelium and conidia. When the fungus overwinters as mycelium in dormant buds, shoots arising from such buds become infected and provide inoculum for subsequent secondary mycelial or spore infection and disease development on foliage and flowers.

When the fungus overwinters as cleistothecia the discharged mature ascospores also serve as primary inoculum. Ascospores or conidia are carried by wind to young green tissues, and if temperature and relative humidity are sufficiently high the spores germinate by putting out a germ tube. The germ tube quickly produces a short, fine hypha growing directly through the cuticle and the epidermal cell wall into the epidermal cells.

The penetrating hypha enlarges immediately upon entrance into the cell lumen and forms a globose haustorium by which the fungus obtains its nutrients. The germ tube continues to grow and branch on the surface of the plant tissue producing a network of superficial mycelium. As the mycelium spreads on the plant, it continues to send haustoria into the epidermal cells.

The absorption of nutrients from the cells depletes their food supply, weakens them, and may sometimes lead to their death. Photosynthesis in the affected areas is greatly reduced, and the other functions of the cells are also impaired. Infection of young leaves also causes irritation and uneven growth of the affected and the surrounding cells, resulting in slight raised areas on the leaf and distortion of the leaf.

The aerial mycelium produces short, erect conidiophores, each bearing a chain Of 5 - 10 conidia. The conidia are disseminated by air currents and cause new infections on the expanding leaves and shoots.

Greenhouse roses are susceptible throughout the year. In the field, however, expanding tissues seem to be the most susceptible ones, and only under quite favorable humidity and temperature do fully developed tissues become infected. Growth of severely infected shoots is inhibited. Infected buds often do not open. If they do open, the flowers become infected and do not develop.

Control. Many new rose varieties show a moderately high level of resistance, but the resistance is not stable since some of them are resistant in some geographical areas but susceptible in others, or even in the same location, they are resistant some years and susceptible others. The variable resistance is presumably due to the presence or prevalence of different races of the pathogen in different geographical areas or during different seasons. Most popular rose varieties are highly susceptible to powdery mildew, and therefore additional protection by fungicides is necessary.

Powdery mildew has been controlled in the past by application of sulfur, dinocap, benomyl, and certain other fungicides. Sulfur may be used as a spray, as a dust, and in the greenhouse, as a vapor. Dinocap, benomyl, and cycloheximide are used as sprays. Under most conditions weekly applications give adequate protection, but during rapid de temperature fluctuations, and frequent rains, more frequent applications may be necessary. In the last few years, newer, more effective systemic fungicides such as triforine, fenarimol, triadimefon, dodemorph, and etaconazole have replaced many of the older fungicides in the control of powdery mildew. Some of these, for example, fenarimol, triadimefon, and etaconazole, are excellent for controlling powdery mildew in greenhouses by volatilization at normal greenhouse temperatures or after heating.

Several fungi such as *Ampelomyces quisqualis,*

Cladosporium oxysporum, *Tilletiopsis* sp., and *Verticillium lecanii*, and the insect *Thrips tabaci* have been reported to parasitize or antagonize the rose powdery mildew and the powdery mildew fungi of several other crops. Although this control approach appears promising, so far it has not been developed sufficiently to be used for practical control of powdery mildews.

Alternaria diseases

The Alternaria diseases are among the most common diseases of many kinds of plants throughout the world. They affect primarily the leaves, stems, flowers, and fruits of annual plants, especially vegetables and ornamentals, but also may affect parts of trees such as citrus and apple. Alternaria diseases appear usually as leaf spots and blights, but they may also cause damping off of seedlings, collar rots, and tuber and fruit rots. Some of the most common diseases caused by *Alternaria* include early blight of potato and tomato, leaf spot of bean, tobacco, geranium, and stock, blight of carrot, carnation, chrysanthemum, petunia and zinnia, leaf spot and blight of crucifers, onion, purple blotch, leaf spot and fruit spot on squash and on apple, core rot of apple, and rot of lemons and oranges.

The leaf spots are generally dark brown to black, often numerous and enlarging and usually developing in concentric rings, which give the spots a targetlike appearance. Lower, senescent leaves are usually attacked first, but the disease progresses upward and makes affected leaves go into a yellowish, senescent condition and either dry up and droop or fall off. Dark, often targetlike, sunken spots develop on branches and stems of plants such as tomato.

Stem lesions developing on seedlings may form cankers, which may enlarge, girdle the stem, and kill the plant, or if present near the soil line they may develop into a collar rot. In belowground parts, such as potato tubers, dark, slightly sunken, circular, or irregular lesions develop that may be Up to 2 cm in diameter and 5 - 6 mm in depth.

Fruits affected by Afternaria are usually attacked when they approach maturity, in some hosts at the stem end while in others at the blossom end or at other points through wounds, growth cracks, and so on. The spots are brown to black and may be small, sunken, with well-defined margins, or they- may enlarge to cover most of the fruit, have a leathery consistency and a black, velvety surface layer of fungus growth and spores.

In some fruits, such as citrus and tomato, a small lesion at the surface may indicate an extensive spread of the infection in the central core and the segments of the fruit. The pathogen, Afternaria sp., has dark-colored mycelium and in older diseased tissue it produces short, simple, erect conidiophores that bear single or branched chains of conidia. The conidia are large, dark, long, or pear shaped and multicellular, with both tranverse and longitudinal cross walls.

The conidia are detached easily and are carried by air currents. Alternaria occurs in many species throughout the world. Their spores are present in the 'air and dust everywhere and are one of the most common fungal causes of hay fever allergies. *Alternaria* spores also land and grow as contaminants in laboratory cultures of other microorganisms and on dead plant tissue killed by other pathogens or other causes. Actually, many species of Alternaria are mostly saprophytic, that is, they cannot infect living plant tissues but they grow only on dead or decaying plant tissues and, at most, on senescent or old tissues such as old petals, old leaves, and ripe fruit. Therefore, it is often difficult to decide whether an Alternaria fungus found on a diseased tissue is the cause of the disease or a secondary contaminant.

Many species of *Alternaria* produce toxins, some of which, such as tentoxin, produced by *A. tenuis* are host nonspecific, while others, such as AK-toxin and AM-toxin, produced by *A. kikuchiana* and *A. mali*, respectively, are host specific. Plant pathogenic species of Afternaria overwinter as mycelium in infected plant debris and as mycelium or spores in or on seeds. If the fungus is carried with the seed, it may attack the seedling, usually after emergence, and cause damping off or stem lesions and collar rot. More frequently, however, spores that are produced abundantly, especially during heavy dews and frequent rains, are blown in from mycelium growing on debris, infected cultivated plants, or weeds.

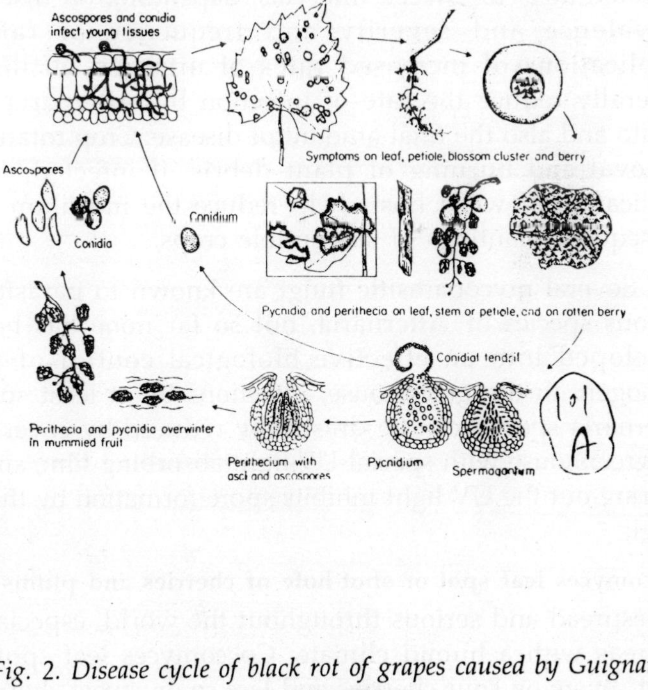

Fig. 2. Disease cycle of black rot of grapes caused by Guignardia bidwellii.

The germinating spores penetrate susceptible tissue directly or through wounds and soon produce new conidia that are further spread by wind, splashing rain, or tools. With few exceptions, Alternaria diseases are more prevalent on older, senescing tissues and particularly on plants of low vigor or poor nutrition or those under some other kind of stress caused by unfavorable environmental conditions, insects, or other diseases.

Alternaria diseases are controlled primarily through the use of resistant varieties, of disease-free or treated seed, and through chemical sprays with fungicides such as chlorothalonil, maneb, captafol, mancozeb, and fentin hydroxide. The sprays should begin soon after the seedlings emerge or are transplanted and should be repeated at 1- to 2-week intervals, depending on disease prevalence and severity and frequency of rains. Applications of increased rates of nitrogen fertilizer generally reduce the rate of infection by Alternaria on potato and also the final amount of disease. Crop rotation, removal and burning of plant debris, if infected, and eradication of weed hosts help reduce the inoculum for subsequent plantings of susceptible crops.

Several mycoparasitic fungi are known to parasitize various species of Alternaria, but so far none has been developed into an effective biological control of the pathogen. In the greenhouse, infections by at least some Alternaria species can be drastically reduced by covering the greenhouse with special UV-light-absorbing film, since filtering out the UV light inhibits spore formation by these fungi.

Coccomyces leaf spot or shot-hole of cherries and plums

Widespread and serious throughout the world, especially in areas with a humid climate, Coccomyces leaf spot is most severe on sour cherries and less so on sweet cherries and plums. In cherries, the symptoms appear as numerous minute, red to purplish-black spots on the upper sides of leaves and, in severe infections, on the petioles, fruit, and pedicels. On the under sides of the spots on the leaves, slightly raised, waxy pustules appear that after heavy dews or rains produce a white, mildewlike growth. Infected leaves usually turn yellow and fall, or the spots may drop out and the leaves have a shot-hole appearance.

The shot-hole effect is even more common and more pronounced on plum and prune leaves, which may appear completely skeletonized. Severe leaf drop and shot-holing early in the season are common and weaken the trees, which may die back during the same or subsequent years. The disease is especially common and serious In nursery plantings. The fungus, *Coccomyces* sp. (or *Higginsia* sp.), produces ascospores in apothecia formed in fallen infected leaves and *Cylindrosporium*-type conidia formed in acervuli on the under side of infected leaves.

The conidia are colorless, threadlike, straight, or curved and consist of one or several cells. The ascospores are produced in the spring over a period of 6 - 7 weeks and are forcibly ejected when the leaves are thoroughly soaked. The ascospores are then carried by air currents and cause the primary infections on the leaves, which then produce large numbers of conidia that are spread by rain from leaf to leaf and cause all subsequent infections. Control of the disease is achieved by 4 - 5 sprays starting at petal-fall, and one postharvest spray with benomyl, captan, thiophanate methyl, or certain other fungicides such as dodine, sulfur, and ferbam.

Black rot of grape

Black rot of grape is present in Europe and in the United States and Canada east of the Rocky Mountains. It is probably the most serious disease of grapes where it commonly occurs, particularly in warm, humid regions. In the absence of control measures and in favorable weather, the crop is usually destroyed completely, either through direct rotting of the berries or through blasting of the blossom clusters. The disease causes numerous scattered, circular, red necrotic spots on leaves in late spring.

The spots form usually between the veins and are most apparent on the upper side of the leaves. Later, when the spots are about 2-6 mm or more in diameter, the main area of the spots appears brown to grayish-tan, while the margins appear as a black line. Black dotlike, Phyllosticta-type pycnidia are formed on the upper side of the spots in a ring near the outer edge of the brown area of the spot. On the shoots, tendrils, the leaf and flower stalks, and on leaf veins, the spots are purple to black, somewhat depressed and elongated, and bear scattered pycnidia. Spots begin to appear on berries when the berries are about half grown. These spots are at first whitish but are soon surrounded by a rapidly widening brown ring with a black margin.

The central area of the spot remains flat or becomes depressed, and dark pycnidia appear near the center. The whole berry soon becomes rotten and shrinks, and it becomes coal black as the surface becomes studded with numerous black pycnidia. The fungus, *Guignardia bidwellii*, in addition to conidia-bearing pycnidia, also produces ascospores in globose perithecia forming in rotten, mummified fruit. The perithecia supposedly develop from transformed pycnidia.

The fungus overwinters mostly as ascospores in perithecia, but conidia can also survive the winter in most locations where grapes grow, so both ascospores and conidia can cause primary infections in the spring. The release of ascospores and conidia takes place only when the perithecia and pycnidia become thoroughly wet, but while the ascospores are shot out forcibly and may then be carried by air currents, the conidia are exuded in a viscid mass from which they can be washed down or splashed away by rain.

Ascospores may be discharged continually through the spring and summer, although most of them are discharged in the spring. Primary infections, whether from ascospores or conidia, take place on young, rapidly growing leaves and on fruit pedicels. In the ensuing spots, pycnidia are produced rapidly, and these pycnidia provide the conidia for the secondary infections of berries, stems, and so on. Control of the grape leaf spot and black rot depends primarily sprays of grapevines with fungicides. Sprays with ferbarn or benomyl just before bloom, immediately after bloom, and 10- 14 days later give good control of the disease.

Captan, folpet, triadimefon, and copper fungicides are also effective against black rot and are used when downy mildew or powdery mildew are also to be controlled. Where black rot has been severe, another ferbam or captan application should be made during the first part of June.

Banana leaf spot, or sigatoka disease

Banana leaf spot, or Sigatoka disease occurs throughout the world and is one of the most destructive diseases of banana, although its economic importance varies with the region. If causes losses by reducing the functional leaf surface of the plant, which results in small, unevenly ripened bananas that may fall and fail to ripen.

The disease first appears as small, indistinct, longitudinal, light yellow spots parallel to the side veins of leaves that unfurled about a month earlier. A few days later, the spots become 1-2 cm long, turn brown with light grey centers, and become readily visible. Such spots cause little damage, but they soon enlarge further, the tissue around them turns yellow and dies, and adjacent spots coalesce forming large dead areas on the leaf. In severe infections, entire leaves die within a few weeks.

Since it takes at least 12 healthy leaves on mature banana plants to carry fruit to maturity, destruction of most mature leaves by the leaf spot disease may leave only a few functioning leaves that are insufficient to bring the fruit to maturity. As a result, immature fruit bunches on such plants fail to fill out and ripen and may fall. If the fruit is nearing maturity at the time of heavy infection, the flesh ripens unevenly, individual bananas appear undersized and angular in shape, their flesh develops a buff pinkish color, and they store poorly. The causal fungus is *Mycosphaerella musicola*. It produces spermatia in spermogonia, ascospores in perithecia, and conidia of the Cercospora type in sporodochia.

Sporodochia appear while the spots are still light yellow, but successive crops of abundant conidia are produced by the same sporodochia only during the brown spot stage of the disease. Conidia are produced on both sides of the leaf but are usually more abundant on the upper side and are spread by wind and dripping or splashing water. Although conidia are produced throughout the year, their release and germination depends on water or high humidity. Perithecia, formed as a result of fertilization of sexual hyphae by compatible spermatia, are produced during warm humid weather, and their ascospores are shot out violently in response to wetting of the perithecia.

Ascospores are spread by air currents and are responsible for the long-distance spread of the disease, while conidia are generally the most important means of the local spread of the disease. Infection by either ascospores or conidia produces the same type of spot and subsequent development of the disease. In addition to the common Sigatoka disease, caused by Mycosphaerella musicola, there is also the black leaf streak disease caused by *M. fijiensis*, and the black Sigatoka disease caused by *M. fijiensis* var. *difformis*.

The three fungi have similar life cycles and morphology except that *M. f.* var. *difformis* produces sporodochia in young spots and its hyphae move from one stoma to another and cause lesions over entire leaves much more commonly than *M. musicola*. The Sigatoka diseases are controlled by a combination of measures including quarantine, sanitation by removal and destruction of badly infected leaves, and mainly by frequent, year-round application of fungicidal sprays. For many years Bordeaux mixture or copper oxychloride with or without zineb were the fungicides used. Later it was shown that zineb or copper oxychloride suspended in mineral oil or mineral oil alone (consisting largely of saturated hydrocarbons) gave better and cheaper control than Bordeaux.

The oil sprays, however, are phytotoxic under certain conditions, may reduce fruit yields by as much as io percent, may cause patchy, retarded ripening when applied directly to fruit, and have resulted in an increase of certain other leaf spot and fruit spot and rot diseases previously controlled by Bordeaux mixture. To date, chlorothalonil, mancozeb, or other fungicides are routinely included in oil - water- fungicide emulsions for best all-around results. In some areas it is necessary to apply ground or airplane sprays every 10- 12 days throughout the year, especially for control of black leaf streak and black Sigatoka diseases, while in other areas one application every 3, 4 or even 6 weeks suffices to maintain control.

Cucurbit leaf spot, gummy stem blight, and black rot

Cucurbit leaf spot, gummy stem blight, and black rot is probably worldwide in distribution, and in favorable weather the pathogen infects all parts of all cucurbits. Usually, however, it attacks the leaves and stems of watermelons, cucumber, and cantaloupe and the fruit of squash, pumpkin, and gourd. When the fungus is carried in the seed it also causes damping off, killing the seedlings. On the leaves, petioles, and stems, pale brown or gray spots develop. On the stems, the spots usually start at the joints, become elongated and cracked, and exude an amber-colored gummy material.

The spots on the leaves enlarge along with the spots on stems and petioles and make the leaves turn yellow and die. Even the whole plant may wilt and die. On the fruit, the spots appear at first as yellowish, irregularly circular areas that later turn gray to brown and may have a droplet of gummy exudate in the center.

The spot finally turns black. In some kinds of squash the black rot lesions are superficial and spread over the surface or appear as a dry, brownish, circular mass, the enlargement of which is arrested by a defensive barrier of squash tissue. Very often, however, especially in storage, the fungus penetrates through the rind and spreads widely throughout the squash and into the seed cavity. On all the spots, whether on the leaf, stem, or fruit, the fungus produces closely spaced groups of pale-colored pycnidia and dark, globular perithecia that are sometimes arranged in rings and are visible with the naked eye. The fungus, *Didymella bryoniae* (*Mycosphaerella melonis*), produces ascospores in perithecia and conidia in pycnidia. Both conidia and ascospores are short-lived after they are released, and the fungus generally overwinters in diseased plant refuse as chlarnydospores and in or on the seed.

Thus, either type of spore or infected seed can result in primary infections, with the subsequently profusely produced conidia causing the secondary infections. Cucurbit plants seem to be predisposed to infection by

Mycosphaerella melonis by previous infestation with beetles or infection with powdery mildew. The striped cucumber beetle, in addition, appears to serve as a vector of *M. melonis* among cucurbit plants in the field. Control of black rot of cucurbits is difficult, requiring the use of clean or treated seed, long crop rotations, and frequent applications of such fungicides as mancozeb, chlorothalonil, and captan.

Good control of the leaf and stem infections reduces fruit infections both in the field and in storage. However, further care is needed to avoid infection in storage. Wounding of stored fruit must be avoided. Curing of squash at 23-29°C for two weeks to heal the wounds and subsequent storage at 10 - 12°C are very helpful. If the inoculum present in the field is heavy, dipping the squash fruit in formaldehyde or Clorox before curing and storage is also helpful.

Helminthosporium diseases

Helminthosporium diseases occur throughout the world and are very common and severe on many important crop plants of the grass family (Grammeae), and in some areas, they also cause diseases on apple (black pox) and on pear (blister canker). Thus, different species of *Helminthosporium*, of which several are now known under the names *Bipolaris, Drechslera*, or *Exserohilum*, cause corn leaf blights, brown spot or blight of rice; crown and root rot of wheat, and the leaf spot of wheat; net blotch of barley, stripe disease of barley, and the spot blotch of barley; the Victoria blight and the leaf blotch of oats, eye spot and the brown stripe of sugarcane; and leaf spots or blights of turf grasses, and the crown and root rots (melting out) of turf grasses.

The leaf spots and blights and also the crown and root rot diseases caused by *Helminthosporium* on the various hosts have many similarities but also some significant differences. Three of them, brown spot or blight of rice, southern corn leaf blight, and *Helminthosporium* blight of oats, caused sudden and catastrophic epidemics that resulted in huge crop losses, human suffering, and new approaches to disease control. All *Helminthosporium* diseases destroy various percentages of the leaf area, or they may attack and destroy part of the stem or roots, or attack the kernels directly, in every case causing considerable yield loss. Of the diseases on corn, southern corn leaf blight causes rather small (0.6 × 2.5 cm), tan lesions that may be parallel or elliptical and may be so numerous that they almost cover the entire leaf. Some races of the species causing these diseases also attack the stalks, leaf sheaths, ear husks, shanks, ears, and cobs. Affected kernels are covered with a black, felty mold, and cobs may rot or, if the shank is infected early, the ear may be killed prematurely or drop. Seedlings from infected kernels may wilt and die within a few weeks of planting. The monetary value of the lost crop was estimated at one billion dollars. In the northern corn leaf blight, only the leaves are affected; the lesions are grayish-green or tan and range in length from 2 to 15 cm and are 1 - 3 cm wide. The same fungus causes similar but smaller and darker spots on sorghum.

The brown spot or blight disease of rice appears at first as small, purplish-brown spots on the leaves and glumes. Later the spots grow larger and have a grey center and brown border. Entire glumes may b covered by several small or one large spot on which a dark brown, velvety felt of conidiophores and conidia is present. The fungus causes damage by infecting the seed directly, which then germinates poorly and produces weak seedlings, but primarily by attacking the leaves during the seedling stage either in the seed beds or in the field. In such infections the young foliage is severely damaged, the plants are weakened, and the yield drastically reduced.

The Helminthosporium diseases on barley, wheat, and oats are common, similar, widespread, and cause considerable losses year after year, although the amount of loss varies with the crop, the variety, and the prevailing weather conditions in a particular year. The diseases seem to be more common and more severe on barley than on the other crops. In the net blotch of barley, small, brown, almost square-shaped, netlike blotches appear near the tip of the seedling leaf.

The spots enlarge as the leaf grows and spread along the entire leaf blade, and as they become more elongate, the leaf develops a netted appearance. In barley stripe, yellow stripes develop along leaf blades and sheaths of the older leaves. Later, these stripes become brown, and near the end of the season, the leaves often split along the stripe lesions and become shredded. Infected plants are stunted and usually do not produce normal heads. In the crown rot and common root rot of wheat, barley, and other grasses, spots develop on seedlings, plant crowns, stems, leaves, floral parts, and kernels. Dark brown to black lesions develop on seedlings near the soil line and may spread into the leaves.

The seedlings may be blighted and killed before or after emergence, or they may survive but their growth is retarded. Crowns are infected at or just below the soil line and show a reddish-brown decay that destroys the tiller buds and advances into the root system, which it kills. Winter survival of root rot-infected wheat and barley plants is reduced considerably, in some cases by 10-30 percent in wheat and 20-60 percent in barley.

The leaf spots are brown and elongate with definite margins and frequently enlarge and coalesce to form brown irregular stripes or blotches that cover large areas of the leaf blade. Older lesions are covered with a layer of olive-colored conidiophores and conidia of the fungus. Floral parts and kernels also develop lesions, or their entire surface may appear dark brown.

The embryo end of the kernel is often black, and this symptom is characteristic of this disease. Due to crown and root rot and to leaf blotch, surviving plants are shorter; the spikes may be only partially emerged and may be sterile or have poorly filled kernels. Blight of floral parts and kernels also causes sterility or death of individual kernels.

In the *Victoria blight of oats,* which affects only types of oats bred from the cultivar "Victoria," the fungus causes necrotic lesions at the base of the shoot of seedlings, which then develop reddish stripes on the young leaves. Severely affected seedlings die. Those that survive later develop a rot at the base of the stem and in the root and brown lesions on the leaves. The stem is weakened in the infected region and is easily toppled over, while a velvety spore mass develops on its lower blackened nodes.

The fungus causing Victoria blight of oats produces the specific toxin victorin that affects and produces the typical stunting and chlorosis symptoms of the disease only on "Victoria" oats. Lawn and fine golf course grasses are frequently attacked by various *Helminthosporium* species, which cause the most common and serious group of diseases known as leaf spots, blights, crown (foot) rots and root rots-melting out-of these grasses. These diseases resemble in most respects those described above for the small grain crops, although on turf grasses one or more leaf spots often merge and girdle the leaf blade, which then turns yellow or reddish-brown and dies back from the tip. In severe infections leaves become completely blighted, wither, die, and drop off. Furthermore, the perennial nature of the turf grasses and the fact that they are mowed and irrigated several times each year create additional opportunities for the diseases to be spread and to become established.

The diseases are usually most destructive during wet or humid weather or where the turf is sprinkle-irrigated frequently, especially late in the day. In advanced cases of infection turf areas of various sizes and shapes turn yellow, then brown to straw colored, the plants in these areas are killed and thinned out, and finally all plants die and decay (melting out).

The disease, if unchecked and if the weather is favorable, may spread and kill the entire turf in the area. Quite distinctly from the above diseases, another species of Helminthosporium causes a pitted or scaly bark condition and small, black, sunken spots on apple and pear and a blister canker on pear. The pathogen in the above diseases is one or several of the many species of "*Helminthosporium*" affecting plants. The fungus produces large, cylindrical, dark, 3- to many-celled (usually 5 - 10) conidia that have thick walls and sometimes are slightly curved.

The conidia are produced successively on new growing tips of quite dark, septate, irregular conidiophores. In the last several years, most plant pathogenic species of Helininthosporium have been reclassified under different genera, depending on the shape and manner of germination on of the conidium and on the kind of perfect (ascomycetous) stage they produce. Several species have been shown to produce, with more or less regularity, black perithecia containing cylindrical asci, within which are formed colorless, threadlike, 4- to 9-celled, coiled ascospores. Thus, former *Helminthosporium* species that produce a *Cochliobolus* perfect stage are now known as Bipolaris species, those that produce a *Pyrenophora* perfect stage are known as Drechslera species, and those that produce a *Setosphaeria* perfect stage are known as *Exserohilum*.

Only species that do not produce a perfect stage are still called *Helminthosporium*, but only one such species (*H. solani*) is a plant pathogen. However, because this classification has not yet been universally accepted, because all the older and much of the recent literature can be found under Helminthosporium, and more importantly, because of the biological and plant pathological similarities of all these species and genera, the diseases can be effectively discussed under the name "*Helminthosporium*" diseases.

The various "*Helminthosporium*" species survive the winter as mycelium or spores in or on infected or contaminated seed, in plant debris, and in infected crowns or roots of susceptible plants. Some species of the fungus are weak parasites, but several are potent pathogens. When in the soil, however, all of them are weak as saprophytes, probably because of antagonism by soil microorganisms, especially at high nitrogen content. Many *Helminthosporium* species, for example, *H. victoriae* and *H. maydis* race T, produce potent host-specific toxins such as victorin and HM T-toxin that play important roles in the development of the respective diseases.

Most "Helminthosporium " species are favored by moderate to warm (18-32°C) temperatures and particularly by humid, damp weather. Most Helminthosporium diseases, especially leaf spots, are retarded by dry weather, while crown- and root-affecting fungi may continue their invasion of diseased plants, killing out the plants (melting out) in irregular areas. Spread of the fungus is through the seed and infected debris blown or carried away. Over short distances during the growing season the fungus spreads through its numerous conidia, which may be carried by air currents, splashing rain, or by clinging to cultivating equipment, feet, animals, and so on.

Control of *Helminthosporium* diseases depends on the use of resistant varieties, pathgen-free seed, seed treatment with fungicides, proper crop rotation and fertilization, plowing under of infected plant debris, and by fungicides. In turf grasses, control of Helminthosporium diseases is facilitated by mowing at the recommended maximum height, reducing or removing the accumulated dense thatch, supplying sufficient fertilizer, and by irrigating quickly and sufficiently but in widely spaced (7- to io-day) intervals. If fungicides are necessary, several of them, including cycloheximide, cycloheximide-thiram, chlorothalonil, Dyrene, and maneb, can be applied beginning in early spring and continuing at I- to 2-week intervals for as long as necessary to get the disease under control. Several systemic fungicides, such as imazalil, nuarimol, etaconazole, and fenapanil, when applied as seed treatments or, in turf grasses, with the irrigation water, give good control of the root rot and several of the other symptoms and are being tested for grower application.

Dothichiza canker of poplar

One of the most important diseases of poplar, especially black, Lombardy, and Simon poplar, and of cottonwood, in Europe and North America, Dothichiza canker of poplar causes cankers on twigs, branches, and stems. All the young trees in nurseries and plantations may be killed rapidly by cankers that girdle the stem. On older trees, branch and stem cankers result in a typical dieback.

The fungus enters the tree through lenticels, buds, and bark cracks. The developing canker is discolored and sunken. The host checks the advance of the fungus during favorable conditions, but during low temperatures or drought when the host vigor is reduced, the fungus resumes its activity, the canker enlarges, and may girdle and kill the branch or tree.

The fungus produces conidia in pycnidia on the diseased parts throughout the growing season. The conidia are spread by rain, water, and wind and can probably cause new infections throughout the season, but most infections seem to occur in late spring when conidia are also most abundant. Perithecia and ascospores are seldom produced.

Black knot of plum and cherry

Black knot of plum and cherry occurs on cultivated and wild plums and cherries, primarily in the eastern half of the United States and New Zealand. It causes conspicuous, 2 - 25 cm or more long, coal-black knotty swellings on one side of, or encircling, twigs and branches. They may be several times the diameter of the limbs and make heavily infected trees appear quite grotesque. Infected plants become worthless after a few years as a result of limb death and stunting of the trees.

The fungus, Plowrightia (Dibotryon) morbosum, produces conidia on free hyphae and ascospores in perithecia formed on the black knots. Both conidia and ascospores are spread by wind and rain, and in early spring they can penetrate healthy and injured woody tissue of the current season's growth. Large limbs are also attacked, especially at points of developing small twigs.

The fungus grows into the cambium and xylem parenchyma and along the axis of the twig. After 5 or 6 months, excessive parenchyma cells are produced and pushed outward forming the swelling. The following spring conidia are produced on the knot surface, giving it a temporary olive-green velvety appearance. The knots enlarge rapidly during the second summer, and in their surface iayer, perithecia are formed that develop during the winter and release ascospores the following spring. The knots continue to expand in following years.

The disease can be controlled by pruning and burning of all black knots and destruction of black knots or of all affected wild plums and cherries near the orchard. Spraying the orchard trees before and during bloom with sulfur or captan, each alone or combined with thiophanate methyl, or with fixed copper fungicides to which hydrated lime is added, protects trees from infection,

Chestnut blight

American chestnuts killed by the blight composed 50 percent of the overall value of eastern hardwood timber stands. The fungus, *Endothia parasitica,* which some call *Cryphonectria parasitica,* also attacks oak, red maple, hickory, and, sporadically, other trees, but not nearly as severely as it attacks the American chestnut. It is now present throughout North America, Europe, and Asia. The fungus penetrates the bark of stems through wounds and then grows into the inner bark and cambium. Soon a swollen or sunken canker develops, the bark of which is reddish-orange to yellow-green and covered by pimplelike pycnidia and perithecia. Cankers often have long cracks on their surface, may be several inches to many feet long, and eventually girdle the stem or branch causing wilting and death of the parts beyond the canker.

The pycnidia produce tiny conidia that ooze out as long orange curllike masses during moist weather and are spread by birds, crawling or flying insects, or splashing rain. The perithecia produce ascospores that are shot forcibly into the air and may be carried by wind over long distances. The fungus survives and continues to invade and produce its spores in trees or parts of trees already killed by the blight. Blighted trees almost always produce sprouts below the basal cankers, but the resulting saplings become blighted in turn by new infections. No control is available against chestnut blight, although some new systemic fungicides appear promising for isolated trees.

In recent years several strains with reduced virulence (hypovirulence) have been found in Europe and the United States.

All of these strains contain double stranded RNA, which is the kind of RNA present in many viruses that infect fungi. When a chestnut tree canker caused by the typical virulent, wild, dsRNA-free *Endothia parasitica* is also inoculated with a hypovirulent dsRNA-containing strain of the fungus, the dsRNA passes through mycelial anastomoses into the mycelium of the virulent strain. The acquisition of the dsRNA changes this strain into a hypovirulent one, and further development of the canker slows down or stops completely. Although this type of biological control of chestnut blight works well on isolated trees, it has not yet been possible to use it on a large scale in the forest. So far, no completely resistant American chestnuts have been found.

Nectria canker

Nectria canker is one of the most important diseases of apples and pears and of many species of hardwood forest trees in most parts of the world. Losses are greater in young trees because in these the fungus girdles the trunk or scaffold branches, while in older trees only small branches are usually killed directly. Cankers on the main stem of older trees, however, reduce the vigor and value or productivity of the tree, and such trees are subject to wind breakage.

Nectria cankers usually develop around bud scars, .wounds, twig stubs, or in the crotches of limbs. Young cankers are small, circular, brown areas. Later, the central area becomes sunken and black, while the edges are raised above the surrounding healthy bark. In many hosts and under favorable conditions for the host, the fungus grows slowly, the host produces callus tissue around the canker, and the margin of the canker cracks. The tissues under the black bark in the canker are dead, dry and spongy, flake off, and fall out, revealing the dead wood and the callus ridge around the cavity.

In subsequent years the fungus invades more healthy tissue and new, closely packed, roughly concentric ridges of callus tissue are produced every year, resulting in the typical open, target-shaped *Nectria* canker. In some hosts, however, and under conditions that favor the fungus, invasion of the host is more rapid, the bark in the cankered area is roughened and cracked but does not fall off, and the successive callus ridges are some distance apart. In hosts such as apple and pear, fruits are also infected and develop a circular, sunken, brown rot. White or yellowish pustules producing numerous conidia form on rotted areas. Internally the rotted tissue is soft and has a striated appearance.

The fungi, Nectria galligena and some related species, attack the many different tree hosts. All Nectria species produce similar, two-celled ascospores in brightly colored perithecia on the surface of a cushion-shaped stroma, but different Nectria species produce conidia, which in themselves do not appear to be related and are classified as various species of Imperfect fungi. Thus, the conidia of *N. galligena* are either single-celled macroconidia or more commonly 2- to 4-celled, cylindrical to crescent-shaped macroconidia of the *Cylindrocarpon* type.

The conidia are produced soon after infection on small, white, or creamy-yellow or bright orange-pink sporodochia, which appear on the surface of the bark over the infected area or on fruit. The conidia are produced more commonly early in the season but also in the summer and early fall. They are spread by wind and by washing during rainy periods and perhaps by insects. Perithecia appear in the cankers in late summer and fall and in the same stroma that earlier produced the conidia, which they eventually -replace.

The ascospores are either forcibly discharged and carried by wind or, in moist weather, they ooze from the perithecium and are washed by rain or carried by insects. Ascospores are dispersed more abundantly in late summer and fall but are also released at other times of the year. Sanitation, that is, removal, and burning of cankered limbs or trees where possible, is often the only control measure possible. Spraying with a fungicide such as captafol or 8:8: 100 Bordeaux mixture immediately after leaf fall helps reduce Nectria infections in fruit trees.

Valsa, or cytospora, canker and dieback

Valsa, or Cytospora, canker and dieback is a worldwide canker disease that probably affects more species of trees than any of the canker diseases previously described. It is estimated that more than 70 species of fruit trees, harwood forest and shade trees, shrubs, and conifers are attacked by one of several species of the pathogen.

The fungus, Valsa sp., which some call *Leucostoma* sp., is most commonly found in its Imperfect stage, *Cytospora* sp., and therefore the disease is usually known as *Cytospora* canker.

Cytospora canker is most serious on peach and the other stone fruits, on apple and pear, and on poplar and willow, but it is often serious on many other shade or forest trees. Actually, few orchards are free from its damaging effects. Many trees are seriously injured by cankers on the trunk, in the main crotch, on the limbs, and on the branches. Infected branches of fruit trees often break from the weight of the crop or during storms.

Cytospora canker is most severe on fruit or shade trees growing under stress, such as those growing on an unfavorable site, or injured by drought, frost, fire, or severe pruning. The fungus is mostly a saprophyte living on dead bark but becomes parasitic when the tree is weakened. However, the presence of *Cytospora* on a dead twig or branch does not mean that this fungus has killed it.

Infection of small twigs and branches results in dieback without definite cankers. The cankers occur and are most pronounced on trunks and large branches. A canker appears first as a gradual circular killing of the bark of a limb or stem. The infected area soon becomes brownish and sunken, and the host often produces raised callus tissue around it. In some hosts, particularly the stone fruit trees, the inner diseased bark becomes dark and odorous, and a copious flow of gum exudes from the dead tissues.

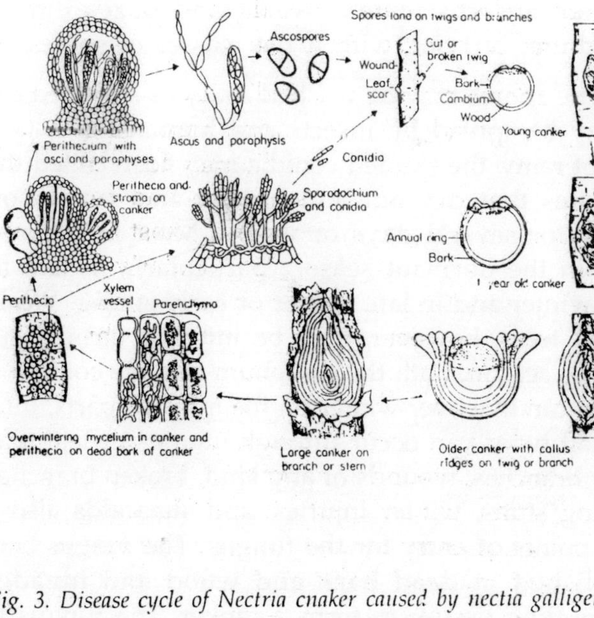

Fig. 3. Disease cycle of Nectria cnaker caused by nectia galligena.

The cankers may be long and slightly sunken or short,

deeply sunken, with conspicuously raised callus borders. Later the bark shrivels and separates from the underlying wood and from the surrounding healthy bark. Small, pimplelike pycnidia of the fungus appear on the dead bark, and later the shriveled bark may slough off exposing dead wood beneath. The cankers increase in size each year and become unsightly, rough swellings. Many twigs and branches die back as a result of cankers that girdle them completely.

Cytospora cankers result from infections by conidia of the fungus *Cytospora*. The fungus produces *Valsa*-type ascospores in perithecia, but the perithecial stage is not common. The conidia are produced inside pycnidia consisting of many connecting cavities and one pore through which the conidia are exuded. The spores are small, hyaline, one-celled, and slightly curved. They are produced In a gelatinous matrix, which during wet weather, absorbs water, swells, and oozes out of the pycnidium, carrying with it the masses of spores.

The spores may be washed away or splashed by rain or may be spread by insects and humans. If it is moist but not rainy, the exuded conidia may form coiled threads of spores that dry out and harden and remain on the canker for several days or weeks. Most infections take place in the dormant season, particularly in late fall or early winter and in late winter or early spring. Weakened injured trees, however, may be infected throughout the growing season. Both the mycelium and the conidia of the fungus can live over winter on the infected parts. Infection of small twigs can occur through injuries or leaf scars. In larger branches, wounds of any kind, broken branches and pruning stubs, winter injuries, and sunscalds also make ideal points of entry for the fungus. The fungus becomes established in dead bark and wood and invades the surrounding tissues to form a canker. The fungus grows through the cells in the bark and the outer few rings of the wood.

Control measures for the *Cytospora* canker depend on: good cultural practices such as watering and fertilization to keep the trees in good vigor; avoiding wounding and severe pruning of trees; removing cankers from trunks and large branches during dry weather and treating the wound and all pruning cuts with a disinfectant and a wound dressing; removing and burning cankered and dead branches and twigs; pruning as late in the spring as possible and spraying with Phygon XL immediately after pruning and before it rains.

Anthracnose diseases by ascomycetes and imperfect fungi

Anthracnoses are diseases of the foliage, stems, or fruits that typically appear as small or large, dark-colored spots or slightly sunken lesions with a slightly raised rim. In addition to leaf spots, anthracnoses often have a prolonged latent stage in fruit infection and may cause twig or branch dieback. In some anthracnoses, particularly serious on some fruit crops, the symptoms appear as small spots with raised, corky surfaces. Anthracnose diseases of fruit often result in fruit drop and fruit rot. Anthracnoses are caused by fungi that produce their asexual spores, conidia, within small, black acervuli arranged in the lesion concentrically or in a scattered manner.

Four ascomycetous fungi, *Diplocarpon, Elsinoe Glomerella,* and *Gnomonia,* belong to this group, although a few of their species produce conidia in pycnidia rather than acervuli. Actually, these fungi are found in nature mostly in their conidial stage and can overwinter as mycelium or conidia, yet, some more frequently than others also produce ascospores in perithecia, which may overwinter.

The acervulus-producing Imperfect Fungi make up

the order Melanconiales. The most important plant pathogenic fungi that produce acervuli are *Colletotrichum* (*Gloeosporium*), *Coryneum*, *Cylindrosporium*, *Marssonina*, *Melanconium*, and *Sphaceloma*. Some of these are the conidial stages of some of the Ascomycetes that cause anthracnose diseases. Thus, several Colletotrichum or *Gloeosporium* species produce a *Glomerella*-type perfect stage, and the diseases caused by these species are discussed as Glomerella diseases-, some *Cylindrosporium* species have a *Higginsia*-type perfect stage and some a *Mycosphaerella*-type perfect stage; some *Marssonina* species have a *Diplocaron*- or *Gnomonia*-type perfect stage; and most *Sphaceloma* species have an *Elsinoe*-type perfect stage. For some species of these same fungi, however, and for all species of *Coryneum* and *Melanconium*, no perfect stage is yet known.

Anthracnose diseases, particularly those caused by *Colletorichum* (*Gloeosporium*) or *Glomerella* group, are very common and destructive on numerous crop and ornamental plants, and their geographic distribution is in most cases worldwide. Although severe everywhere, anthracnose diseases cause their most severe losses in the tropics and subtropics.

Black spot of rose

The black spot of rose appears as small to large circular, black lesions on the leaves, and on susceptible varieties, as raised, purple-red, later blackened and blistered irregular blotches on immature wood of first-year canes. The leaf spots are consistently black, have fringed margins and may coalesce to produce large, irregular, black lesions. The leaf tissue around the lesions turns yellow, and often, when severely infected, entire leaves become yellow and fall off prematurely, leaving the canes almost completely defoliated. The fungus, *Diplocarpon rosae*, produces ascospores in tiny apothecia formed in old lesions, and

Marssonina-type conidia in acervuli forming between the outer wall and cuticle of the epidermis.

The conidiophores arise from a thin black stroma, are short, and give rise to successive crops of conidia. The abundant conidia production pushes up and ruptures the cuticle. The fungus overwinters as mycelium or as ascospores and conidia in infected leaves and canes. Both kinds of spores can cause primary infections of leaves in the spring by direct penetration. The mycelium grows in the mesophyll but within two weeks forms acervuli and conidia at the upper surface. Conidia are produced throughout the growing season and cause repeated infections during warm, wet weather.

Control of *Diplocarpon* diseases is through sanitation, such as removing and burning infected leaves, cutting back the canes of diseased rose plants, and spraying with benomyl, chlorothalonil, zineb, or mancozeb or applying sulfur-copper dust. Applications should begin as soon as new leaves appear in the spring or at the first appearance of black spot on the foliage and then repeated at 7- to io-day intervals or within 24 hours after each rain.

Glomerella diseases

At least four species of *Glomerella* cause serious anthracnose diseases of numerous important annual crop and ornamental plants, while one. *G. cingulata*, also causes cankers and dieback of woody plants such as camellia and privet, bitter rot of apples, and ripe rot of grape, pears, peaches, and other fruits.

Glomerella Anthracnose Diseases of Annual Plants. The most important Glornerella anthracnose diseases are those on bean, cotton, soybean, and sweet pea. Although different species of the fungus are responsible for the disease on each of these hosts, the life cycles of the fungi, the symptoms, the disease development, and control are approximately the same in all cases. The diseases are present wherever their hosts are grown, although they are more severe in warm to cool, humid areas, and generally are not a problem under dry conditions. Plants in all stages of growth are subject to anthracnose. The fungus is often present in or on the seed produced in infected pods or bolls. Infected seed may show yellowish to brown sunken lesions of various sizes. When infected seeds are planted, many of the germinating seedlings are killed before emergence.

Dark-brown, sunken lesions with pink mass of spores in the center are often present on the cotyledons of young seedlings. The fungus may destroy one or both of the cotyledons, while its spores spread onto the hypocotyl and the mycelium moves into the stem. On the stem the fungus produces numerous small, shallow, reddish-brown specks that subsequently enlarge, become elongated, and finally sunken. The lesions are covered with myriads of pink- to rust-colored spores. If conditions are humid, the lesions may be so numerous that they girdle and weaken the stem to the point where it cannot support the top of the plant.

The fungus also attacks the petioles and the veins' of the under side of the leaves, on which it causes long, dark, brick-red to purplish colored lesions that later turn dark brown to almost black, Few lesions are produced between the veins in bean, but they are rather common on cotton, and in sweet pea they may involve the entire leaf.

The anthracnose fungi also attack and cause their most characteristic symptoms on the bean pods and on the cotton bolls. On the latter, the fungus seems to produce numerous lesions that spread and coalesce and cover most or all the surface of young cotton bolls, with almost continuous masses of spores covering the infected area. On pods, small flesh- to rust-colored elongated lesions appear, which later become sunken, circular, and about 5-8 mm in diameter. Lesions developing on young pods may extend through the pod and even to the seed, while in older pods the lesions do not extend beyond the pod. As the pods mature, the margin of the lesions is generally slightly raised, while the pink spore masses of the lesions dry down to gray, brown, or black granulations or to small pimplelike protrusions.

Glomerella Fruit Rots. The most important of the Glomerella fruit rots are bitter rot of apple and ripe rot of grape.

Bitter rot is worldwide in distribution and in warm, humid weather may cause enormous losses by destroying an entire crop of apples just a few weeks before harvest, Bitter rot symptoms may appear when the fruit is half grown ,but more frequently when it approaches its full size. The rot starts as small, light brown areas that enlarge rapidly and become circular and somewhat sunken in the center. The surface of the spots is smooth at first and may be dark brown or black until the spots are 1 - 2 CM In diameter. Then numerous, slightly raised cushions appear mostly near the center 4 the spots and some extending outward toward the edge of the spots. In humid weather, the cushions produce creamy masses of pink-colored spores, sometimes arranged in concentric circles, the rotted area expands rapidly, and more rings of spore masses appear. In older rotted areas the pink masses disappear and the tissue becomes dark brown to black, wrinkled, and sunken. The rot also spreads inward toward the apple core forming a cone of somewhat watery, rotted tissue that may or may not be bitter. When, as it is common, several spots develop on a fruit, they usually enlarge, fuse, and rot the entire fruit, which may drop and mummify or mummify and cling on the twig. Bitter rot infections may occur in the fall but fail to develop appreciably during cold storage. When, however, the fruit is marketed and kept at room temperature, bitter rot may develop very rapidly. Bitter rot cankers on the limbs are rare and resemble those produced on branches and stems described above.

Ripe rot of grape and other fruits is also worldwide in distribution but is most serious in areas with warm, humid weather during the ripening of the fruit. Ripe rot appears when the fruit is nearly mature and may continue its destruction of fruit after it has been picked and during shipment and marketing. On white or light-colored grapes, a small reddish-brown spot appears at first. It soon spreads to over half the berry and becomes darker with a purplish center and a light-brown border. In dark-colored grapes no appreciable change of color is caused by the rot on the berries. As the disease progresses, the whole berry rots, usually in a continuous manner but sometimes, marked by a series of concentric zones. By this time, the rotted berry becomes more or less densely covered with numerous, small, slightly raised pustules from which, in humid weather, pinkish slimy masses of spores ooze out. Later, the spore masses become darker, almost reddish-brown. The rotted berries then develop a sunken area at the point of infection and gradually become more or less shriveled and mummified, while the pustules continue to produce spores. Infected berries often "shell" or drop off before the rot causes them to dry up.

The fungus, *Glomerella* sp., occasionally produces ascospores in perithecia on overwintering fruit and cankers of some hosts, but in other hosts ascospores and perithecia almost never develop. In all hosts, however, the fungus reproduces profusely by forming pink masses of *Colletotrichum*- or *Gloeosporium*-type conidia in acervuli.

The acervuli consist of a cushion stroma of mycelium

several to many cells thick and develop just beneath the cuticle, which is ruptured by the upward pressure of the developing mass of conidiophores and conidia. The conidia are held together in a sticky mass, which is firm and horny in dry weather, but under humid, moist weather the conidia are released in a pinkish mass and may be washed or spattered by raindrops or carried by wind-blown mist and insects. The fungus usually overwinters in diseased stems, leaves, and fruit as mycelium or spores, in the seed of most affected annual hosts, and in cankers of perennial hosts.

In the cases in which ascospores are produced in mummified fruit, cankers, and so on, they may cause primary infections in the spring, but generally these are not necessary. The surviving mycelium quickly produces conidia in the spring that can themselves cause primary infections and subsequent continuous secondary infections during the entire season as long as temperature and humidity are favorable. Infection is by direct penetration of uninjured tissue, and the mycelium grows intercellularly and may remain latent for some time before the cells begin to collapse and rot. The mycelium then produces acervuli and conidia just below the cuticle, which upon rupture again release conidia that cause more infections.

The fungus generally requires high temperatures and humidity for best activity, and although it can attack young cotyledons, stems, leaves, and fruit, attacks of young fruit generally remain latent until the fruit are past a certain stage of development and maturity, at which point the infections develop fully.

Control of *Glomerella* diseases depends on the use of disease-free seed grown in the arid west or use of treated seed and also crop rotation of hosts like bean, soybean, sweet pea, and cotton, the use of resistant varieties when available, removal and burning of dead twigs, branches, and fruit infected with the fungus in woody plants, and finally, on spraying with fungicides. The fungicides most commonly used include Bordeaux mixture, captan, ferbam, Dikar, mancozeb, captafol, benomyl, and thiophanate-methyl. The kind of fungicide used and the timing of its application vary considerably with the host treated.

Colletotrichum (Gloeosporium) diseases

Colletotrichum diseases are the most common anthracnoses and are very similar, if not identical, to the diseases caused by Glomerella. The latter is probably the sexual stage of most or all species of *Colletotrichum* (Gloeosporium). On cereals and grasses, the fungus, which lives saprophytically on crop residue, may attack young seedlings, but usually it attacks the tissues at the crown and the bases of stems of more developed plants. Infected areas first appear bleached but later become brown. Brownish blotches often develop at or near diseased joints. Toward maturity of the-plant, numerous small black acervuli appear on the stems, lower leaf sheaths, and sometimes on the leaves and on the chaff and spikes of diseased heads.

Depending on how early the plant is attacked and on the severity of the disease, the plant may show a general reduction in vigor, premature ripening or dying of the head, and shriveled grain. The fungus occasionally causes superficial infection on seeds, and it can also overwinter as mycelium on the seed. When seed-borne, the fungus may result in root rot and crown rot of the developing plant. Anthracnose of corn and other cereals has become a major problem in areas where reduced tillage, practiced to minimize loss of soil or water, allows greater survival of inoculum of the pathogen on the crop residue.

Anthracnose of cucurbits is probably the most

destructive disease of these crops everywhere, being most severe on watermelon, cantaloupe, and cucumber. All aboveground parts of the plants are affected. Symptoms appear first on the leaves as small, water-soaked, yellowish areas that enlarge from several millimeters to i - 2 cm and become black in watermelon, while in all other cucurbits they turn brown. Infected tissues dry up and break. Lesions also develop on the petioles, which may result in defoliation of the vine-, on the fruit pedicel, which causes the fruit to turn dark, shrivel, and die; and on the stem, which weaken or kill whole vines. The fruit becomes susceptible to infection at about the time of ripening. Circular, watery, dark, sunken lesions appear on the surface of the fruit that may be from 5 mm to io cm in diameter and up to 8 mm in depth.

The lesions expand rapidly in the field and during transit or storage and may coalesce to form larger ones. The sunken lesions have dark centers, which in moist weather are filled with pink spore masses exuding from acervuli that break through the cuticle. Severely affected fruits are often tasteless or even bitter and are often invaded by soft-rotting bacteria and fungi that enter through the broken find. The fungus overwinters in infected debris in the soil and on or in the seed.

Anthracnose or ripe rot of tomato, and other vegetables and fruits results in serious losses of fruit and occasionally in damage to stems and foliage. Canning tomatoes are particularly susceptible to anthracnose before and after harvest, but other tomatoes, as well as eggplant, pepper, apple, pear, and banana, may be attacked in a similar manner from the time ripening begins through harvest and in storage. In early stages of tomato infection, the symptoms appear as small, circular, sunken, water-soaked spots resembling indentations caused by burnt circular objects. As the fruit softens, the spots enlarge Up to 2 - 3 cm in diameter, and their central portion becomes dark and slightly roughened as a result of black acervuli developing just beneath the skin.

The spots are often numerous and coalesce, leading to the eventual watery softening of the fruit and finally rotting of the fruit, sometimes accelerated by other invading microorganisms. Enormous numbers of conidia are present in acervuli below the skin even in the smallest spots, and under some conditions, pink or salmon-colored masses of spores are also produced on the surface of the spots. The fungus overwinters in infected plant debris and in or on the seed. The fungus may cause light infections of foliage and young stems that may go unnoticed, but they enable the fungus to survive and multiply somewhat until the fruit begins to ripen and become susceptible to infection. High temperatures and high relative humidity or wet weather at the time of ripening favor infection and spread of the fungus and often lead to destructive epidemics. In onion smudge, dark-green or black smudges appear on the outer scales or neck of the bulbs primarily of white onions, although most colored varieties are also partially susceptible, especially in the colorless region of the bulb neck.

The smudgy spots first appear as tiny black stromata or visible-mycelium beneath the cuticle of the scale and may be scattered over the surface of the bulb; more commonly, they congregate in uniformly black, smudgy, circular areas or are arranged in concentric circles, the outer one being up to two or more centimeters in diameter. In moist weather the stromata produce acervuli filled with cream-colored spore masses and containing numerous black, stiff, bristlelike hairs (setae) visible with a hand lens. The fungus attacks inner, living scales only under conditions of favorable high moisture and temperature and, usually, underneath spots on outer scales or where the outer scales have cracked and exposed the inner scales to the soil. The fungus overwinters as mycelium or stromata on infected onions, on sets, and in the soil as a saprophyte.

In citrus anthracnose, especially of orange, grapefruit, and lemon, the disease affects all mature, weakened, or injured aboveground plant parts, including leaves, twigs, and fruit. Anthracnose may occur on trees of any size, in the nursery or in the orchard, but it rarely develops on vigorously growing trees. Anthracnose is common, however, on trees that are weakened or injured from inadequate fertilization, drought, low temperatures, spray injury, insects, other diseases, and so on.

Anthracnose leaf spots bring about death and drying of infected tissues with minute black acervuli produced in concentric circles in the dead areas. During severe infections, defoliation may occur. Weakened twigs are invaded by the anthracnose fungus and die back slowly or rapidly, resulting in what is called withertip. Leaves in affected twigs turn yellow, wither and drop, or they die quickly and dry before they can fall off. Affected branches also lose fruit.

Numerous, small, black, pimplelike acervuli develop on the dead portions of twigs. On dying or dead areas of the surface of citrus fruits, anthracnose fruit spots develop that are circular and sunken and vary from tiny specks to dark-brown or black areas 5 - 10 mm in diameter. The spots become dry and hard and sometimes are dotted with small black acervuli that in humid weather exude masses of pinkish spores. Although anthracnose fruit spots generally affect only the rind, the disease often extends into the pulp and gives it a disagreeable or bitter taste. Some strains of the anthracnose fungus cause a soft decay that results in fruit drop. Also,, often other fungi invade the fruit through anthracnose spots and speed up the rate of fruit decay. Overripe fruit is particularly susceptible to anthracnose infection. When spores of the anthracnose fungus from dead twigs are washed over fruits and then germinate on the fruit, they cause anthracnose russeting of the fruit. The russeting may appear as a large blotch or as a tear stain.

The fungus, *Colletotrichum*, or *Gloeosporium* sp., produces colorless, one-celled, ovoid, cylindrical, and sometimes curved or dumbbell-shaped conidia in acervuli. Masses of conidia appear pink or salmon colored. The acervuli are subepidermal and break out through the surface of the plant tissue; they are disk- or cushion-shaped and waxy, with simple short, erect conidiophores.

Colletotrichum has been distinguished from Gloeosporium by the fact that *Colletotrichum* acervuli have dark, long spines, or sterile hairlike hyphae while *Gloeosporium* acervuli do not. Because, however, this is not always so, the distinction of the two genera is often-impossible, and they are often considered as the same fungus. As mentioned earlier, many *Colletotrichum* species also produce an ascigerous perfect stage, usually *Glomerella*, occasionally *Physalospora* or others, while many *Gloeosporium* species have as perfect stage the ascomycetes *Glomerella* or *Gnomonia*, and occasionally others. The fungus is favored by high temperatures and humid or moist weather.

The conidia are released and spread only when the acervuli are wet and are generally spread by splashing and blowing rain or by coming in contact with insects, other animals, tools, and so on. The conidia germinate only in the presence of water. Upon germination they produce an appressorium and penetration peg and penetrate the host tissues directly. In the beginning the hyphae may grow rapidly, both intercellularly and intracellularly, but cause little or no visible discoloration or other symptoms of disturbance. Then more or less suddenly, especially when fruits begin to ripen, the fungus becomes more aggressive, and symptoms appear. In many hosts the fungus reaches the seed and is either carried on the seeds or in some, it may even invade a small number of seeds without causing any apparent injury to them. There is considerable variability in the kinds of host plants each species of *Colletotrichum* or *Cloeosporium* can attack, and there may be several races with varying pathogenicity within each species of the fungus.

Control of *Colletotrichum* or *Gloeosporium* diseases depends on the use of disease-free seed or seed treated with chemicals and hot water, on a two- to three-year crop rotation when possible, on the use of resistant varieties that are available for several annual crops, and the use of fungicides such as benomyl, maneb, zineb, mancozeb, chlorotholonil, captafol, and folpet.

Fruit and general diseases by ascomycetes and imperfect fungi

These groups of diseases are caused by Ascomycetes and Imperfect Fungi other than those already described and are most commonly found on the fruit or cause most of their damage by their effect on the fruit although they may affect other parts of the plant as well. Most of these fungi differ considerably from each other in fruiting structures, life cycles, and in the diseases they cause. Most of these Ascomycetes produce ascospores in perithecia and both, Ascomycetes and Imperfects, produce conidia on free hyphae.and berry rot of grape, and stem-end rot of citrus fruits.

Ergot of cereals and grasses

Ergot occurs throughout the world, most commonly on rye but also on wheat and less frequently on barley and oats. It is also very common on certain wild and cultivated grasses. An ergot disease affecting corn Occurs, in Mexico.

The disease causes loss of some of the grains in infected heads, occasionally, resulting in losses of up to 5 percent in rye and 10 percent in wheat, but its main importance is due to the fact that the characteristic fungal sclerotia that replace the grains are poisonous to humans and animals that eat feed or bread made from grain contaminated with sclerotia.

The symptoms of ergot appear at first as creamy to golden-colored droplets of a sticky liquid exuding from young florets of infected heads. These droplets may go unnoticed, but they are each soon replaced by a hard, horn-shaped, purplish-black fungal mass that is usually a few millimeters in diameter but may be from 0.2 to 5.0 cm long. These are the sclerotia of the fungus, sometimes called ergots, that grow in place of the kernel and consist of a hard compact mass of fungal tissue, which in cross section appears white or faintly purple.

Ergot is caused by *Claviceps purpurea* and other *Claviceps* species. The fungus overwinters as sclerotia on or in the ground, or mixed with the seed. In the spring, about the time cereals are in bloom, sclerotia on or near the surface of the soil germinate by forming from one to sixty flesh-colored stalks 0.5 - 2.5 cm tall. The tip of each stalk consists of a spherical head at the periphery of which are embedded numerous perithecia, each containing many asci. Each ascus contains eight long, multicellular ascospores. The ascospores are either extruded in a viscous fluid in humid weather and are spread to flowers by insects or are discharged forcibly into the air, are picked up by air currents, and are carried by wind to young open flowers. There they germinate and infect the ovaries directly or by way of the stigma. Within about a week the fungus in the ovary tissues produces spreading, stromalike sporodochia that produce numerous conidia of the *Sphacelia* type. The conidia are floating in a sticky liquid and exude from the young florets as creamy or golden droplets, which are known as the "honey dew" stage.

The liquid of the "honey dew" stage is sugary and attractive to insects, which visit such infected flowers, become smeared with the conidia of the fungus present in the "honey dew," and carry them to other healthy flowers, which the conidia promptly infect. Conidia are probably spread to other flowers by splashing rain, resulting in more infections. Gradually, the secretion of the "honey dew" ceases and each infected ovary, instead of producing normal seed, becomes replaced by a hard mass of fungal mycelium, which eventfully forms the characteristic ergot sclerotium. The sclerotia mature about the same time as the healthy seeds and either fall to the ground where they overwinter, or they are harvested with the grain and may be returned to the land with the seed.

Susceptibility of the various hosts and varieties seems to be related to the duration the flowers remain open. This characteristic has gained significance in the last few years because of the efforts of breeders to produce hybrid varieties in several cereal crops, since the flowers of male-sterile lines of self-pollinated cereals remain open, and therefore susceptible to ergot infection, for a long time. For example, in some experimental Plots, 76 percent of the heads and 36 percent of the flowers of male-sterile barley lines became infected with ergot.

Although ergot does not cause ergotism in humans nearly as often or as severely as it used to, it is probable that it is involved in many otherwise unexplainable poisonings of humans, and it certainly continues to be of economic importance as an animal disease. Grain containing more than 0.3 percent by weight of the ergot sclerotia is classed as ergoty, that is,, can cause ergotism and therefore it may not legally be sold and milled for flour and human consumption. Although most of the sclerotia can be removed from ergoty grain with modern cleaning machinery, it is costly and quite often difficult to remove enough sclerotia to meet the legal standards, particularly in poorer countries, and the remaining traces have often proven toxic to livestock. Feeding livestock with cleanings from contaminated grain or grazing pastures that have infected grass heads can also lead to reproductive failure or gangrene of the peripheral parts of the animals.

Control of ergot depends entirely on cultural and sanitary procedures. Only clean seed or seed that has been freed from ergot should be sown. Sclerotia may be removed from seed by machinery or by soaking contaminated seed for 3 hours in water and then floating off the sclerotia in a solution of about 18 kg salt in 100 liters of water. Ergot sclerotia do not survive for more than a year and do not germinate if buried deep in the ground. Therefore, deep ploughing or crop rotation with a noncereal for at least a year helps eliminate the pathogen from a particular field.

Wild grasses should be mowed or grazed before flowering to prevent production of ergot sclerotia on them and avoid poisoning of livestock through them and also to prevent the spread of the fungus to cultivated cereals and grasses. On male-sterile barley, reasonable control of ergot was obtained with benomyl sprays before and during flowering. Some fungi, for example, *Fusarium roseum*, are hyperparasites of the ergot fungus and appear promising as biological control agents but have yet to be developed.

Apple scab

Apple scab exists in every country where apples are grown. It Is most severe in areas with cool, moist springs and summers, however, and may be completely absent in areas with very dry or warm climates. In the United States it is most serious in the north central and northeastern states.

The disease affects all apples in the genus *Malus*, but similar scab diseases affect pears and hawthorns. Scab is the most important disease of apples. Its primary effect is the reduction of the quality of infected fruit, but it also reduces fruit size and the length of time infected fruit can be kept in storage. Infection of the stem of young fruit results in premature fruit drop. Severe leaf infections result in reduction of the functioning leaf surface, defoliation, and poor fruit bud development for the next year's crop. Losses from apple scab may be 70 percent or more of the total fruit value, and in many apple-producing areas marketable fruit can be harvested if scab control measures are not taken.

Symptoms. The first symptoms of apple scab appear on the under surface of sepals or young leaves of the flower buds as light, somewhat olive-colored, irregular; spots. Soon after, the lesions become olive green with a velvety grayish-dark surface and more circular in outline. Later, the velvety surface disappears and the lesions appear metallic black in color and may be slightly raised. Lesions on leaves that have already unfolded are generally on the upper surface of the leave. The number of lesions per leaf varies with the severity of infection. Lesions may remain distinct or they may coalesce. After severe early leaf infection, leaves may become dwarfed and curled and may later fall off.

Infections of the fruit appear as distinct, almost circular scab lesions, which at first are velvety and olive green but later become darker, scabby, and sometimes cracked. The cuticle of the fruit is ruptured at the margin of the lesions. Severe early fruit infections result in misshapen, cracked fruits, which frequently drop prematurely. Infections late in the season when the fruit approaches maturity result in small lesions that may even be too small to be visible at harvest but develop into dark scab spots during storage.

Twig and blossom infections appear as small scab spots, but they are uncommon and of little importance.

The pathogen: Venturia inaequalis. The mycelium is at first light in color, but later turns brownish in the host tissues. In young leaf lesions the mycelium develops radially in branched ribbons of hyphae, but in older leaves and on the fruit the mycelial strands are compact and thick and in several superimposed layers. In living tissues the mycelium is located only between the cuticle and the epidermal cells and produces short, erect, brownish conidiophores, which successively give rise to several, one- or two-celled, reddish brown *Spilocaea* (Fusicladium)-type conidia of variable, but rather characteristic, shape. In dead leaves the mycelium grows through the leaf tissues.

Fertilization takes place by means of ascogonia and antheridia and perithecia form. The latter, when mature, are dark brown to black with a slight beak and a distinct opening (ostiole). Inside the perithecium 50- 100 asci are formed, each containing eight ascospores. Each ascospore consists of two cells of unequal size, which are hyaline at first but turn brown when mature.

Development of disease. The pathogen overwinters in dead leaves on the ground as immature pseudothecia. Pseudothecia initially develop in the fall and early winter and probably continue to grow during warm periods in the winter and early spring, but rapid growth and ascospore maturation occur with the resumption of favorable weather for growth and development of the host. Neither all the pseudothecia nor all the asci of a pseudothecium mature simultaneously, and some may have ascospores before the apple buds start to open in the spring. Most of the ascospores in the pseudothecia, however, mature in the period during which the fruit buds open.

When dead leaves containing pseudothecia become thoroughly soaked in the spring, the asci elongate, push through the ostiole, and forcibly discharge the ascospores into the air; air currents may carry them to susceptible green apple tissues. Ascospore discharge may continue for 3 - 5 weeks after petal fall.

The ascospores can germinate and cause infection only when they are kept wet over a certain minimum period of time at temperatures ranging roughly from 6 to 26°C. Thus, for infection to occur, the spores must be continuously wet for 28 hours at 6°C, for 14 hours at 10°C, for 9 hours at 18 - 24°C, or 12 hours at 26°C.

Upon germination on an apple leaf or fruit, the ascospore produces a disklike appressorium from which a slender mycelial tube pierces the cuticle, and after developing into a hypha of normal diameter, grows between the cuticle and the outer cell wall of the epidermal cells.

For a few days after infection, the epidermal cells show no injury at all, but by the time the lesion appears these cells show a gradual depletion of their contents, and they eventually collapse and die. Soon the palisade, and later the mesophyll, cells exhibit the same reactions, while the fungus remains largely in the subcuticular position. It is assumed that the fungus obtains its nutrients and causes the death of the cells by secreting enzymes (and possibly toxic substances) that alter the permeability of the cell membranes and break down macromolecular components of the cell into small molecules, which then move along osmotic pressure gradients, reach the mycelium and are absorbed by it.

Once the mycelium is established in the host, it produces enormous numbers of conidia, which push outward, rupture the cuticle, and within 8 - 15 days of inoculation, form the olive-green, velvety scab lesions. Conidia remain attached to the conidiophores in dry weather, but upon wetting during a rain they are easily detached and may be washed down or blown away to other leaves or fruit on which they germinate and cause infection in the same way ascospores do.

Additional infections by conidia continue throughout the growing season following a rain of sufficient duration. Infections, however, are more abundant in the cool, wet periods of spring and early summer and again in the fall. They are infrequent, if not entirely absent, in the dry, hot summer weather. After infected leaves fall to the ground, the mycelium penetrates into the interior of the leaf and forms pseudothecia, which carry the fungus through the winter.

Control: Several apple varieties resistant to scab are available, but all the popular ones are moderately to highly susceptible. A number of fungi are antagonistic to the apple scab fungus, and some of them, such as *Athelia bombasina* and *Chaetomium globosum*, when applied to scab-infected apple leaves on the orchard floor decrease production of ascospores by the apple scab fungus. So far, no effective practical biological control of apple scab has been developed. Apple scab, however, can be thoroughly controlled by timely sprays with the proper fungicides.

For an effective apple scab control program, apple trees must be diligently sprayed or dusted before, during, or immediately after a rain from the time of budbreak until all the ascospores are discharged from the pseudothecia. If these primary infections from ascospores are prevented, there will be less need to spray for scab during the remainder of the season. If primary infections do develop, spraying will have to be continued throughout the season. In most areas application of fungicides for scab control is based on the phenological development of the trees, buds, and flowers, and the first application is made when buds show a slight green tip, the second when 1- 2 CM green leaf shows, the third at tight bud cluster, the fourth when some pink shows, at full bloom, and the fifth at go percent petal fall.

Sprays begin in the spring when a rainy period is sufficiently long at the existing temperature to produce an infection, and are repeated every 5-7 days, or according to rainfall, until petal fall. One must make sure that the new tissues on rapidly expanding young leaves and fruit are always covered with fungicide during an infection period. After petal fall, and depending on the success of the control program to that point, sprays are usually repeated every 10- 14 days for several more times.

In recent years, considerable progress has been made in developing simple or computerized apple scab prediction systems for scheduling fungicide applications for scab control. All these systems are based on the interactions between temperature, amount and duration of rainfall, and duration of leaf wetness on the one hand, with the period required for the pathogen to initiate infection on the other. When conditions favorable to infection are predicted to prevail or have prevailed for sufficiently long periods, the recommendation to apply fungicides is made. The availability of fungicides with protectant or curative activity (or both) against apple scab makes possible the use of apple scab-predicting systems with excellent control results and with reduced numbers of fungicide applications.

Several fungicides that give, excellent control of apple scab are available. Some of them are protectant, since they can protect a plant from becoming infected, but they cannot cure an infection, although some have so-called "kickback" action, that is, the ability to stop infections that may have started, and some have an eradicant action, that is, they can "burn out" young scab spots early in the season. Dodine gives excellent scab control and is one of the fungicides exhibiting eradicant action. It reduces spore formation on scab spots and inhibits germination of spores produced on such spots.

Excellent scab control is also obtained with captan, ferbam, mancozeb, dichlone, thiram, sulfur, captafol, and the systemic fungicides benomyl and thiophanate-methyl. These fungicides may be used alone or in combinations since they differ in their ability to control scab and other diseases, in duration of "kickback" action, in compatibility with other fungicides, and in phytotoxicity. Captafol has recently been used as a single application treatment at the green tip stage of bud development and has been shown to protect new growth from scab until petal fall.

Several newer fungicides, most of them systemics and acting by inhibiting ergosterol biosynthesis in the fungus, show excellent protectant as well as curative control of apple scab. They include etaconazole, bitertanol, fenarinol, and triforine. As with all systemic fungicides, because of their specific mechanism of action against the fungus and the quick appearance of fungus strains resistant to the fungicide, it is recommended that they be applied only in combination with captan, mancozeb, or another broad-spectrum fungicide.

In some areas, new strains of *Venturia inaequalis* have now appeared that are resistant to dodine, benomyl, and some other systemics. These chemicals, therefore, can no longer be relied on to control the disease by themselves.

Brown rot of stone fruits

Brown rot occurs throughout the world where stone fruits

are grown and where there is sufficient rainfall during blossoming and fruit ripening periods. It affects peaches, cherries, plums, apricots, and almonds with about equal severity.

Losses from brown rot result primarily by rotting of the fruit in the orchard, although serious losses may also appear during transit and marketing of the fruit. Yields may be reduced also by destruction of the flowers during the blossom blight stage of the disease. In severe infections, and in the absence of good control measures, 50 - 75 percent of the fruit may rot in the orchard, and the remainder may become infected before it reaches the market.

Symptoms. The first symptoms of the disease appear on the blossoms. Brown spots appear on petals, stamens, or pistils, and they spread rapidly, involving the entire flower and its stem. In humid weather the infected organs are covered with the grayish-brown conidia of the fungus and later shrivel and dry up, the rotting mass clinging to the twigs for some time. Twigs bearing infected flowers develop small, elliptical, sunken, brown cankers around the flower stem, which sometimes may encircle the stem and cause twig blight. In humid weather, gum and also gray tufts of conidia appear on the bark surface.

Fruit symptoms appear when the fruit approaches maturity. Small, circular, brown spots appear, which spread rapidly in all directions. Depending on the humidity, they are sooner or later covered with ash-colored tufts of conidia, which break through the skin and are either scattered or arranged in concentric rings on the fruit surface. One large or several small rotten areas may be present on the fruit, which finally becomes completely rotted and either dries up into a mummy and remains hanging from the tree or falls to the ground, where it also forms a mummy. Sometimes small cankers also develop on twigs or branches bearing infected fruit.

The pathogen: Mondinia (Sclerotinia) fructicola. In addition to *M. fructicola*, two other species, *M. laxa* and *M. fructigena*, cause brown rot of stone fruits. The former occurs in the west coast and the Wisconsin -Michigan area of the United States; the latter is found exclusively in Europe, where it is as serious on apples as it is on stone fruits. With slight differences, the development of the disease caused by each species is essentially the same.

The mycelium produces chains of elliptical *Monilia*-type conidia on hyphal branches arranged in groups or tufts (sporodochia). The fungus also produces microconidia (spermatia) in culture and on mummied fruit. The micronidia are borne in chains on bottle-shaped condlophores, and they do not germinate, but seem to be involved in the fertilization of the fungus. The sexual stage (apothecium) originates from pseudosclerotia formed in mummified fruit partly or wholly buried in the soil or debris.

More than 20 apothecia may form on one mummy. Small, bulblike protrusions appear on the mummy, and they, extend to form the stipe of the fruiting body. As the stipe emerges above ground, its upper portion becomes swollen and a depression appears at the tip. Subsequent growth of the sides of the swelling forms the apothecial "cup," which is usually funnel or, later, disk shaped. The inside or upper surface of the apothecium is lined with thousands of cylindrical asci interspersed with paraphyses. Each ascus contains eight single-celled ascospores.

Development of Disease. The pathogen overwinters as mycelium in mummified fruit on the tree and in cankers of affected twigs, or as pseudosclerotia in mummies in the ground. In the spring the mycelium in mummified fruit on the tree and in the twig cankers produces new conidia, while the pseudosclerotia in mummified fruit buried in the ground produce several apothecia, which will form asci and ascospores.

Both conidia and ascospores can cause blossom infections. The conidia are windblown or may be carried by rainwater and splashes or insects to floral parts. The ascospores are forcibly discharged by the ascus, forming a whitish "cloud" over the apothecium. Air currents then carry the ascospores to the flowers, Conidia and ascospores germinate and can cause infection within a few hours.

The mycelium, especially in humid weather, produces short hyphae, which group together, push outward through the epidermis, and form numerous conidial tufts on the rotten, shriveled floral parts from which new masses of conidia are released. In the meantime, the mycelium advances rapidly down the tissues of the blossom petioles and from there into the fruit spurs and the twigs. In the twig the mycelium causes disintegration and collapse of the cells around the fruit spur, and a depressed, reddish-brown, shield-shaped canker forms. The advance of the mycelium may encircle the twig, which then becomes girdled and dies.

The surface of the canker is soon covered with conidial tufts, and conidia from these serve as inoculum for fruit infection later in the season. The brown rot fungus does not infect leaves or bark directly, and the new conidia and ascospores are short lived. The apothecia themselves soon disintegrate, and therefore no ascospores are present when the fruit becomes susceptible. The gap between the time the blossoms are infected and when the fruit on the same tree can become infected is bridged by the conidia, which are formed on twig cankers during humid weather in the summer. Also, the fruit of some early blooming stone fruits begins to ripen, and therefore becomes susceptible to infection, when some late-blooming ones are still in bloom or have just finished. In the latter case, conidia produced on the flowers of late-blooming trees can be carried to and infect the fruit of early ripening trees. The susceptibility of the fruit to infection increases with its maturity.

Conidia usually penetrate fruit through wounds made by insects, twig punctures, or hail, but on some, fruit penetration can take place through stomata or directly through the cuticle. The fungus grows intercellularly at first and through secretion of enzymes causes the maceration and browning of the infected tissues. The invasion of the fruit by the fungus is quite rapid. As the fungus advances into the fruit, it also produces conidial tufts on the already rotted area, and the conidia may be carried away and infect more fruit.

The entire fruit may become completely rotten within a few days, and it either clings to and hangs from the tree, or falls to the ground. Fruit falling to the ground soon after infection usually disintegrates under the action of saprophytic fungi and bacteria. Fruit left hanging on the tree soon loses moisture and shrivels, and by the end of the season it becomes a dry, distorted mummy with a corrugated surface. The skin remains as a covering, and beneath it the remains of the fruit cells are held in place by the mycelial threads, which are closely interwoven and form a hard rind. Once the fruit has dried into a mummy, it may fall to the ground, but it is not affected by soil microorganisms and may persist there for two or more years.

Fruit infection also takes place after harvest, in storage, and in transit. Infected fruit will continue to rot after harvest, and the mycelium will attack directly healthy fruit in contact with infected ones. Healthy fruit may also be attacked by conidia at any time between harvest and use by the consumer.

Control. Brown rot of stone fruits can be controlled best by completely controlling the blossom blight phase of the disease. This can be done by spraying two to four times with an effective fungicide from the time the blossom buds show pink until the petals fall. Captan, benomyl, thiophanatemethyl, triforine, chlorothalonil, dichlone, sulfur, and thiram are the fungicides used for brown rot control. Several newer fungicides that provide excellent control of brown rot are now being tested. They Include the contact fungicides iprodione and vinclozolin and the systemic bitertand and etaconazole. Resistant strains of the brown rot fungus have developed to each of the systemic fungicides, and therefore, these chemicals are generally used in combination with one of the broad-spectrum fungicides such as captan, thiram, or sulfur.

Twigs bearing infected blossoms or cankers should be removed as early as possible to reduce the inoculum available for fruit infections later on in the season and to eliminate one of the sources of overwintering mycelium and spores that cause blossom infections the following season.

To control brown rot in ripening fruit, the fungicides are applied to the trees a few weeks before harvest, and applications continue weekly or biweekly until just before harvest. Since most infections of immature fruit and many of mature fruit orginate in wounds made by insect punctures, control of insects will also help control the disease.

To prevent infections at harvest and during storage and transit, fruit should be picked and handled with the greatest care to avoid punctures and skin abrasions on the fruit, which enable the brown rot fungus to gain entrance more easily. All fruit with brown rot spots should be discarded. Postharvest brown rot can be reduced by dipping or drenching fruit in a dichloran-benomyl or a dichloran-triforine-benomyl solution before storing and again during the sorting operation; and by hydrocooling or cooling fruit in air before refrigeration at 0 - 3°C. Recently, biological control of brown rot with the bacterium *Bacillus subtilis* has been reported and is being tested for prevention of pre- and postharvest decay of stone fruits.

Botrytis diseases

Botrytis diseases are probably the most common and most widely distributed diseases of vegetables, ornamentals, fruits, and even field crops throughout the world. They are the most common diseases of greenhouse-grown crops. Botrytis diseases appear primarily as blossom blights and fruit rots but also as damping-off, stem cankers or rots, leaf spots and tuber, corm, bulb, and root rots. Under humid conditions, the fungus produces a noticeable gray-mold fruiting layer on the affected tissues that is characteristic of the Botrytis diseases.

Some of the most serious diseases caused by *Botrytis* include gray mold of strawberry, gray mold rot of vegetables such as artichoke, bean, beet, cabbage, carrot, cucumber, eggplant, tip-end rot of bananas, lettuce, pepper, squash, tomato, onion blast and neck rot, calyx end rot of apples, blossom and twig blight of blueberries, blight or gray mold of ornamentals such as African violet, begonia, cyclamen, chrysanthemum, dahlia, geranium, hyacinth, Illy, peony, rose, snapdragon, stock and tulip, bulb rot of amaryllis, corm rot and also leaf spot and stem rot of gladiolus. *Botrytis* also causes secondary soft rots of fruits and vegetables in storage, transit, and market.

In the field, blossom blights often precede and lead to fruit rots and stem rots. The fungus becomes established in flower petals, which are particularly susceptible when they begin to age, and there it produces abundant mycelium. In cool, humid weather the mycelium produces large numbers of conidia, which may cause further infections, but the mycelium itself also grows and penetrates and invades the rest of the inflorescence, which becomes filled and covered with a whitish-gray or light brown cobwebby mold.

The fungus then spreads to the pedicel, which rots and lets the buds and flowers lop over. If any fruit has developed, the fungus moves from the petals into the green or ripe fruit and causes a blossom-end rot of the fruit, which advances and may destroy part or all of the fruit and may spread to other fruits touching the diseased one. Infected fruit and succulent stems become soft and watery, and later, invaded tissues appear light brown. As the tissue rots, the epidermis cracks open and the fungus fruits abundantly.

The tissues then become wrinkled and dry, and flat black sclerotia may appear on the surface or are sunken within the tissue. Damping off of seedlings due to Botrytis occurs primarily in cold frames, where the humidity is high, but also in the field if the seed is contaminated with sclerotia of the fungus, or fungus mycelium or sclerotia are present in the soil.

Some species of Botrytis cause leaf spots on their hosts, for example, on gladiolus, onions, and tulip, the spots being small and yellowish at first but later becoming larger, whitish gray or tan, sunken, coalescing, and frequently involving the entire leaf. In many hosts, however, foliage infection occurs only after the fungus has grown on dying parts of the plants or in decaying matter on the soil that comes into contact with healthy leaves.

Stem lesions usually appear on succulent stems or stalks and may be either dark, sunken, elongated lesions with a definite outline or may spread through the stalk and cause it to weaken and break over at the point of infection, as happens with peony, rose, and tulip. Such stalks are usually susceptible to attack by the fungus along their entire length, and in wet weather the diseased parts become covered with the grayish-brown felty coat of fungus spores. Sclerotia may also be produced on infected stems.

Infection of belowground parts, such as bulbs, corms, tubers, and roots, may begin while these organs are still in the ground or upon harvest. Lesions may develop at any point of their surface, but in most hosts they are more likely to begin at the crown or at the base of these organs. Infected tissues usually appear soft and watery at first, but as the infection progresses, these areas enlarge, turn tan to brown and finally dark brown, and become spongy or corky and light in weight. Pockets of mycelium may develop between decayed bulb scales, under the husks of decayed corms, or on the surface of the lesions of such organs. Black sclerotia are often found on the surface or intermingled with the rotted tissues and mycelium.

The pathogen, *Botrytis* sp., produces abundant gray mycelium and long, branched conidiophores with rounded apical cells bearing clusters of colorless or gray, one-celled, ovoid conidia. The conidiophores and clusters of conidia resemble-a grapelike cluster. The conidia are released readily in humid weather and are carried by air currents. The fungus frequently produces black, hard, flat, irregular sclerotia. Some species of *Botrytis* occasionally produce a Sclerotinia perfect stage in which ascospores are produced in an apothecium.

Botrytis overwinters in the soil as mycelium growing on decaying plant debris and as sclerotia. The fungus does not seem to infect seeds, but it can be spread with seed contaminated with sclerotia the size of the seed or with bits of plant debris infected with the fungus. The overwintering stages can also be spread by anything that moves soil or plant debris that may carry sclerotia or mycelium. The fungus requires cool (18-23°C), damp weather for best growth, sporulation, spore release and germination, and establishment of infection.

The pathogen is active at low temperatures and causes considerable losses on crops kept for long periods in storage, even if the temperatures are between 0 and 10°C. Germinating spores seldom penetrate actively growing tissue directly, but they can penetrate tissues through wounds or after they have grown for a while and produced mycelium on old flower petals, dying foliage, dead bulb scales, and so on. Botrytis sclerotia usually germinate by producing mycelial threads that can infect directly, but in a few cases sclerotia germinated by producing apothecia and ascospores.

Control of *Botrytis* diseases is aided by the removal of infected and infested debris from the field and storage rooms, and by providing conditions for proper aeration and quick drying of plants and plant products. In greenhouses, humidity should be reduced by ventilation and heating. Storage organs such as onion bulbs can be protected by keeping them at 32 - 50°C for 2-4 days to remove excess moisture and then keeping them at 3°C in as dry an environment as possible. Biological control of *Botrytis* gray mold of apple fruit was obtained by spraying the flowers with a spore suspension of the antagonistic fungus *Trichoderma harzianum*, but this is not used in practice yet. Control of Botrytis in the field through chemical sprays has been only partially successful, especially in cool, damp weather. For *Botrytis* rot of lettuce, sprays with dichloran or zineb are recommended, while difolatan, dyrene, maneb-zinc, maneb, and chlorothalonil seem to give better control on crops such as onion and tomatoes. To control fruit rots, such as gray mold of strawberry, sprays or dusts with captan, thiram, or benomyl are recommended.

Two newer contact fungicides, iprodione and vinclozolin, give excellent control of Botrytis and are now being tested on a wide variety of crops. Botrytis strains resistant to benomyl, dichloran, iprodione, and even captan have been found in various crops sprayed with these chemicals. Therefore, the use of different fungicides and fungicide combinations is recommended to reduce appearance and establishment of resistant strains.

Vascular wilts by ascomycetes and imperfect fungi

Vascular wilts are widespread, very destructive, spectacular, and frightening plant diseases appearing as more or less rapid wilting, browning, and dying of leaves and succulent shoots of plants followed by plant death. Wilts occur as a result of the presence and activities of the pathogen in the xylem vascular tissues of the plant. Entire plants or plant parts above the point of vascular invasion by the pathogen may die within a matter of weeks in most annuals and some perennials, although in certain perennials death may not occur until several years after infection.

The pathogen usually continues to spread internally through the xylem vessels as mycelium or conidia until the entire plant is killed. As long as the infected plant is alive, the fungi that cause vascular wilts remain limited to the vascular (xylem) tissues and a few surrounding cells and never come to the surface of the plant-not even to produce spores. Only when the infected plant is killed by the disease do these fungi move into other tissues and sporulate at or near the surface of the dead plant. There are three genera of fungi that cause vascular wilts: *Ceratocystis*, *Fusarium*, and *Verticillium*. Each of them causes widespread and severe disease on several important crop, forest, and ornamental plants.

Ceratocystis causes vascular wilts primarily of trees, such as Dutch elm disease (*C. ulmi*) and oak wilt (*C. fagacearum*).

Fusarium causes vascular wilts primarily of annual vegetables and flowers, herbaceous perennial ornamentals, plantation crops, weeds, and of the mimosa tree (silk tree). Most of the vascular wilt-causing *Fusaria* belong to the species *Fusarium oxysporum*. Different host plants are attacked by special forms or races of the fungus. Thus, the fungus that attacks tomato is designated as F. *oxysporum* f. *lycopersici*, cucurbits *F.* o. f. *niveum*, sweet potato *F. o.* f. *batatas*, onion *F. o.* f *cepae*, cabbage *F.* o. f. *conglutinans*, banana *F* o. f. *cubense*, cotton *F. o.* f. *vasinfectum*, carnation *F. o.* f. *dianthii*, chrysanthemum *F. o.* f. *chrysanthemi*, and so on.

Verticillium causes vascular wilts of annual vegetables, flowers, crop plants, and weeds, and of perennial ornamentals, fruit trees, forest trees, and weeds. It exists as two species, *Verticillium albo-atrum* and *V. dahliae*, and it attacks hundreds of kinds of plants causing wilts and losses of varying severity.

All vascular wilts, regardless of which pathogen causes them, have certain characteristics in common. The leaves of infected plants or of parts of infected plants lose turgidity, become flaccid, lighter green to greenish yellow, droop and finally wilt, turn yellow, then brown, and die. Wilted leaves may be flat or curled. Young, tender shoots also wilt and die. In cross sections of infected stems and twigs, discolored brown areas appear as a complete or interrupted ring consisting of discolored vascular tissues. In the xylem vessels of infected stems and roots, mycelium and spores of the causal fungus may be present. Some of the vessels may be clogged with mycelium, spores, or polysaccharides produced by the fungus. Clogging is further increased by gels and gums formed by the accumulation and oxidation of breakdown products of plant cells attacked by fungal enzymes.

The oxidation and translocation of some such breakdown products seems to also be responsible for the brown discoloration of affected vascular tissues. In newly infected young stems the number of xylem vessels formed is reduced, and their cell walls are thinner than normal. Often the parenchyma cells surrounding xylem vessels are stimulated by secretions of the pathogen to divide excessively, and this, combined with the thinner and weaker vessel walls, results in reduction of the diameter or complete collapse of the vessels. In some hosts, tyloses are produced by parenchyma cells adjoining some xylem vessels.

The balloonlike tyloses protrude into the vessels and contribute to their clogging. Toxins secreted in the vessels by the wilt-causing fungi are carried upward in the water stream and affect living parenchyma cells adjacent to the xylem, thus causing some of the effects described above. Toxins may also be carried to the leaves in which they cause reduced chlorophyll synthesis along the veins (vein clearing) and reduced photosynthesis, disrupt the permeability of the leaf cell membranes and their ability to control water loss through transpiration and thereby result in leaf epinasty, wilting, interveinal necrosis, browning and death.

Of the wilt fungi, *Fusarium* is a soil inhabitant, while *Verticillium* is more of a soil invader. Both infect plants through the roots, which they penetrate directly or through wounds. Large numbers of parasitic nematodes in the soil usually increase the incidence of *Fusarium* and *Verticillium* wilts, presumably by providing effective penetration points. Once in the root, the mycelium reaches the xylem vessels, where it may produce microconidia (*Fusarium*) or conidia (*Verticillium*), and subsequently mycelium and spores spread upward through the vessels, the spores being carried by the transpiration stream. Both fungi produce only asexual spores.

Fusarium overwinters; in the soil or plant debris as thick-walled asexual spores called chlamydospores, or as mycelium and spores in plant debris. *Verticillium* overwinters in the soil as microsclerotia or as mycelium in perennial hosts and in plant debris. Both are effective saprophytes, and once introduced into a field, they become established there forever, although their populations may vary considerably depending on the susceptibility and the duration of cultivation of the host plant grown in the field. *Fusarium* and *Verticillium* spread through the soil to a small extent as mycelium growing through roots or plant debris, but primarily as mycelium, spores, or sclerotia carried in soil water, on farm equipment, transplants, tubers, seeds of some hosts, cuttings of infected plants and in some cases as wind-blown spores or sclerotia.

The two wilt-causing species of the third fungus, *Ceratocystis,* live primarily in the xylem vessels and adjacent parenchyma cells of infected elm and oak trees and in the outer layers of wood and inner layers of bark in elms and oaks killed by them. The fungus produces both ascospores and conidia and spreads from tree to tree either as spores carried by certain bark-feeding beetles or by natural root grafts. The beetles introduce the fungus into the xylem of young, vigorously growing twigs or larger branches on which they feed, and from there, as well as from the natural root grafts, the fungus spreads as mycelium or conidia into the vascular system of the tree and induces wilt. The spores of Ceratocystis are not soil-borne.

Vascular wilts are more or less worldwide in distribution, causing tremendous losses on most kinds of vegetables and flowers and on field crops such as cotton, alfalfa (*Fusarium* and *Verticillium*), on fruit "trees" such as banana (*Fusarium*) and stone fruits (*Verticillium*), on forest and shade trees (*Verticillium*), and on elm and oak trees, in particular (*Ceratocystis*). *Fusarium* wilts are much more common and destructive in the warmer temperate regions and in the tropics and subtropics, becoming less damaging or rare in colder climates except for greenhouse crops in these areas. *Verticillium* is much more common in the temperate zones and is considerably more coldresistant than *Fusarium*, especially in its tree hosts and causes diseases in greater latitudes than the latter. *Ceratocystis* wilts are less widespread than the others, their distribution depending on the availability of the hosts (elms and oaks), of the pathogen, and of contaminated insect vectors.

Vascular wilts are among the most difficult to control. The fact that only a single infection of a plant by one spore is sufficient to introduce the pathogen into the plant, in which it then grows and spreads internally, makes prevention of infection and subsequent control with surface fungicides practically impossible. Also the fact that *Fusarium* and *Verticillium* can survive in the soil of a field saprophytically almost forever, makes control through crop rotation or other cultural practices impractical or ineffective. On the other hand, the dissemination of Ceratocystis spores over long distances by insect vectors feeding on trees of all sizes makes its control even more problematic.

The most effective means of controlling *Fusarium* and *Verticillium* wilts has been the use of resistant varieties. Due to the relative immobility of the pathogens and therefore slow development and distribution of any new pathogen races, varieties remain resistant for rather long periods of time. Cultural practices such as deep plowing, crop rotation, leaving the soil fallow, and flooding the field have been helpful in reducing the pathogen populations in the soil but do not eliminate it completely. Soil fumigation has been used with success in some cases, but it is too expensive and its effect does not last long enough to make its use profitable.

In the greenhouse, soil sterilization gives effective control of both diseases. Control of Ceratocystis wilts has been attempted by efforts to control the insect vectors of the pathogen by insecticides sprayed on or injected into the trees, removal and burning of infected trees and logs to eliminate the fungus and the breeding grounds of the insect vectors and through selection of resistant trees. None of these measures has been successful against the *Ceratocystis* wilts, and the diseases keep on spreading.

An apparent breakthrough in the control of fungal vascular wilts seems to have been made by the discovery of the systemic fungicides containing thiabendazole or its derivatives, including, and particularly, benomyl in its various formulations. These chemicals, although not yet proven to give complete control of any of these wilts, when injected into elm trees before and sometimes after infection have given promising results with *Ceratocystis* wilts, the cause of Dutch elm disease.

Fusarium wilt of tomato

Fusarium wilt is one of the most prevalent and damaging diseases of tomato wherever tomatoes are grown intensively. The disease is most destructive in warm climates and warm, sandy soils of temperate regions. In the United States the disease is most severe in the central states and in the southern regions, whereas in the northern states it can become important only on greenhouse tomatoes. Great losses may be caused by the disease, especially on susceptible varieties and under favorable weather conditions. Fusarium wilt damages plants by causing stunting of plants, which soon wilt and finally die.

Occasionally entire fields of tomatoes are killed or severely damaged before a crop can be harvested. Generally, however, the disease does not cause serious losses unless soil and air temperatures are rather high during much of the season.

Symptoms. The first symptoms appear as slight vein clearing on the outer, younger leaflets, followed by epinasty of the older leaves caused by drooping of the petioles. When plants are infected at the seedling stage, they usually wilt and die soon after appearance of the first symptoms. Older plants I n the field may wilt and die suddenly if the infection is severe and if the weather is favorable for the pathogen.

More commonly, however, in older plants vein clearing and leaf epinasty are followed by stunting of the plants, yellowing of the lower leaves, occasional formation of adventitious roots, wilting of leaves and young stems, defoliation, marginal necrosis of the remaining leaves, and finally death of the plan. Often these symptoms appear on only one side of the stem and progress upward until the foliage is killed and the stem dies. While the plant is still living, no fungus mycelium or fructifications appear only its surface. Fruit may occasionally become infected, and then it rots and drops off without becoming spotted. Roots also become infected, and after an initial period of stunting, the smaller side roots rot.

In cross sections of the stem near the base of the infected plant a brown ring is evident in the area of the vascular bundles, and the upward extent of the discoloration depends on the severity of the disease.

The pathogen: Fusarium oxysporum f lycopersici. The mycelium is colorless at first, but becomes cream-colored or pale yellow with age, and under certain conditions it produces a pale pink or somewhat purplish coloration. The fungus produces three kinds of asexual spores. Microconidia, which are one or two celled, are usually the most frequently and abundantly produced spores under all conditions. They are the spores most frequently produced by the fungus inside the vessels of infected host plants.

Macroconidia are the typical "Fusarium" spores, three to five celled, gradually pointed, and curved toward both ends. They are common on the surface of plants killed by the pathogen and usually appear, in sporodochialike groups. Chlamydospores are one- or two-celled, thick-walled, round spores produced terminally or intercalary on older mycelium or in macroconidia. All three types of spores are produced in cultures of the fungus and probably in the soil, although only chlarnydospores can survive in the soil for long.

Development of disease. The pathogen is a soil inhabitant that survives between crops in infected plant debris in the soil as mycelium and in all its spore forms but most commonly, especially in the cooler temperate regions, as chlarnydospore. It spreads over short distances by means of water and contaminated farm equipment, and over long distances primarily in infected transplants or in the soil carried with them. Usually, once an area becomes infested with Fusarium, it remains so indefinitely.

When healthy plants grow in contaminated soil, the germ tube of spores or the mycelium penetrate root tips directly, or enter the roots through wounds or at the point of formation of lateral roots. The mycelium advances through the root cortex intercellularly and, when it reaches the xylem vessels, enters them through the pits. The mycelium then remains exclusively in the vessels and travels through them, mostly upward, toward the stem and crown of the plant. While in the vessels, the mycelium branches and produces microconidia, which are detached and carried upward in the sap stream. The microconidia germinate at the point where their upward movement Is stopped, the mycelium penetrates the upper wall of the vessel, and more microconidia are produced in the next vessel. The mycelium also advances laterally into the adjacent vessels penetrating them through the pits.

Presumably a combination of the processes discussed earlier-of vessel clogging by mycelium, spores, gells, gums, and tylosis and crushing of the vessels by proliferating adjacent parenchyma cells-is responsible for the breakdown of the water economy of the infected plant. When the amount of water available to the leaves is below the required minimum for their function, the stomata close and the leaves wilt and finally die, followed in death by the rest of the plant.

The fungus then invades the parenchymatous tissues of the plant extensively, reaches the surface of the dead tissues, and there it sporulates profusely. The spores may be disseminated to new plants or areas by wind, water, and so on. Occasionally, the fungus may reach the fruit of infected plants and penetrate or contaminate the seed. This happens primarily when the soil moisture is high and the temperature relatively low, conditions that allow plants to produce good yields although infected with the fungus. Usually, however, infected fruits decay and drop, and even if harvested, infected seeds are so light that they are eliminated in the procedures of extraction and cleaning of the seed and therefore play little role in the spread of the fungus. Control. Use of tomato varieties resistant to the fungus is the only practical measure for controlling the disease in the field. Several such varieties are available today. The fungus is so widespread and so persistent in soils that seedbed sterilization and crop rotation, although always sound practices, are of limited value. Soil sterilization is too expensive for field application, but should be always practiced for greenhouse-grown tomato plants. Use of healthy seed and transplants is of course mandatory, and hot-water treatment of seed suspected of being infected should precede planting.

A great deal of research has been done in the last several years regarding the possibility of biological control of Fusarial wilt of tomatoes and of many other crops. Encouraging results have been obtained by prior inoculation of plants with formae specialis of *F. oxysporum* not pathogenic to each crop, by the use of antagonistic fungi, such as *Trichoderma*, and of siderophore-producing Pseudomonas bacteria. Solar heating (solarization) of field soil by covering with transparent plastic film during the summer also reduces disease incidence. Although promising, none of these methods is used for practical control of Fusarial wilts so far.

Verticillium wilts

Verticillium wilts are worldwide in distribution but most important in areas of the temperate zones. *Verticillium* attacks more than 200 species of plants, most of them vegetables (such as tomato, eggplant, pepper, cantaloupe, and watermelon), flowers (such as chrysanthemum, aster, and dahlia), fruit trees (such as apricot, cherry, and peach); also strawberries, raspberries and roses, field crops (such as cotton, potato, alfalfa, peanuts, and mint); and shade and forest trees (such as maple and elm).

The symptoms of *Verticillium* wilts are almost indentical to those of Fusarium wilts, and on hosts affected by both, the two pathogens cannot be distinguished except by laboratory examinations. In many hosts and most areas, however, *Verticillium* induces wilt at lower temperatures than *Fusarium*, the symptoms develop more slowly, and often appear only on the lower or outer part of the plant or on only a few of its branches. In some hosts,

Verticillium wilt develops primarily in seedlings, which usually die shortly after infection, but more common are late infections, which cause epinasty of the upper leaves followed by the appearance in leaves of irregular chlorotic patches that become necrotic.

Older plants infected with *Verticillium* are usually stunted in various degrees, and their vascular tissues show characteristic discoloration. In many hosts, Verticillium infection results in defoliation, gradual wilting and death of successive branches, or an abrupt collapse and death of the entire plant.

Initial outbreaks of *Verticillium* wilt in a field are typically mild and local. In subsequent years, attacks become severe and widespread until the crop has to be discontinued or is replaced with resistant varieties. The increasing severity of the disease from year to year is brought on by a greater build-up in inoculum potential, by the appearance of strains of the fungus more virulent than the original, or by both.

Two species of *Verticillium*, *V. albo-atrum* and *V. dahliae*, are the causes of verticillium wilts in most plants. Both produce conidia that are short lived. *Verticillium dahliae* also produces microsclerotia, while *V. albo-atrum* produced microsclerotial-like dark thick-walled mycelium but not microsclerotia. *V. albo-atrum* grows best at 20-25°C, while *V. dahliae* prefers slightly higher temperatures (25-28°C) and is somewhat more common in warmer regions. There is, however, considerable variability in virulence and other characteristics of strains within each species. Although some *Verticillium* strains show host specialization, most of them show little host specialization and attack a wide range of host plants. *V. dahliae* overwinters in the soil as microsclerotia, which can survive up to fifteen years. Both, however, can overwinter as mycelium within perennial hosts, in propagative organs, or in plant debris. *Verticillium* penetrates young roots of host plants directly or through wounds.

The fungus is spread by contaminated seed, by vegetative cuttings and tubers, by scions and buds, by wind and surface groundwater, and by the soil itself, which may contain up to 100 or more microsclerotia per gram; 6-50 microsclerotia per gram are sufficient to give 100 percent infection in most susceptible crops. Many fields have become contaminated with *Verticillium* for the first time by planting infected potato tubers or other crops, and it is known that solanaceous crops such as potato, eggplant, and tomato increase the inoculum level in the soil. However, *Verticillium* is often found in uncultivated areas, indicating that the fungus is native to the soils and can attack susceptible crops as soon as they are planted.

Control of *Verticillium* wilts depends on the use of disease-free plants in disease-free soil, the use of resistant varieties, and on avoiding the planting of susceptible crops where solanaceous crops have been grown repeatedly. Soil fumigation can be profitable when used to protect high-value crops, but it is too expensive on large areas. Thermal inactivation via soil solarization is proving useful for control of *Verticillium* in regions with high summer temperatures and low rainfall, such as California and Israel,

Ceratocystis wilts

The Ceratocystis wilts include mainly the Dutch elm disease and oak wilt.

Dutch elm disease

Dutch elm disease Is the most destructive shade tree disease in the United States today. It affects all elm species but most severely the American elm. The disease may kill branches and entire trees within a few weeks or a few years from the time of infection. Hundreds of thousands of elm trees in towns across the country die from Dutch elm disease every year. The cost of cutting down diseased and dead elm trees amounts to many millions of dollars per year. And, of course, no one can estimate the value of the natural beauty destroyed by the diease in countless communities.

Symptoms. The first symptoms of Dutch elm disease appear as sudden or prolonged wilting of the leaves of individual branches or of the entire tree. Wilted leaves frequently curl, turn yellow, then brown, and finally fall off the tree earlier than normal. Most affected branches die immediately after defoliation.

The disease usually appears first on one or several branches and then spreads to other portions of the tree. Thus, many dead branches may appear on a tree or a portion of a tree. Such trees may die gradually, branch by branch, over a period of several years or they may recover. Sometimes, however, entire trees suddenly develop disease symptoms and may die within a few weeks. Usually trees that become infected in the spring or early summer die quickly, while those infected in late summer are much less seriously affected and may even recover, unless they become reinfected.

When the bark of infected twigs or branches is peeled back, brown streaking or mottling appears on the outer layer of wood. In cross section of the branch, the browning appears as a broken or continuous ring in the outer rings of the wood.

The pathogen: Ceratocystis ulmi. The mycelium is creamy white. While in the vessels, the mycelium produces short hyphal branches on which clusters of *Sporothrix (Cephalosporium)*-type conidia are formed. In dying or dead trees, the mycelium produces some *Sporothrix*, but mostly *Pesotum (Graphium)-type* spores on coremia developing on bark which is somewhat loose from the wood and in tunnels made in the bark by insects. The coremia consist of hyphae grouped into an erect, dark, solid stalk, and a colorless, flaring head to which the spores adhere, forming a sticky glistening, whitish at first, and later slightly yellowish, droplet.

The fungus is heterothallic and requires the contact of two sexually compatible strains for sexual reproduction. Since, frequently, only one of the mating types is found in large areas in nature, sexual reproduction is extremely rare. In the United States, for example, the fungus rarely reproduces sexually, but it does so rather frequently in Europe. When the two mating types do come in contact, perithecia develop. The perithecia are spherical and black, about 120 μm in diameter, and have a long (about 300-400 μm) neck. Perithecia form singly or in groups and in the same areas in the bark as the coremia.

Inside the perithecium, many asci develop but as the asci mature, they disintegrate, leaving the ascospores free in the perithecial cavity. The ascospores are discharged through the neck canal and accumulate in a sticky droplet.

Development of disease. Dutch elm disease is the result of an unusual partnership between a fungus and an insect. Although the fungus alone is responsible for the disease, the insect is the indispensable vector of the fungus, carrying the fungus spores from infected elm wood to healthy elm trees. The insects responsible for the spread of the disease are the European elm bark beetle (*Scolytus multistriatus*) and the native elm bark beetle (*Hylurgopinus rufipes*).

The fungus overwinters in the bark of dying or dead elm trees and logs as mycelium and as spore-bearing coremia. Elm bark beetles prefer to lay their eggs in the intersurface between bark and wood of trees weakened or dying by drought or disease. The adult female beetle tunnels through the bark and opens a gallery either parallel with the grain of the wood (*Scolytus*) or at an angle or perpendicular (*Hylurgopinus*).

The female lays eggs along the sides of the gallery, the eggs soon hatch, and the larvae open tunnels at right angles to the maternal gallery. If the tree was already infected with the fungus, the fungus produces mycelium and sticky, *Graphium*-type spores in the beetle tunnels. When the adult beetles emerge, they carry thousands of fungus spores on and in their bodies. *Scolytus* beetles feed in the crotches of living, vigorous elm twigs. *Hylurgopinus* beetles feed on stems 5-30 cm in diameter.As the beetles burrow into the bark and wood, the spores are deposited in the wounded tissues of the tree, germinate, and grow rapidly into the injured bark and the wood. When the fungus reaches the large xylem vessels of the spring wood, it may produce Sporothrix-type spores, which are carried up by the sap stream. These spores reproduce by yeastlike budding, germinate, and start new infections.

The extent of symptoms in the crown is correlated with the extent of vascular invasion. In early stages of infection, the mycelium invades primarily the vessels, and only occasionally tracheids, fibers, and the surrounding parenchyma cells. General invasion of tissue begins at the terminal or extensive dieback phase of the disease, at which time there is also considerable intercellular growth of the fungus between the parenchyma cells. Gums and tyloses are produced in the larger vessels, and sometimes isolated areas of the sapwood are blocked by a combination of gums, tyloses, and fungal growth. Infection also induces browning of the water-conducting vessels. Infected twigs and branches soon wilt and die. Infections that take place in the spring or early summer result in invasion of the long vessels of the elm springwood through which the spores can be carried rapidly to all parts of the tree. If vascular invasion becomes general, the tree may die within a few weeks.

During later infections, vascular invasion is limited to the outer, shorter vessels of the summerwood in which they move only for short distances. As a result, late infections may produce only localized infections and seldom cause serious immediate damage to the tree but may kill the tree the next year. The elm bark beetles feed on living trees for only a few days and then fly back to dying or weakened elm wood in which they construct new galleries and lay eggs. There are usually two generations of beetles per season. In each generation the young adult goes from dead or weakened elm trees to living, vigorous ones on which it feeds and then returns to the dead or weakened trees to lay its eggs. Therefore, once an insect becomes contaminated with fungus spores, it may carry them either to healthy or diseased wood, in both of which the fungus grows and multiplies and may contaminate all the offspring of the insect as well as any other insects that visit the infected wood.

Control Great efforts have been made and are being continued to find resistant clones within the susceptible American elm species and in other species. Certain Asiatic species, such as the Siberian and the Chinese elm, are resistant to Dutch elm disease but produce poor shade trees. Hybrids between various species have shown resistance in varying degrees and some of them look promising, but so far none of them has been planted widely or proved completely resistant. For a long time, control of Dutch elm disease in the United States was attempted primarily through sanitation measures and through chemical control of the insect vectors of the fungus. Sanitation involves the removal and destruction of weakened or dead elm trees and elm logs, thus destroying the larvae contained in them or denying the insect and the fungus their overwintering habitat. Pruning out infected twigs and branches sometimes eliminates the disease. Naturally grafted roots of elm trees can be cut or killed with chemicals to prevent spread of the fungus to adjacent trees.

Control of the insect vector by chemicals involves spraying the healthy elm trees while dormant and in the spring with methoxychlor and other insecticides, but spraying has been only partially effective. In some areas trap logs and pheromone traps are being tested as a means of reducing the number of insect vectors of Dutch elm disease but so far with little success. The most promising results for Dutch elm disease control in individual trees have been obtained with trunk or root injections of healthy or diseased elm trees with solubilized benomyl or thiabendazole. These systemic fungicides, in various chemical formulations, have in some cases arrested the advance of the disease in infected trees and reduced the appearance of new infections on treated healthy trees, but they are not particularly dependable.

Root and stem rots by ascomycetes and imperfect fungi

Several Ascomycetous fungi attack primarily the roots and lower stems of plants, particularly of cereals. Another fungus, *Sclerotinia*, causes crown rots and blights of nearly all kinds of succulent plants, primarily flowers and vegetables, and also root and crown rot of turf grasses, a disease known as dollar spot.

In few, if any, of the diseases caused by the first two fungi, *Cochliobolus* and *Gibberella*, does the ascigerous stage play a role of any consequence. In almost all cases, the diseases are caused strictly by the asexual stages of these fungi, which are primarily species of *Helminthosporium* for *Cochhobolus* and species of *Fusarium* for *Gibberella*. Therefore, the diseases caused by *Cochhobolus* are discussed as diseases caused by *Helminthosporium* (see pages 359-366) and all but one *Gibberella* disease are discussed as diseases caused by *Fusarium*.

As a general rule, the root and stem rot diseases caused by the above and by other Ascomycetes and Imperfect Fungi appear on the affected plant organs at first as water-soaked areas that later turn brown to black, although in some diseases they are frequently covered by white fungal mycelium. The roots and stems are killed more or less rapidly, and the entire plant grows poorly or is killed. The fungi that cause these diseases are nonobligate parasites that live, grow, and multiply in the soil as soil inhabitants, usually in association with dead organic matter, and they are favored by high soil moisture and high relative humidity in the air.

Most of them produce conidia, and some produce ascospores occasionally or regularly. Several produce sclerotia. In all of the above fungi the fungus can overwinter as mycelium in infected plant tissues or debris, as sclerotia, or as any of the kinds of spores the fungus may produce. These same stages also serve as inoculum that can be spread and start new infections. In recent years, considerable progress has been made in biological control of several root and stem rot fungi by treating the seed with antagonistic fungi and bacteria. Such treatments, however, are still at the experimental stage.

Fusarium root and stem rots

Several *Fusarium* species, but primarily *F. solani* and its formae specialis, and also some formae specialis of *F. oxysporum* cause, instead of vascular wilts, rotting of seeds and seedlings (damping off), rotting of roots, lower stems and crowns, and rots of corms, bulbs, and tubers. The plants affected belong to widely separated families and may be vegetables, flowers, field crops, and weeds. These diseases are worldwide in distribution and cause severe losses by reducing stands and the growth and yield of infected plants.

In root rots, as those of bean, peanut, soybean, and asparagus, tap roots of young plants at first show a slightly reddish discoloration; this later becomes darker red to brown and larger, more or less covering the tap root and the stem below the soil line without a definite margin, or appearing as streaks extending up to the soil line. Longitudinal fissures appear along the main root, while the small lateral roots are killed. Plant growth is generally retarded, and in dry weather the leaves may turn yellow and even fall off. Sometimes, infected plants develop secondary roots and a large number of rootlets just below the soil line, and these roots, under favorable moisture conditions, may be sufficient to carry the plant to maturity and to production of a fairly good crop. In many cases, however, infected plants decline and die with or without wilt symptoms. In stem rots, such as those of carnation and chrysanthemum, infected plants wilt and die from a stem rot at the base of the plant. Lesions develop on the stem at or, below the soil line, and their edges often have pink or red discolorations.

The lesions develop inward from the outside, and usually there is no internal stem discoloration, but in some plants a brown discoloration may extend in the wood of the stem for a considerable distance above the ground. In older plants the roots may have also rotted and may have sloughed off. Rots of bulbs, corms, and tubers by species of Fusarium can occur in the field and in storage. They are common on plants such as onion, iris, Illy, and gladiolus. The rot can start at uninjured sides of bulbs, corms, or tubers, but it often starts at wounds, at the base of these organs, at injured or diseased roots or foliage, or through the cuts formed on such tissues during harvest. Invaded bulbs and corms may or may not show outward symptoms, although usually the basal plate and fleshy scales, as well as the roots, are brown to black, sunken and decaying, and often containing mats of mycelium.

The rot is generally dry and firm. The foliage turns yellow, purple, or brown and dies prematurely. Tubers usually develop small brown patches that soon enlarge, become sunken, and show concentric wrinkles that contain cavities lined with white mycelium. Eventually large parts of the tuber or entire tubers are destroyed and become hard and mummified, unless it is humid and then they are invaded by soft rotting bacteria.

Fusarium root and stem rots increase greatly in severity when plants exposed to the pathogen are stressed by low temperature, by intermittent drought or excessive soil water, by herbicides, by surface soil compaction by tractor wheels, and by subsurface tillage pans, which restrict root growth. The fungus, Fusarium solani, generally produces only asexual spores, although under certain conditions a perithecial stage identified as Nectria *haematococca* is produced. The asexual spores are produced in sporodochia and include one- to two-celled microconidia, and the typical *Fusarium*-type macroconidia consisting of 3 - 9 (usually 4 - 5) cells, slightly curved, with more or less pointed ends.

Fusarium also produces one- to two-celled, thick-walled chlarnydospores that can withstand drought and low temperatures. The fungus can live on dead plant tissue and can overwinter as mycelium or spores in infected or dead tissues or seed. The spores are easily spread by air, equipment, water, and contact, and the fungus is already present in many soils as spores.

Control of *Fusarium* rots of root, stem, and corms is generally possible in the greenhouse through soil sterilization and use of healthy propagative stock. Because of rapid reestablishment of the pathogen in the soil from airborne spores, however, it may be necessary to eliminate such spores within the greenhouse by fumigation, and the soil may have to be treated with chemicals such as captafol after soil sterilization to inhibit recolonization of the steamed soil by the pathogen. There are currently no adequate control measures for these diseases in the field.

Loosening compacted soil with subsoiler chisels to a depth Of 25-50 cm in the last tillage before planting has been the most dependable method in reducing Fusarium root rot of bean. Rotation with nonsusceptible crops, good soil drainage, and the use of disease-free or fungicide-treated seed or other propagative stock may help reduce losses. Fertilization with the nitrate form of nitrogen also helps reduce disease as does the use of resistant varieties when available. Treatment of propagative stock with benomyl or application of benomyl sprays on the plants in the field or greenhouse has helped reduce the incidence of Fusarium rots on some kinds of plants.

Biological control of Fusarium root and stem rots has been attempted with some success by incorporating organic materials such as barley straw, lettuce, and chitin in the soil, thus favoring the increase of several fungi and bacteria antagonistic to Fusarium, or by treating seeds or transplants with spores of fungal antagonists, mycorrhizal fungi, or antagonistic Pseudomonas bacteria. None of the biological controls is used in practice so far.

Take-all of wheat, other cereals, and grasses

Take-all is a wide-spread and destructive disease of wheat and of the other cereals and grasses in temperate climates around the world. It is primarily, a root and basal stem disease of winter wheat, particularly in areas of intensive, continuous cultivation of cereals. Losses may vary from negligible to 50 percent. The presence of take-all in a wheat field is often suggested early in the season by the appearance of patches of poorly developed, yellowish seedlings or stunted and unthrifty plants producing few tillers. Later, as plants approach maturity, affected plants ripen prematurely and produce heads that have sterile, bleached spikelets and are known as white-heads. Infected plants are easily pulled from the soil because much of their root system has been destroyed by the fungus and the remaining few roots are short, brown-black, and brittle.

The brown-black dry rot usually extends to the crown and the base of the stem up to the lower leaf bases. A dark mat of mycelium develops between the stem and the lowest leaf sheath, and the necks of fungal perithecia appear on the leaf sheath as small black raised spots. A diagnostic feature of the disease is the presence on the surface of roots of thick brown strands of runner hyphae.

The pathogen of take-all is the fungus *Gaeumannomyces* (*Ophiobolus*) *graminis*, of which var. *tritici* attacks most cereals and grasses but not oats, while var. *avenae* attacks all cereals, including oats. The fungus produces runner hyphae, which grow superficially on roots and produce short, darker, haustoriumlike feeder hyphae called hyphopodia. The hyphopodia grow toward the host, are flattened, and have a pore through which a hyphal peg grows into the root.

The fungus produces only one kind of spores in nature, ascospores in asci in perithecia. In culture, however, it also produces phialospores (conidia) from phialids (bottle-shaped terminal hyphal cells). The perithecia are black and embedded in basal leaf sheaths, with protruding black necks.

The fungus overwinters in infected wheat and grass plant roots and stems and in host debris. The ascospores are discharged forcibly from the asci in wet weather but rarely seem to cause infection. By far the most infections are caused by mycelium coming in contact with roots of growing plants. The superficial mycelium produces feeder hyphae that penetrate root tissues directly through pegs. The fungus invades the cortex and the vascular system but does not grow systemically through the latter. Invaded roots are killed. In young plants, the fungus extends into the crown and base of the stem, while in more mature plants its spread is slower and usually remains confined to the roots.

The fungus can infect plants throughout the growing season but is more active at temperatures between 12 and 18°C. Take-all is most severe in infertile, compacted, alkaline, and poorly drained soils. Its severity increases for several (3 - 6) years in fields cultivated continuously with wheat, but then it declines (take-all decline) and stabilizes at a lower level.

Control of take-all depends primarily on cultural practices, particularly crop rotation with nonhost plants. Other control measures include destruction of grassy weeds and volunteer wheat plants that can harbor the fungus, application of adequate potassium, phosphorus, and ammonium- but not nitrate-type nitrogen fertilizer, and the use of tolerant varieties since no highly resistant ones are available. Recently, yield losses due to take-all were reduced by 60-75 percent through seed treatment with the systemic fungicide triadimenol.

In recent years, a great deal of research has been carried out to discover and to develop biological controls of take-all. It was observed that some soils were suppressive to take-all, while others were conducive to the disease and that suppressiveness could be transferred from field to field and could be eliminated by high (60°C) temperatures and by fumigation. It was later shown that take-all decline (soil suppressiveness) was brought about by root-colonizing fluorescent pseudomonad bacteria that are antagonistic to *Gaeumannomyces* and inhibit its growth on the root surface or in the lesion formed after infection. It appears that the antagonistic bacteria are favored by wheat root exudates and multiply 5 - 10 times faster than other bacteria. Through their increased populations, and increased inhibitory action on the pathogen by means of their antibiotics, siderophores, and so on, the antagonistic bacteria bring about the decline of take-all. Many bacterial strains have now been found that effectively inhibit the fungus in laboratory tests. When the same bacteria are applied on the seed, however, and the seed is planted in *Gaeumannomyces*-infested soil in the greenhouse and in field plots, control is only partial-and frequently falls completely. Therefore, biological control of take all in the field is not yet possible, but it is likely that, through research, the obstacles will soon be overcome.

Sclerotinia diseases

Fungi of the genus *Sclerotinia*, especially *S. sclerotiorum* and *S. minor*, cause destructive diseases of numerous succulent plants, particularly vegetables and flowers and some shrubs. *S. minor* attacks primarily peanuts and lettuce, while another species, *S. trifoliorum*, attacks forage legumes, and *S. homeocarpa* causes a destructive disease of turf grasses. Sclerotinia diseases are worldwide in distribution and affect plants in all stages of growth, including seedlings, mature plants, and harvested products in transit and storage.

Sclerotinia diseases of vegetables and flowers

The symptoms caused by *Sclerotinia* vary somewhat with the host or host part affected and with the environmental conditions. The *Sclerotinia* diseases are known under a variety of names. The most common of these along with some of the host plants most seriously affected, are the following: cottony rot, white mold, or watery soft rot of bean, cabbage, carrot, eggplant, citrus, peanut, potato, stock, tobacco: stem rot and timber rot of cucumber, squash, bean, artichoke, asparagus, chrysanthemum, dahlia, delphinium, peony, potato, tomato, soybean, sweet potato, drop of lettuce, broad bean, beet, cabbage; damping off of celery, lettuce; crown rot or wilt of columbine, snapdragon; blossom blight of narcissus, camellia; pink joint of red pepper, stem canker of hollyhock, and root and crown rot of clover.

The most obvious and typical early symptom of Sclerotinia diseases is the appearance on the infected plant of a white fluffy mycelial growth in which soon afterwards develop large, compact resting bodies or sclerotia. The sclerotia are white at first but later become black and hard on the outside and may vary in size from 0.5 - i mm in *S. minor* to 2- 10 mm in diameter in *S. sclerotiortun*, although they are usually more flattened and elongated than spherical. *Steins* of infected succulent, herbaceous plants at first develop pale or dark brown lesions at their base. The lesions are often quickly covered by white cottony patches of fungal mycelium. In the early stages of lesion development in the stem, the foliage may show little sign of attack, and infected plants are easily overlooked until the fungus grows completely through the stem and the stem rots. Then the foliage above the lesion wilts and dies more or less quickly. In some cases the infection may begin on a leaf and then move into the stem through the leaf. The sclerotia of the fungus may be formed either internally in the pith of the stem, giving no outward signs of their presence there, or they may be formed on the outside of the stem where they are quite apparent.

Leaves and petioles of plants such as lettuce, celery, and beets suddenly collapse and die as the fungus infects the base of the stem and the lower leaves. Rapidly the fungus invades and spreads through the stem, and the entire plant dies and collapses, each leaf dropping downward until it rests on the one below. Mycelium and sclerotia usually appear on the lower surface of the outer leaves, but under moist conditions the fungus invades the plant completely and causes it to rot, producing a white, fluffy, mycelial growth over the entire plant. If dry weather follows infection, the fungus forms cankers in the stem that kill the plant without a soft rot. Attack of celery produces a characteristic pink or reddish-brown, water-soaked area at the base of the affected petioles that is often covered by the white mycelium, and the rot may spread through the stalks causing the collapse of the whole plant.

Fleshy storage organs, such as carrots, infected by *Sclerotinia* develop a white, cottony growth on their-surface whether they are still in the field or in storage. Black sclerotia are formed externally and invaded tissues appear darker than healthy ones and become soft and watery. If the disease develops after harvest in the storage house, the rot spreads to adjacent roots or whatever the storage organs are and produces pockets of rotted organs, or all the organs in the crate may become infected and collapse producing a watery soft rot, covered by fungus growth.

Fleshy fruits, such as cucumber, squash, and eggplant, and seed pods of bean, are also attacked by *Sclerotinia* through their closest point to the ground, at the point of their contact with the ground, or through their senescent flower parts. The fungus causes a wet rot that spreads from the tip of the fruit or pod to the rest of the organ, which eventually becomes completely rotted and disintegrated. The white fungal mycelium and the black sclerotia can usually be seen both externally and within the affected pods and fruits.

Chapter 4

Characteristics of Nematodes

Nematodes are wormlike in appearance but quite distinct taxonomically from the true worms. Numerous species of nematodes attack and parasitize humans and animals, in which they cause various diseases. Several hundred species, however, are known to feed on living plants, causing a variety of plant diseases. Plant-parasitic nematodes are small, 300-1000 µm, with some up to 4 mm long, by 15-35 µm wide. Their small diameter makes them invisible to the naked eye, but they can be easily observed under the microscope. Nematodes are, in general, eel-shaped, and round in cross section, with smooth, unsegmented bodies, without legs or other appendages. The females of some species, however, become swollen at maturity and have pear-shaped or spheroid bodies.

The nematode body is more or less transparent. It is covered by a colorless cuticle, which is usually marked by striations or other markings. The cuticle molts when a nematode goes through Its successive larval stages.

The cuticle is produced by the hypodermis, which consists of living cells and extends into the body cavity as four chords separating four bands of longitudinal muscles. These muscles enable the nematode to move. Additional specialized muscles exist at the mouth and along the digestive tract and the reproductive structures. The body cavity contains a fluid through which circulation and respiration take place. The digestive system is a hollow tube extending from the mouth through the esophagus, intestine, rectum, and anus. Lips, usually six in number, surround the mouth. All plant-parasitic nematodes have a hollow stylet or spear, which is used to puncture plant cells. The reproductive systems are well developed. Female nematodes have one or two ovaries, followed by an oviduct and uterus terminating in a vulva. The male reproductive structure is similar to the female, but there is a testis, seminal vesicle, and a terminus in a common opening with the intestine. A pair of protrusible, copulatory spicules are also present in the male.

The life histories of most plant parasitic nematodes are, in general, quite similar. Eggs hatch into larvae, whose appearance and structure are usually similar to those of the adult nematodes. Larvae grow In size, and each larval stage is terminated by a molt. All nematodes have four larval stages, with the first molt usually occurring in the egg. After the final molt the nematodes differentiate into adult males and females. The female can then produce fertile eggs either after mating with a male or, in the absence of males, parthenogenetically, or can produce sperm herself. A life cycle from egg to egg may be completed within 3 or 4 weeks under optimum environmental, especially temperature, conditions but will take longer in cooler temperatures. In some species of nematodes the first or second larval stages cannot infect plants and depend for their metabolic functions on the energy stored in the egg. When the infective stages are produced, however, they must feed on a susceptible host or starve to death. Absence of suitable hosts may result in the death of all individuals of certain nematode species within a few months, but in other species the larval stages may dry up and remain quiescent, or the eggs may remain dormant in the soil for years.

Almost all plant-pathogenic nematodes live part of their lives in the soil. Many of these live freely in the soil, feeding superficially on roots and underground stems, but even in the specialized sedentary parasites, the eggs, the preparasitic larval stages, and the males are found in the soil for all or part of their lives. Soil temperature, moisture, and aeration affect survival and movement of nematodes in the soil.

Nematodes occur in greatest abundance in a layer of soil from 0 to 15 cm deep, although distribution of nematodes in cultivated soil is irregular and is greatest in or around the roots of susceptible plants, which they follow sometimes to considerable depths (30-150 cm or more). The greater concentration of nematodes in the region of host plant roots is due primarily to their more rapid reproduction on the food supply available and also to attraction of nematodes by substances released into the rhizosphere.

To these must be added the so-called hatching factor effect of substances originating from the root that diffuse into the surrounding soil, markedly stimulating the hatching of eggs of certain species. Most nematode eggs, however, hatch freely in water in the absence of any special stimulus. Nematodes spread through the soil very slowly under their own power. The overall distance traveled by a nematode probably does not exceed a meter per season. Nematodes move faster in the soil when the pores are lined with a thin film of water than when the soil is waterlogged. In addition to their own movement, however, nematodes can be easily spread by anything that moves and can carry particles of soil. Farm equipment, irrigation, flood or drainage water, animal feet, and dust storms spread nematodes in local areas, while over long distances nematodes are spread primarily with farm produce and nursery plants. A few nematodes that attack the above ground parts of plants not only spread through the soil as described above, but they are also splashed to the plants by falling rain or overhead watering, or they ascend wet plant stem or leaf surfaces on their own power. Further spread takes place upon contact of infected plant parts with adjacent healthy plants. Three genera of the family Aphelenchoididae, that is *Aphelenchoides* (bud and leaf nematodes), *Bursaphelenchus* (the pine wilt nematode), and *Rhadinaphelenchus* (the coconut red-ring nematode), seldom, if ever, enter the soil. They survive instead in the tissues of the plants they infect and, the last two, in their insect vector.

All plant-parasitic nematodes belong to the phylum Nematoda. Most of the important parasitic genera belong to the order Tylenchida, but a few belong to the order Dorylaimida.

Phylum: NEMATODA

Order: Tylenchida.

Suborder: Tylenchina

Superfamily: Tylenchoidea

Family: Tylenchidae

Genus: *Anguina*, wheat or seed-gall nematode

Ditylenchus, stem or bulb nematode of alfalfa, onion, narcissus, etc.

Family: Tylenchorhynchidae

Genus: *Tylenchorhynchus*, stunt nematode of tobacco, corn, cotton, etc.

Family: Pratylenchidae

Genus: *Pratylenchus*, lesion nematode of almost all crop plants and trees

Radopholus, burrowing nematode of banana, citrus, coffee, sugarcane, etc.

Family: Hoplolaimidae

Genus: *Hoplolaimus*, lance nematode of corn, sugarcane, cotton, alfàlfa, etc.

Rotylenchus, Spiral nematode of various plants

Helicotylenchus, spiral nematode of various plants

Family: Belonolaimidae

Genus: *Belonolaimus*, sting nematode of cereals, legumes, cucurbits, etc.

Superfamily: Heteroderoidea

Family: Heteroderidae

Genus: *Globodera*, cyst nematode of potato

Heterodera, cyst nematode of tobacco, soybean, sugar beets, cereals

Meloidogyne, root-knot nematode of almost all crop plants

Family: Nacobbidae

Genus: *Nacobbus*, false root-knot nematode

Rotylenchulus, reniform nematode of cotton, papaya, tea, tomato, etc.

Superfamily: Criconematoidea

Family: Criconematidae

Genus: *Criconemella*, ring nematode of woody plants

Hemicychophora, sheath nematode of various plants

Family: Paratylenchidae

Genus: *Paratylenchus*, pin nematode of various plants

Family: Tylenchulidae

Genus: *Tylenchulus*, citrus nematode of citrus, grapes, olive, lilac, etc.

Suborder: Aphelenchina

Superfamily: Aphelenchoidea

Family: Aphelenchoididae

Genus: *Aphelenchoides*, foliar nematode of chrysanthemum, straw berry, begonia, rice, coconut, etc.

Bursaphelenchus, the pine wood nematode

Rhadinaphelenchus, the coconut red ring nematode

Order: Dorylaimida

Family: Longidoridae

Genus: *Longidorus*, needle nematode of some plants

Xiphinema, dagger nematode of trees, woody vines, and of many annuals

Family: Trichodoridae

Genus: *Paratrichodorus*, stubby root nematode of cereals, vegetables, cranberry, apple

Trichodorus, stubby root nematode of sugar beet, potato, cereals, apple

In terms of habitat, pathogenic nematodes are either *ectoparasites*, that is species that do not normally enter root tissue but feed only on the cells near the root surfaces, or *endoparasites*, that is, species that enter the host and feed from within. Both of these can be either *migratory*, that is, they live freely in the soil and feed on plants without becoming attached, or move around inside the plant, or *sedentary*, that is, species that, once within a root, do not move about. The ectoparasitic nematodes include the ring nematodes (sedentary) and the dagger, stubby root, and sting nematodes (all migratory). The endoparasitic nematodes include the root knot, cyst, and citrus nematodes (all sedentary), and the lesion, stem and bulb, burrowing, leaf, stunt, lance, and spiral nematodes (all somewhat migratory).

Plant-parasitic nematodes are generally isolated from the roots of plants they infect or from the soil surrounding the roots on which they feed. A few kinds of nematodes, however, attack above ground plant parts, for example, chrysanthemum foliar nematode, grass seed gall nematode, and the stem, leaf, and bulb nematode, and these nematodes can be isolated primarily from the plant parts they infect.

From a freshly collected soil sample of about 100 - 300 CM^3, the nematodes in it can be isolated by either the Baermann funnel method or by sieving. A Baermann funnel consists of a fairly large (12- to 15-cm diameter) glass funnel to which a piece of rubber tubing is attached, with a pinchcock placed on the tubing.

The funnel is placed on a stand and filled with water. The soil sample is placed in the funnel on porous, wet-strength paper, sometimes supported by a 5- to 6-cm circular piece of screen, or in a beaker over which a piece of cloth is fastened with a rubber band. The beaker is then inverted in the funnel with the cloth and all the soil below the surface of the water and allowed to stand overnight or for several hours.

The live nematodes move actively and migrate through the cloth or porous paper into the water and sink to the bottom of the rubber tubing Just above the pinchcock. More than go per cent of the live nematodes are recovered in the first 5-8 ml of water drawn from the rubber tubing, and this sample is placed in a shallow dish for examination and, if desired, single nematode isolation.

The sieving method is based on the fact that when a small soil sample, such as 300 cm^3 is mixed with considerably more water, for example, 2 liters, the nematodes float in the water and can be collected on sieves with pores of certain sizes. Thus, the sol 1-water mixture is stirred and then allowed to stand for 30 seconds.

The supernatant is poured through a 20-mesh sieve (20 holes per square inch), which holds large debris but allows the nematodes to pass into a bucket. The liquid containing the nematodes is then poured through a 60-mesh sieve, which holds the larger nematodes and some debris but lets the smaller ones pass through into another bucket. The latter is then passed through a 200-mesh sieve, which holds the small nematodes and some debris. Both the 60- and the 200-mesh sieves are washed two or three times to remove as much of the debris as possible, and the nematodes are then washed into shallow dishes for direct examination and further isolation.

Regardless of the type of plant material containing nematodes, the material is cut into very small pieces by hand or with the use of a blender for a few seconds, and is then placed in the Baermann funnel as described above. The nematodes leave the tissue and move into the water in the tubing, from which they are collected in a shallow dish.

Nematode infections of plants result in the appearance of symptoms on roots as well as on the above ground parts of plants. Root symptoms may appear as root knots or root galls, root lesions, excessive root branching, injured root tips, and root rots when nematode infections are accompanied by plant-pathogenic or saprophytic bacteria and fungi. These root symptoms are usually accompanied by noncharacteristic symptoms in the aboveground parts of plants, appearing primarily as reduced growth, symptoms of nutrient deficiencies such as yellowing of foliage, excessive wilting in hot or dry weather, reduced yields, and poor quality of products. Certain species of nematodes invade the aboveground portions of plants rather than the roots, and on these they cause galls, necrotic lesions and rots, twisting or distortion of leaves and stems, and abnormal development of the floral parts. Certain nematodes attack grains or grasses forming galls full of nematodes in place of seed.

The direct mechanical injury inflicted by nematodes while feeding causes only slight damage to plants. Most of the damage seems to be caused by a secretion of saliva injected into the plants while the nematodes are feeding. Some nematode species are rapid feeders. They puncture a cell wall, inject saliva into the cell, suck part of the cell contents, and move on within a few seconds. Others feed much more slowly and may remain at the same puncture for several hours or days. These, as well as the females of species that become permanently established in or on roots, inject saliva intermittently as long as they are feeding.

The feeding process causes the affected plant cells to react, resulting in dead or devitalized root tips and buds, lesion formation and tissue breakdown, swellings and galls of various kinds, and crinkled and distorted stems and foliage. Some of these manifestations are caused by dissolution of infected tissues by nematode enzymes, which, with or without the help of toxic metabolites, cause tissue disintegration and the death of cells. Others are caused by abnormal cell enlargement (hypertrophy), by suppression of cell divisions, or by stimulation of cell division proceeding in a controlled manner and resulting in the formation of galls or of large numbers of lateral roots at or near the points of infection.

Plant disease syndromes caused by nematodes are complex. Root-feeding species often decrease the ability of plants to take up water and nutrients from soil 'and thus cause symptoms of water and nutrient deficiencies in the aboveground parts of plants.

In some cases, however, it is the plant -nematode biochemical interactions that impair the overall physiology of plants, and the role nematodes play in providing courts for entry of other pathogens that are primarily responsible for plant injury. The mechanical damage or withdrawal of food from plants by nematodes is generally less significant but may become all-important when nematode populations become very large.

Although nematodes can cause diseases to plants by themselves, most of them live and operate in the soil, where they are constantly surrounded by fungi and bacteria, many of which can also cause plant diseases. In many cases an association develops between nematodes and certain of the other pathogens.

Nematodes then become a part of an etiological complex resulting in a combined pathogenic potential far greater than the sum of the damage either of the pathogens can produce individually. Several nematode-fungus disease complexes are known. *Fusarium* wilt of several plants increases in incidence and severity when the plants are also infected by the root knot, lesion, sting, reniform, burrowing, or stunt nematodes. Similar effects have also been noted in disease complexes involving nematodes and *Verticillium* wilt, *Pythium* damping off, *Rhizoctonia* and *Phytophthora* root rots, and in some other instances. In none of these cases is the fungus transmitted by the nematode. However, plant varieties susceptible to the respective fungi are damaged even more when the plants are infected with the nematodes, the combined damage being considerably greater than the sum of the damage caused by each pathogen acting alone. Also, varieties ordinarily resistant to the fungi apparently become infected by them after previous infection by nematodes.

The importance of nematodes in these complexes in indicated by the fact that soil fumigation aimed at eliminating the nematode but not the fungus greatly reduces the incidence and the damage caused by the fungus-induced disease.

Although it seems quite probable that the mechanical wounding caused to plants by nematodes is an important factor in providing avenues of entry for the fungus, the continuation of the effect that nematodes have on host susceptibility in later stages of plant development suggests that the nematodes may also cause some host response that lowers natural resistance to the fungus.

It should also be noted that, in at least some such complexes, there is a greater mass of mycelium present in nematode-infected than in nematodefree tissues of the same plant and also that higher populations of nematodes are present in fungus-infected than in fungus-free tissues of a diseased plant. Relatively few cases of nematode-bacterial disease complexes are known. Thus, root-rot nematode increases the frequency and severity of the bacterial wilt of tobacco caused by *Pseudomonas solanacearum* of the bacterial wilt of alfalfa caused by *Clavibacter michiganense subsp. insidiosum*, and of the bacterial scab of gladiolus caused by *Pseudomonas marginata*. In most of these the nematode role seems to be that of providing the bacteria with an infection court and to assist bacterial infection by wounding the host.

On the other hand, root infection of plum trees with the ring nematode *Criconemella xenoplax* changed the physiology of the trees and resulted in the development of more extensive cankers by the bacterium *Pseudomonas syringae* pv. *syringae* on branches of nematode-infected trees than on nematode-free trees. Much better known are the interrelationships between nematodes and viruses. Several plant viruses such as grapevine fanleaf, arabis mosaic, tobacco ring spot, tomato ring spot, tomato black ring, raspberry ring spot, tobacco rattle, and pea early browning virus are transmitted through the soil by means of nematode vectors. All these viruses, however, are transmitted by only one or more of the four genera of dagger, needle, and stubby root nematodes: *Xiphinema*,

Longidorus, *Trichodorus*, and *Paratrichodorus*. *Xiphinema* and *Longidorus* transmit only round, that is, polyhedral viruses, which include most of the nematode-transmitted viruses, while *Trichodorus* and *Paratrichodorus* transmit two rod-shaped viruses, tobacco rattle and pea early browning viruses. These nematodes can transmit some of the viruses after feeding on infected plants for as short a time as one hour, but the percentage of transmission increases with longer feedings up to four days. Once they have acquired virus from an infected plant the nematodes remain infective for periods of 2-4 months and sometimes even longer.

All stages, larval and adult nematodes, can transmit viruses, but the virus is not carried from one larval stage to another and to adults through molts nor does the virus pass from adults, through eggs, to larvae.

Although nematodes can ingest and carry, within them several plant viruses, they can only transmit certain of them to healthy plants, which suggests that there is a close biological association between the nematode vectors and the viruses they can transmit.

Several methods of effectively controlling nematodes are available, although certain factors, such as expense and types of crops, limit their applicability in some cases. Four general types of control methods are employed.

Control through cultural practices, biological control through resistant varieties and certain other means, control by means of physical agents, such as heat, and control through chemicals. In practice, a combination of several of these methods is usually employed for controlling nematode diseases of plants.

Root-knot nematodes occur throughout the world but are found more frequently and in greater numbers in areas with warm or hot climates and short or mild winters. Root-knot nematodes are also found in greenhouses everywhere when nonsterilized soil is used. They attack more than 2000 species of plants, including almost all cultivated plants. Root-knot nematodes damage plants by devitalizing root tips and either stopping their growth or causing excessive root production, but primarily by causing formation of swellings of the roots, which not only deprive plants of nutrients but also disfigure and reduce the market value of many root crops. When susceptible plants are infected at the seedling stage, losses are heavy and may result in complete destruction of the crop. Infections of older plants may have only slight effects on yield or they may reduce yields considerably.

The aboveground symptoms are similar to those caused by many other root diseases or environmental factors that result in reduced amounts of water available to the plant. Infected plants show reduced growth and fewer, small, pale green, or yellowish leaves that tend to wilt in warm weather. The most characteristic symptoms of the disease are those appearing on the underground parts of the plants. Infected roots swell at the point of invasion and develop into the typical root-knot galls which are two or three times as large in diameter as the healthy root. Several infections take place along the same root, and the developing galls give the root a rough, clubbed appearance.

Usually, however, infected roots remain smaller and show 5 various stages of necrosis. Rotting of the roots frequently develops, particularly late in the season. When tubers or other fleshy underground organs are attacked, they produce small swellings over their surface, which become quite prominent at times and may cause distortion of the organs or cracking of their skin.

The Pathogen: Meloidogyne sp. The adult male and

female root-knot nematodes are easily distinguishable morphologically. The males are wormlike and about 1. 2-1.5 mm long by 30-36 μm in diameter. The females are pear shaped and about 0.40-1.30 min long by 0. 2 7-0.7 5 Turn wide. Each female lays approximately 500 eggs in a gelatinous substance produced by the nematode. The first-stage larva develops inside each egg, and after undergoing the first molt within the egg it becomes second-stage larva. The latter emerges from the egg into the soil, where it moves until it finds a susceptible root.

The second-stage larva is wormlike and is the only infective stage of this nematode. If a susceptible host is present in its vicinity, the larva centers the root, becomes sedentary, and grows in thickness, assuming a sausage-shaped form. The nematode feeds on the cells around its head by inserting its stylet and secreting saliva into these cells.

The saliva stimulates cell enlargement and also liquefies part of the contents of the cells, which are then sucked by the nematode through its stylet. The nematode undergoes a second molt and gives rise to the third-stage larva, which is similar to the second-stage larva but lacks a stylet and is stouter. The third-stage larva goes through the third molt and gives rise to the fourth-stage larva, which can be distinguished as either male or female.

A male fourth-stage larva becomes wormlike and is coiled within the third cuticle. It undergoes the fourth and final molt and emerges from the root as the wormlike adult male, which becomes free living in the soil. The fourth-stage female larva continues to grow in thickness and somewhat in length, undergoes the fourth and final molt, and becomes an adult female, which appears pear shaped.

The eggs may be laid inside or outside the root tissues, depending on the position of the female. Eggs may hatch immediately or they may overwinter and hatch in the spring. A life cycle is completed in 25 days at 27°C, but it takes longer at lower or higher temperatures.

When the eggs hatch, the infective second-stage larvae may Migrate from within galls to adjacent parts of the root and cause new infections in the same root, or they may emerge from the root and infect other roots of the same plants or roots of other plants. The greatest numbers of root-knot nematodes are usually in the root zone from 5 to 25 cm below the surface, but galls have been found on peach and other roots 2-2.5 in deep. The ability of root-knot nematodes to move on their own power is limited, but they can be spread by water or by soil clinging to farm equipment or otherwise transported into uninfested areas.

Development of disease

Infected second-stage larvae usually enter roots behind the root tip and push their way between or through cells until they reach positions behind the growing point. There they become permanently established with their head in the plerome. In older roots the head is usually in the pericycle. Some cell damage occurs along the path of the larva and, if several larvae have entered, the cells near the root tip cease to divide and growth of the root stops. On the other hand, cortical cells near the point of entry begin to enlarge as sometimes do cells of the pericycle and endodermis near the path of the larvae. Two or three days after the larva has become established, some of the cells around its head begin to enlarge. Their nuclei divide, but no cell walls are laid down. The existing walls between some of the cells break down and disappear, and the protoplasmic contents of several coalesce, giving rise to giant cells. Enlargement and coalescing of cells continues for 2-3 weeks, and the giant cells invade the surrounding tissues irregularly. Each gall usually contains 3–6 giant cells, which may form in the cortex as well as in the stele.

The enlargement of the cells seems to be brought about by the substances contained in the saliva secreted by the nematode in the giant cells during feeding.

The giant cells degenerate when nematodes cease to feed or die. When giant cells form in the stele, irregular xylem elements develop or their development may be interrupted. Xylem elements already present may be crushed by the mechanical pressure exerted by the enlarging cells. In the early stages of gall development the cortical cells enlarge in size but, during the later stages, they also divide rapidly.

Swelling of the root results also from hypertrophy and hyperplasia of the vascular parenchyma, pericycle, and endodermis cells surrounding the giant cells and from enlargement of the nematode. As the females enlarge and egg sacs are formed, they push outward, split the cortex, and may become exposed on the surface of the root or may remain completely covered, depending on the position of the nematode in relation to the root surface. In addition to the disturbance caused to plants by the nematode galls themselves, frequently damage to infected plants is increased by certain parasitic fungi, which can easily attack the weakened root tissues and the hypertrophied, undifferentiated cells of the galls.

Root knot can be effectively controlled in the greenhouse with steam sterilization of the soil or soil fumigation with nematicides. In the field the best control of root knot is obtained by fumigating the soil with chemicals such as methyl bromide plus chloropicrin, metam sodium, or methyl isothiocyanate. Several newer nematicides such as aldicarb, oxamyl, and fenamiphos are being used effectively. Each treatment usually gives satisfactory control of root knot for one season. In recent years, good experimental control of root knot has been obtained by application to the soil of granular formulations of avermectins, which are antibiotic substances produced by the actinomycete *Streptomyces avermitilis*.

Biological control of root knot has also been obtained by treating nematode-infested soil with spores of *Bacillus* (*Pasteuria*) *penetrans*, which is an obligate parasite of some plant-parasitic nematodes; by treating transplants or infested soils with spores of the fungus *Dactylella oviparasitica*, which parasitizes the eggs of *Meloidogyne* nematodes; and in some experiments by treating transplants or infested soils with spores of the vesicular-arbuscular mycorrhizal fungi *Gigaspora* and *Glomus*. In several crops, varieties resistant to root-knot nematodes are also available.

Cyst nematodes cause a variety of plant diseases, mostly in the temperate regions of the world. Some species of cyst nematodes attack only a few plant species and are present over limited geographic areas, while others attack a large number of plant species and are widely distributed.

A cyst nematode particularly severe on potato but also on tomato and eggplant is Globodera rostochiensi. Other common cyst nematodes and their most important hosts are Heterodera avenae on cereals, H. glycines on soybeans. H. schachtii on sugar beets, crucifers, and spinach, H. tabacum on tobacco, and H. trifolii on clover. The diagnostic feature of cyst nematode infections is the presence of cysts on the roots and usually the proliferation of roots and,production of shallow, bushy root systems.

The soybean cyst nematode has been found in northeastern Asia, Japan, and in the United States in an area from Virginia to Florida to Arkansas to Missouri, Iowa, Minnesota, and Illinois. It continues to spread slowly to new areas in spite of the strict quarantine measures imposed on the currently infested areas. The most severely affected host is soybean, but several other legumes, such as common bean, vetch, lespedeza, lupine, and a few nonleguminous plants are also attacked by this nematode.

Infected soybean plants appear stunted and have an unthrifty appearance. The foliage turns yellow prematurely and falls off early. The plants bear only a few flowers and a few small seeds. Infected plants growing on sandy soil usually die.

Infected plants growing on fertile soils with plenty of moisture may show only slight chlorosis of the older leaves, little or no stunting, and may produce a nearly normal yield for a year or two. In subsequent years, however, due to the tremendous buildup of nematodes in the soil, plants in these areas also become severely chlorotic and dwarfed. The root system of infected plants appears smaller than that of healthy plants, but no macroscopic lesions, galls, or other type of abnormalities are evident on infected roots.

Roots of infected plants bind only a few nodule-inducing Rhizobia and therefore usually have considerably fewer bacterial nodules than those of healthy plants. The most characteristic symptom of this disease is the presence of female nematodes in varying stages of development and of cysts attached on the soybean roots. Young females are small, white, and partly buried in the root, with only part of them protruding on the surface. Older females are larger, almost completely on the surface of the root, and appear yellowish or brown, depending on maturity. Dead, brown cysts are also present on the roots.

The Pathogen: Heterodera glycines. The soybean cyst nematode overwinters as a brown cyst in the upper 90 - 100 cm of soil. The cysts are the leathery skins of the females and are filled with eggs. The eggs contain fully developed second-stage larvae. When temperature and moisture become favorable in the spring, the larvae emerge from the cysts and infect roots of host plants. At least four races of the pathogen are known. At 4-6 days after penetrating the roots, the larvae molt and produce the third-stage larvae. The third-stage larvae are much stouter than the second-stage larvae, and 5-6 days later fourth-stage larvae begin to appear. The adult male is wormlike, about 1.3 mm long by 30-40 µm in diameter. The males remain in the root for a few days, during which they may or may not fertilize the females, then move into the soil and soon die.

The adult females when fully developed are lemon shaped, measuring 0.6-0.8 mm in length and 0.3-0.5 mm in diameter. They are white to pale yellow at first, becoming yellowish-brown as they mature.

The body cavity of the female is almost completely filled by the ovaries, and as the ova gradually develop into fully formed eggs, the body cavity of the female becomes completely filled with eggs. As the female body distends during egg production, it crushes cortical cells, splits the root surface, and protrudes until it is almost entirely exposed through the root surface. A gelatinous mass, usually mixed with dirt and debris, surrounds the posterior end of the females, and the nematodes deposit some of their eggs in it. Each female produces 300-600 eggs, most of which remain inside her body when the female dies. Eggs in the gelatinous matrix may hatch immediately, and the emerging second-stage larvae may cause new infections. Finally, the old body wall, darkening to brown, becomes the cyst.

Approximately 21 - 24 days are required for the completion of a life cycle of this nematode. The cyst consists of the female cuticle transformed through the secretions of the nematode into a tough, brown sac that persists in the soil for many years and protects the eggs, which have been formed within the body.

The infective second-stage larvae penetrate young primary roots or apical meristems of secondary roots directly. The advance into the cortex is mostly intracellular and results in distortion and death of invaded cells. The larvae often pass through the cortex and pierce their stylets into cells of the endodermis or the pericycle.

Within 2 days of penetration larvae come to rest and feed on cells of the cortex and stele tissues, causing the enlargement of these cells. Such groups of enlarged cells, called syncytia, are surrounded by a single layer of small, hyperplastic cells, the walls of which undergo further dissolution and allow enlargement of the syncytia. During the development of the third larval stage cortical cells surrounding the nematode are crushed by the expanding nematode body, especially by developing females. Syncytial development is either restricted largely to pericyclic tissue or occurs in tissues of the phloem and secondary cambium. Syncytia in contact with developing third- or fourth-stage males begin to show signs of degeneration, indicating cessation of feeding. Syncytia in contact with females remain active up to and beyond the stage of egg deposition.

Degeneration of syncytia is accompanied by reduction of syncytial volume and results in the receding and collapse of the syncytial wall. The resulting space is only partly occupied by surrounding parenchymatous tissue. When soybean varieties resistant to the soybean cyst nematode are attacked, there is no apparent inhibition of penetration of the organism into the host tissues. Syncytia are formed within 2-3 days of inoculation, but by day 5 many of them degenerate and most second-stage larvae associated with them are dead. A few nematodes advance to the third stage, but no adult males or females are produced. Development of syncytia and subsequent degeneration and necrosis is restricted to the periphery of the stele and to regions in the cortex that are invaded and stimulated by infective larvae. The root regions vacated by degenerate syncytia are quickly filled by adjacent rejuvenated parenchyma cells. Syncytial development into the secondary cambial region of susceptible varieties results in inhibition of secondary growth of both phloem and xylem.

Control. Soil fumigation of soybean cyst nematode-infested fields with ethylene dibromide (EDB) (the use of which was recently suspended in the United States), or soil treatment with nonfumigant nematicides such as aldicarb and carbofuran, temporarily increases plant growth and soybean yield. Nematode cysts and larvae, however, are almost never eradicated from a field completely by fumigation, and a small nematode population left over after fumigation can build up rapidly on the vigorous soybean grown in newly fumigated soil. In addition, the cost of fumigation per acre makes its use impractical. The most practical method of control of the soybean cyst nematode is through the use of resistant varieties and through a 1- to 2-year crop rotation with nonhost crops, since some legumes are the only other cultivated crops that are hosts of this nematode. The effectiveness of crop rotation is increased by planting the more resistant soybean varieties, which do not allow a quick and excessive buildup of nematode populations.

Cysts and eggs of soybean and other cyst nematodes are often found infected with one of several fungi such as *Fusarium, Verticillium, Nematophthora,* and *Catenona.* In the near future it may be possible to use one of these or another parasite as biological control of the cyst nematodes. Quarantine regulations are currently enforced to prevent the parasite from spreading into nematode-free areas by means of contaminated soil, products, machinery, or other articles.

The sugar beet nematode occurs wherever sugar beets are grown in North America, Europe, the Middle East, and Australia and is the most important nematode pest of sugar beet production. It also affects spinach and crucifers. The sugar beet nematode causes yield losses of 25-50 percent or more, especially in warmer climates or late-planted crops.

The losses on sugar beet are mostly the result of reduced root weight, but in warm climates the sugar content is also reduced and, generally, the nematode aggravates losses caused by other pathogens such as *Cercospora*, *Rhizoctonia*, and beet viruses. In fields infested with the sugar beet nematode, small to large patches of wilting or dead young plants or stunted older sugar beets appear. The latter have an excessive number of hairlike roots. Small white or brownish cysts of female nematodes can be seen clinging to the roots. The morphology, biology, and spread of the sugar beet nematode is similar to that of the soybean cyst nematode.

Control of the sugar beet nematode in red table beets is based on early sowing so that plants can grow as much as possible at temperatures at which the nematodes are more or less inactive, on crop rotations with alfalfa, cereals, or potatoes, which are not hosts of this nematode, and soil fumigation with DCP. No sugar beet varieties resistant to this nematode are commercially available yet.

The citrus nematode is present wherever citrus trees are grown. In some regions, in addition to citrus the nematode also attacks grapevines, olive, lilac, and other plants. Infected trees show a slow decline, that is, they grow poorly, their leaves turn yellowish and drop early, their twigs die back, and fruit production is gradually reduced to unprofitable levels. The pathogen, *Tylenchulus semipenetrans*, is a semiendoparasitic sedentary nematode. The larvae and males are wormlike, but the female body is swollen irregularly behind the neck. The nematodes measure about 0.4 mm long by 18-80 μm in diameter, the larger diameters found only in the maturing and mature females. The females, whose front end of the body is buried in the root tissue while the rear end remains outside, lay eggs in a gelatinous substance.

The life cycle of *T. semipenetrans* is completed within 6-14 weeks at 24°C. The eggs hatch and second-stage larvae emerge. The male larvae and adults do not feed and apparently do not play a role either in the disease or the reproduction of the nematode.

The second-stage female larva is the only infective stage of the nematode and cannot develop without feeding, but it can survive for several years. In the soil, the citrus nematode occurs as deep as 4 meters. The female second-stage larvae usually attack the 4- to 5-week-old feeder roots and feed on the surface cells of the roots. There they undergo the three additional molts and produce adult females.

The young females then penetrate deeper into the cortex and may reach as deep as the pericycle. The head of the nematode develops a tiny cavity around it and feeds on the surrounding 3-4 layers of parenchyma cells known as "nurse cells." Later on, the cells around the feeding site become disorganized and break down. After invasion by secondary fungi and bacteria, the affected areas turn into dark necrotic lesions, which may be so numerous that they give the root a darkened appearance. In severe infections, one hundred or more females may be feeding per centimeter of root. The females, along with soil particles that cling to the gelatinous substance of the egg mass, result in dark, bumpy, and often decayed young roots. The spread of the nematode through the soil is slow, the rate being approximately 1.5 cm per month when the roots of adjacent citrus plants are in contact. The nematode, however, is spread over long distances by movement of nematode-infested soil on equipment, animals, and by irrigation water, and to even longer distances by transfer of infested citrus nursery plants.

The nematodes reach high populations in infected trees, which begin to show decline 3-5 years after the initial infection. When the trees show advanced stages of decline, the nematode populations also decline in numbers. Control of the citrus nematode is based on preventing its introduction into new areas by growing nursery stock in mematode-free fields and by treating nursery stock with hot water at 45°C for 25 minutes or with fensul-fothion. Because of the great depth at which the citrus nematode can survive, soil fumigation is not always effective. Satisfactory control has been obtained by preplant fumigation with DD, or methyl bromide, also by postplant treatment with aldicarb applied by chisel injection, or as granules that are incorporated into the soil immediately. Some citrus clones are resistant to the nematode populations of some regions but not to those of others.

Lesion or meadow nematodes occur in all parts of the world, where they attack the roots of all kinds of plants, such as field crops, cereal crops, vegetable crops, fruit trees, and many ornamentals. The severity of damage caused by lesion nematodes varies with the crop attacked and consists in root reduction or inhibition by formation of local lesions on young roots, which may be followed by root rotting due to secondary fungi, bacteria, and so on. As a result of the root damage, affected plants grow poorly, produce low yields, and may finally die.

Susceptible herbaceous host plants affected by lesion nematodes appear stunted and chlorotic as though they are suffering from mineral deficiencies or lack of water. Usually several plants are affected in one area, producing patches of plants with reduced growth and a yellowish-green color, that can be seen from a distance.

As the season progresses, stunting becomes more pronounced, the foliage wilts during hot summer days, and the color of the leaves becomes yellowish brown. Such plants can be easily pulled from the soil because of the extensive destruction of the root system. Yields of affected plants are reduced in varying degrees, and in severe infections the plants are killed. When shrubs or trees are attacked by lesion nematodes, damage is usually slow to appear; it is less obvious than that on herbaceous hosts, and it rarely kills the plants.

The symptoms usually consist of isolated trees or patches of trees gradually becoming unthrifty and producing poor crops. The leaves are smaller in size, their color being a dull green or yellow. Terminal branches may lose their leaves prematurely and die back.

The whole appearance of affected trees indicates that the trees are weakened and are in a condition of decline. The patches of affected trees may slowly increase in size, although this happens over a rather long period. The root symptoms of affected plants consist of lesions that appear as tiny, elongate, water-soaked, or cloudy yellow spots but that soon turn brown to almost black. The lesions appear mainly on the young feeder roots, and they are most concentrated in the area of the root hairs, but they may appear anywhere along the roots. The lesions enlarge mostly longitudinally following the root axis, and they may coalesce with other lesions, but at the same time they slowly expand laterally until they finally girdle the entire root, which they kill. As the lesions enlarge, the affected cells in the cortex collapse, and the discolored area appears constricted.

Secondary fungi and bacteria usually accompany nematode infections in the soil and contribute to further discoloration and rotting of the affected root areas, which may slough off. Moderately affected plants exhibit varying degrees of root survival, and in some hosts production of adventitious roots may be stimulated by the infection; but generally the individual roots are discolored and stubby, and the whole root system is severely reduced by the root pruning that results from the formation of lesions.

The pathogen: Pratylenchus sp. The nematodes are approximately 0.4-0.7 mm long and 20 - 25 μm in diameter. They appear as stout, cylindroid nematodes with a blunt head, strong, stout spear, and bluntly rounded tail. They are migratory, endoparasitic nematodes affecting the roots of many kinds of plants. Development and reproduction of *Pratylenchus* nematodes is rather slow, the life cycle of the various species being completed within 45 - 65 days. These nematodes overwinter in infected roots or in soil as eggs, larvae, or adults, except for the egg-producing females, which seem to be unable to survive the winter. Adults and larvae of various ages can enter and leave roots of susceptible hosts. The females, with or without fertilization, lay their eggs singly or in small groups inside infected roots. The eggs remain in the roots and hatch there, or when the root tissues break down, they are released into the soil. The first larval stage and the first molt occur in the egg.

The emerging second-stage larva moves about in the soil or enters the root, in either case developing into the subsequent larval stages and the adults. When in the soil the nematodes are susceptible to drying, and during periods of drought they lie quiescent until the moisture increases and the plants resume growth.

Development of disease. Larvae and adult *Pratylenchits* nematodes enter roots usually in a radial direction anywhere along the roots. Intracellular penetration is accomplished by a persistent thrusting of the stylet and head, which seems to soften and break the cell wall. The cell walls and the adherent cytoplasm usually turn light brown in color and appear as small, discolored spots within a few hours after inoculation. The nematodes move into the cortex, where they feed and reproduce. The endodermis is not attacked even when the nematodes completely fill the area between the endodermis and the epidermis.

Necrosis of cortical cells follows the path of nematodes, but discoloration of the affected and adjoining cells varies with the host plant. Sometimes only i or 2 cells on each side of the nematode tunnels are affected, but at other times the lesion involves more than half the circumference of the root. The part of the endodermal layer adjacent to the nematode also takes on a deep brown color, which extends into rather large groups of cells.

As the feeding of the nematode on conical cells continues, cell walls break down, and cavities appear in the cortex with their walls sometimes lined with brown deposits. Each lesion is usually inhabited by more than one nematode, and sometimes single host cells are simultaneously transversed by four or more nematodes. The females lay their eggs in the cortex, and frequently eggs, larvae, and a few adults form "nests"; these nests occur in great numbers in the cortex. Upon hatching of the eggs, the nematodes feed on the parenchyma cells and move mostly lengthwise within the cortex, thus enlarging the lesion. Some of the nematodes leave the lesion, emerge from the root, and travel to other points of the root or other roots where they cause new infections. Necrotic cortical tissues of large lesions are sloughed off or are invaded by secondary fungi and bacteria with resulting rotting and breakdown of the root tissues around the point of infection and subsequent death of the distal part of the root beyond the point of infection. Thus, the number of functioning roots of the plant is drastically reduced, absorption of water and nutrients becomes insufficient, and the aboveground parts of the plant become stunted and chlorotic, showing symptoms of water and nutrient deficiencies.

Root-lesion nematodes can best be controlled by overall or row treatment of the soil with nematicides before the crop is planted. DD and Brozone give good control of these nematodes, but they usually fail to eradicate them completely. Oxamyl, applied as a soil drench or foliar spray, has also given good control of lesion nematodes in some cases.

In hot and dry climates fairly good control of lesion nematodes can be achieved by summer fallow, which reduces nematode populations by exposing them to heat and drying and by eliminating host plants. Control through crop rotation is at present rather unsuccessful due to the wide host ranges of the lesion nematodes and to the lack of information on their precise host preferences.

The burrowing nematode occurs widely in tropical and subtropical regions of the world and in greenhouses in Europe. It is the most important banana root pathogen in most banana-growing areas, where it causes the so-called root rot, blackhead, toppling disease, or decline of banana. Furthermore, it attacks coffee and other fruit, ornamental and forest trees, sugarcane, corn, vegetables, grasses, and weeds. Infected banana plants appear to be growing poorly, have fewer and smaller leaves, show premature defoliation and reduced weight of fruits.

The nematodes, along with fungi and bacteria that invade the cracked roots, cause the roots to rot and eventually only a few short root stubs remain, which cannot anchor the plant sufficiently and the latter topples over. Diffuse black, rotten areas also develop in the rhizome cortex surrounding infected roots. As a result of this disease the profitable life of a banana plantation in many areas is decreased from indefinite to as little as one year, and the costs of annual replanting and losses in production are tremendous. In the spreading decline of citrus, blocks of affected trees also have fewer and smaller leaves and fruits, and many of the twigs and branches die back. Yields of Infected trees are reduced by 40 - 70 percent. Even during periods of mild moisture stress, infected trees wilt readily, but they generally do not die and often recover temporarily after rainy periods. The symptoms of decline spread steadily to more trees each year, the diameter of the decline area increasing approximately 10 - 20 meters per year. The symptoms on the aboveground parts follow infection of the roots by about a year. Infected feeder roots have numerous lesions that appear puffy and cracked and are often invaded by primary and secondary fungal parasites that result in the rotting and destruction of the feeder roots. Feeder roots seem to be attacked and destroyed most at depths Of 50 cm or more, leaving less than half the feeder roots functional.

The pathogen, *Radopholus similis,* usually known as the burrowing nematode, is wormlike, measuring about 0.65 mm long by 25 μm wide. It spends its life and reproduces inside cavities in the root cortex, where it completes a life cycle in about 20 days. All larvae and the adults can infect roots, and although they can emerge from the roots and spread through the soil, most of the spread of the nematode from plant to plant is through root contact or near contact. Long-distance spread of the nematode is primarily with infected plant material, such as infected banana sets. Although the nematodes infecting banana and citrus are morphologically identical, the "banana race" can attack banana but not citrus while the "citrus race" can attack citrus as well as banana and several other hosts. The citrus race, however, is so far known to occur only in Florida. Other races probably exist in other parts of the world. The burrowing nematode enters feeder roots and moves intercellularly in the cortical parenchyma, feeding on nearby cells, destroying them, and causing the formation of cavities.

As the nematodes continue to feed, the cavities enlarge and coalesce with others, forming long and lateral tunnels. In banana, the tunnels are limited to the cortex between the epidermis and the endodermis. From the feeding roots the nematodes also move into the rhizome. In citrus, however, the nematodes not only form cavities in the cortex but they also enter the stele through endodermal passage cells. There they accumulate in the phloem and cambium, which they destroy in time and form nematode-filled cavities.

The cavities within the roots appear externally as brown-reddish lesions throughout the cortex, and three to four weeks from infection the lesions develop one or more deep cracks. Each female lays one or a few eggs per day for many days and as they hatch, develop, and reproduce, nematode populations increase rapidly.

As many as 800 nematodes may be present in a single lesion and a single tree may be supporting hundreds of thousands of burrowing nematodes. Fungi such as *Fusarium* and *Sclerotium* invade nematode-infected roots much more readily and further increase their rotting and destruction. Control of the burrowing nematode in banana can be obtained by removing discolored tissues from banana sets by paring and then dipping the sets in hot water at 55°C for 20 minutes; by flooding the field for 5 -6 months where possible; and by soil fumigation with nematicides. Control of spreading decline of citrus is much more difficult and depends primarily on: (i) preventive regulatory measures that inhibit the spread and establishment of the nematode in new areas by treating nursery trees with hot water at 50°C for io minutes or dipping them in nematicides such as ethoprop and fensulfothion; disinfesting equipment; and fumigating every 6 months with DD 5-meter-wide strips of land around the area of decline and keeping it free of weeds with cultivation or herbicides. (2) Fumigation of decline areas with heavy doses of DD after removal of all declining trees and at least two rows around them. (3) Use of tolerant or resistant rootstocks.

Of the several species of *Ditylenchus* that cause diseases in plants, *D. dipsaci* is the most common and most serious of all and is the one generally referred to as the stem and bulb nematode, while *D. destructor* is known as the potato rot nematode. The stem and bulb nematode is worldwide in distribution but is particularly prevalent and destructive in areas with temperate climate. It is one of the most destructive plant-parasitic nematodes. It attacks a large number of host plants including onions, narcissus, hyacinth, tulip, oats, rye, alfalf, red clover, strawberry, and phlox.

Although all these hosts are attacked by nematodes belonging to one species, different populations or biotypes of the stem and bulb nematode have certain host preferences and when transferred to them, will attack one or a few of these hosts but not the others. On most crops it causes heavy losses by killing seedlings, dwarfing plants, destroying bulbs or making them unfit for propagation or consumption, by causing the development of distorted, swollen and twisted stems and foliage, and, generally, reducing yields greatly.

Symptoms. In fields infested with stem and bulb nematodes, emergence of seedlings such as onion is retarded and stands are reduced considerably. Half or more of the emerging seedlings may be diseased appearing pale, twisted, arched, and with enlarged areas along the cotyledon. Cotyledons are usually puffy with the epidermis cracked in a lacelike fashion.

When bulbs are planted in infested soil, the developing plants within about 3 weeks show stunting, light yellow spots, swellings ("spikkies"), and open lesions on the foliage. Young plants and sprouts develop swellings on the stem and foreshortening and curling of the leaves. Many outer leaves often become flaccid, their leaf tips die back, and the leaves are so weakened that they cannot maintain their erect growth and fall to the ground. The stem and the neck of the bulb become softened, and the softening gradually proceeds downward into individual scales, which become soft, loose, and pale gray in color. Affected scales appear as discolored rings in cross sections of infected bulbs and as discolored, unequal lines in longitudinal sections. In more advanced cases large areas or the whole bulb may be affected. Infected bulbs may also split and become malformed or may produce sprouts and double bulbs.

The outer scales may be loosened and detached by applying a little oblique pressure with the thumb on the upper half of the bulb and reveal the soft mealy, frosty-looking tissue beneath. In dry weather the bulbs become desiccated, odorless, and very light in weight. In wet seasons a soft rot due to secondary invaders sets in, destroying the bulb and giving off a foul odor. Infected bulbs are sometimes superficially healthy, but they continue to decay in storage, where the outer scale often sloughs off exposing the lower puffy, soft scales with the characteristic frosty mealiness.

The Pathogen: ditylenchus dipsaci. The nematode is 1.0 - 1.3 mm long and about 30 µm in diameter. Each female lays 200-500 eggs. Second-stage larvae emerge from, the egg and quickly undergo the second and third molt and produce the preadult or infective larva. The latter can withstand adverse conditions of freezing and of extreme drying for long periods in fragments of plant tissue, stems, leaves, bulbs, seeds, or in the soil.

Under favorable moisture and temperature conditions the preadult larvae become active, enter the host, pass through the fourth molt, and become males and females. The females then lay eggs, mostly after fertilization by the males. A complete cycle from egg to egg usually lasts about 19-25 days. Reproduction takes place in succulent, rapidly growing tissues or in storage organs and continues throughout the year, although it is retarded or stopped by low temperatures.

Ditylenchus dipsaci is an internal parasite of bulbs, stems, and leaves and passes generation after generation in these tissues, escaping to the soil only when living conditions in the plant tissues become unfavorable. When heavily infected bulbs decay, preadult larvae pass out and sometimes accumulate about the basal plates of dried bulbs as grayish-white, cottony masses, called nematode "wool," where they can remain alive for years.

Development of disease. When nematodes attack a germinating seed or young seedlings, they enter near the root cap or at points still within the seed. The nematodes remain mostly intercellular, feeding on the parenchymatous cells of the cortex. Cells near the heads of the nematodes lose all or a portion of their contents, while cells surrounding these divide and enlarge, resulting in development of swellings on the seedlings. The seedling may become malformed. Splitting of the epidermis often follows the enlargement and opens the way to secondary invaders, such as bacteria and fungi.

In older seedlings or young plants, nematodes enter the leaves through stomata or penetrate directly through the epidermis in leaf bases. Cell enlargement, disappearance of chloroplasts, and an increase of intercellular spaces in parenchyma tissue follow penetration.

The nematodes usually remain and reproduce In the Intercellular spaces, feeding on the nearby parenchyma cells whose contents they consume without causing appreciable discoloration on the cell remains. As the bulbs enlarge, the nematodes migrate down from the leaves either intercellularly or by traveling on the surface of the leaves and entering again at the outer sheaths of the stem or neck, through which they infect the outer scales of the bulbs. Heavily infected stems become soft and puffy, due to the formation of large cavities through the breakdown of the middle lamella and of the cells the nematodes feed on. Such stems can no longer remain rigid under the weight of the foliage and they frequently collapse.

The nematodes continue their progress intercellularly through the outer scales of the bulbs by breaking down the parenchymatous tissue. Parenchyma cells are separated from each other and from the vessels, the latter giving a lacy appearance to the scale. The macerated parenchyma cells have a white mealy texture at first, but secondary usually set in and cause them to turn brown. In early stages of infection the nematodes remain within individual scales, and in sections the infection appears as complete or incomplete rings of frosty white or brownish tissue. In later stages of infection the nematodes pass from one scale to the next, and thus more scales may be involved in one ring. The spread of the infection within a bulb continues in the field and in storage until, usually, the entire bulb becomes affected.

Control. Populations of *Ditylenchus dipsaci* parasitic on certain crops can be reduced by long (2-3 years at least) rotations with resistant crops, such as spinach, carrots, potatoes, and lettuce. Since this nematode also overwinters in infected bulbs and seeds, the use of nematode-free sets or seeds is extremely important. Infested seeds or bulbs can be disinfested by treating them in hot water for an hour at 46°C. Onion seed can also be freed from nematodes by enclosing it with methyl bromide gas for 24 hours at 24°C in a gas-tight container, and flower bulbs can be successfully disinfested by placing them in 0.5 percent formaldehyde solution at 43°C for 4 hours. Control of this nematode in large fields, although often too expensive, can be achieved by fall fumigation of the soil, by preplant row treatment, and by treatment at or soon after planting with appropriate nematicides.

Seed-gall nematodes were the first recorded plant-parasitic nematodes. Of the seed-gall nematodes, *A. agrostis* is probably the most widespread in Europe and North American and causes severe injury to bentgrasses (*Agrostis* spp.), but *A. tritici* has been important on wheat and rye in the past and in some areas still is.

The wheat seed gall, which is described below, is present wherever wheat is grown, but in most countries it is quite rare due to the use of fresh and cleaned seed. The wheat seed-gall nematode is still common, however, in some Mediterranean countries, eastern Europe, and Asia. The symptoms appear on plants in all growth stages. Infected seedlings are more or less severely stunted and show characteristic rolling, twisting, curling, or wrinkling of the leaves. A rolled leaf often traps the next emerging leaf or the inflorescence within it and causes it to become looped or bent and badly distorted. Stems are often enlarged near the base, frequently bent, and generally stunted.

Diseased heads are shorter and thicker than healthy ones and the glumes are spread further apart by the nematodefilled seed galls. A diseased head may have one, a few, or all of its kernels turned into nematode galls. The galls are shiny green at first, but turn brown or black as the head matures. Diseased heads remain green longer than healthy ones, and galls are shed off the heads more readily than kernels. Mature galls are hard, dark, rounded, and shorter than normal wheat kernels and often resemble cockle seeds, smutted grains, or ergot sclerotia.

The pathogen, *Anguina tritici*, is a large nematode about 3.2 mm long by 120 µm in diameter. The nematode lays its eggs and produces all its larval stages and the adults in seed galls. The seed-gall nematode overwinters as second-stage larvae in seed galls or in plants infected in the fall. Galls fallen to the ground or sown with the seed soften during warm moist weather and release infective second-stage larvae.

When a film of water is present on the surface of the plants the larvae swim upward and feed ectoparasitically on the tightly compacted leaves near the growing point, causing the leaves and stem to become malformed. When the inflorescence begins to form, the larvae enter the floral primordia and produce the third- and fourth-stage larvae and the adults. Each infected floral primordium becomes a seed gall and may contain 80 or more adults of both sexes. Each of the females then lays up to 2000 eggs over several weeks within the freshly formed gall so that each gall contains 10,000-30,000 eggs. The adults die soon after the eggs are laid. The eggs then hatch and the first-stage larvae emerge, but these soon molt and by harvest produce the second-stage larvae, which are very resistant to desiccation and can survive in the galls for up to 30 years. The seed-gall nematode produces only one generation per year.

The nematode is spread in infected seed. Control of the seed gall nematode depends on the use of clean seed free of nematode-containing galls. Fields infested with seed-gall nematodes should not be planted to wheat or rye for at least a year. In moist weather the seed galls release the second-stage larvae and, if no susceptible hosts are present, they die before they can infect and reproduce. In dry weather, however, nematodes can survive in the seed galls for many years.

Several species of *Aphelenchoides* feed ectoparasitically and endoparasitically on aboveground plant parts. Some of the most important species are: *A. ritzemabosi*, the chrysanthemum foliar nematode; *A. fragariae*, the spring crimp or spring dwarf nematode of strawberry and which also attacks many ornamentals; and *A. besseyi*, the nematode causing summer dwarf or crimp of strawberry and white tip of rice. The foliar nematode of chrysanthemums, also known as chrysanthemum eelworm, is known to be widespread in the United States and Europe. It results in fairly severe losses. In addition to chrysanthemum, the foliar nematode, or closely related species, attacks several other plants, including aster, dahlia, delphinium, phlox, zinnia, and sometimes tobacco and strawberry.

Symptoms. Affected buds or growing points of stems produce short and often abnormally bushy-looking plants with short internodes. The growing point may be so damaged that the shoot does not grow and turns brown. The leaves produced from infested buds are small and distorted. The stem and petioles show brown scars caused by nematodes feeding externally on these tissues while still in the bud. Shoots so infested seldom develop into normal plants. Uninfested shoots may exist on the same stool with infested ones, and they develop into normal new plants. As the season progresses, however, nematodes climb up the stem and attack first the lower and then the upper leaves on which they cause small yellowish spots, later turning brownish black. These spots soon coalesce and form large blotches, which at first are contained between the larger leaf veins. Eventually the entire leaf is covered with spots or blotches, and it soon shrinks, becomes brittle, and falls to the ground. Defoliation, like infection, progresses from the lower to the upper leaves. The nematodes also infest the ray flowers and prevent their development. Severely infected plants die without producing much normal foliage or marketable flowers.

The pathogen: Aphelenchoides Ritzemabosi-Aphelenchoides ritzemabosi is a long, slender nematode measuring about I mm long by 20 µm in diameter. It may live its entire life inside leaves or at the surface of other plant organs. The female adult lays its eggs in the intercellular spaces of leaves. The eggs hatch and produce the four larval stages, and finally adults, all inside the leaf. The life cycle is completed in about 2 weeks. These nematodes do not have to spend any part of their lives in the soil but are frequently found there carried by infected, dead leaves fallen to the ground, or washed down by rain or irrigation water when they happen to be on the surface of plant tissues. The foliar nematodes overwinter as adults in dead leaves or between the scales of buds of infected tissues.

Development of disease. Nematodes overwintering between the bud scales or the growing point of shoots become activated in the spring and feed ectoparasitically by inserting their stylets into the epidermal cells of the organs in their vicinity. Thus, stem areas near infested buds and the petioles and leaves derived from such buds show brown scars consisting of groups of cells killed by the nematodes. In addition to direct killing of cells, the nematodes, through their secretions, cause shortening of the internodes, which results in a bushy appearance of the plant; browning and failure of the shoot to grow (blindness), production of low, premature side-shoots; and development of distorted leaves.

Nematodes infest new, healthy plants by swimming up the stem when it is covered with a film of water during rainy or humid weather. When they reach the leaves, the nematodes enter through the stomata. The presence of nematodes between the leaf cells causes browning in cells. Cells in the mesophyll begin to break down, creating large cavities in the mesophyll. In the early stages of infection the cells of the vein sheath, which in large veins extend from the upper to the lower surface, do not allow penetration of the nematodes through their intercellular spaces and thus block extension of leaf necrosis across the veins. In advanced stages of infection, even these cells break down and the nematodes and leaf necrosis spread across the veins over the entire leaf. In heavily infected leaves the disintegrated cells have a thick layer of brown substance on their walls, the epidermis is broken down in places, and the leaves shrink and, after clinging to the stem for some time, fall to the ground.

Control. Several sanitary practices are quite important in controlling the foliar nematode. The leaves and stem should be kept dry, especially indoors, to prevent movement and spreading of the nematodes. Cuttings should be taken only from the tops of long, vigorous branches, not from shoots near the base of the plant. Early in the spring the soil surface around chrysanthemums should be mulched to cover old infested leaves and prevent nematodes overwintering in them from reaching the lower leaves. Suspected dormant cuttings or stools may be disinfested by dipping in hot water (50°C) for 5 minutes or at 44°C for 30 minutes. Excellent control of this nematode can be obtained by spraying plants with parathion or malathion from July to early September and by applying thionazin as a drench twice with a 2-week interval.

The pine wood nematode has been known to occur in Japan for more than thirty years, in France, and since 1979, in the United States, where it was first found in Missouri and then in most states east of the Rocky Mountains and in California. It affects, with different seventy, more than 28 species of pine and several other conifers, being most severe on Scotch (*Pinus sylvestris*), Austrian (*P. nigra*), Monterey (*P. radiata*) and shortleaf (*P. echinata*) pines. It is the causal agent of pine wilt, a lethal disease of trees of many host species. The disease spread rapidly and caused severe losses of pines in several localities in Japan. The potential threat of this nematode lies in both its ability to kill whole or parts of trees and in the fact that it is transmitted from dead to live pines by certain insects.

Symptoms. Infected branches or whole trees suddenly develop light grayish-green foliage. Resin, which normally flows from the wounds of healthy trees, has ceased to flow from wounds of infected trees. One or two weeks later, the foliage appears generally yellowish green, while random needles turn brown. Soon the foliage turns yellowish brown and only random needles remain light green. At this point, the wood of affected trees shows obvious blue stain 'symptoms. Within 4-6 weeks from the appearance of symptoms, the tree or branch has totally brown foliage, appears witted, or the needles are retained without obvious droop. In many affected tres blue stain in wood is heavy. Infected trees invariably die.

The pathogen: Bursaphelenchus Xylophilus. The nematodes are about 800 μm long by 22 μm in diameter. They develop and reproduce rapidly, completing a life cycle within 4 days during the summer. Each female lays about 80 eggs, which hatch, and the four larval stages develop through the four molts and produce adults in about 4 days. While the tree is still living, the nematodes feed on plant cells, but after its death they feed on fungi that invade the dying or dead tree. In late stages of infection, a different form of third-stage larvae, called the dispersal stage, appear, characterized by large amounts of nutritional reserves and a thick cuticle. These molt to the fourth-stage dispersal larvae, called dauerlarvae, which are especially adapted to survive in the respiratory system of certain cerambycid beetles, by which they are transmitted to healthy trees. *Bursaphelenchus xylophilus* is mycophagous, that is, it feeds and can complete its life cycle feeding on many kinds of fungi, for example, *Botrytis cinerea* and the blue stain fungi (*Ceratocystis* spp.)

Development of disease. The pine wood nematode overwinters in the wood of infected dead trees, which also contain instars (larvae) of one or more cerambycid beetles such as *Monochamus alternatus* in Japan and *M. carolinensis* in the United States. In early spring, the Instars, while still in the wood, excavate small chambers in which they pupate. At the same time, third-stage nematode larvae aggregate around the pupal chambers and molt to produce fourth-stage dauerlarvae. As the adult beetles emerge from the pupae-in mid to late spring, large numbers of dauerlarvae enter the beetles through the metathoracic spiracles and more or less fill many of the tracheae of the insect's respiratory system. The emerging adult beetles bore their way out of the wood, each carrying with it an average of 15,000-20,000 dauerlarvae, although as many as 230,000 dauerlarvae have been obtained from single insects.

The emerging beetles fly to succulent branch tips of healthy trees and feed for about 30 days by stripping the bark to reach cambial tissue. As the beetles feed, the dauerlarvae emerge from the insect through the spiracles and enter the pine tree through the wound. Once in the plant, the dauerlarvae undergo the final molt and produce adult nematodes, which reproduce. The nematodes migrate to the resin canals, where they feed on the epithelial cells lining the canals and cause their death as well as the death of the surrounding parenchyma cells. The nematodes move quickly through resin canals in both the xylem and the cortex, reproduce rapidly, and within a few weeks, build up enormous populations in the host. For example, seedlings of susceptible Scotch pines, inoculated with 2,000 nematodes each, had approximately 50,000 nematodes within 30 days from inoculation and died shortly afterwards.

The destruction of the resin canals leads to the early cessation of resin flow from artificial wounds of branches and trunks within about lo days of inoculation. This is followed by reduced, and later complete cessation of transpiration by the foliage within about 30 days of inoculation, followed by sudden wilting and loss of foliage coloration. Rapid nematode population increases take place primarily after cessation of resin flow, they continue after foliar discoloration and wilting and after the death of the tree, and reach a maximum level about one month after inoculation. From 1,000 to 10,000 nematodes are often present per gram of dry wood of infected trees. In later stages of the disease, and as the condition of the tree deteriorates, nematode populations decline. At the same time, there is a gradual increase in the proportion of the dispersal third-stage larvae in relation to the total population of the nematode in the wood. The third-stage dispersal larvae make up the resting stage of the nematode.

In the meantime, the adult *Monochamus* sp. beetles, that is, the vectors of Bursaphelenchus xylophilus, after they have fed on tender pine twigs for about one month, look for and deposit their eggs under the bark of stressed and dead pine trees, including trees showing symptoms or dying from infection by the pine wood nematode. The first two instars of the insect feed under the bark, but the third penetrates the wood, where, after a molt, it produces the fourth instar, which overwinters in the wood. In early spring, the fourth instar excavates a chamber in the wood, in which it pupates, and attracts numerous third-stage nematode larvae all around it. The latter molt to produce dauerlarvae, which infect the adult insect as soon as it emerges from the pupa -and the cycle is completed. In some temperate regions, primarily pine trees stressed by various diseases and insects are attacked by the pine wood nematode, and typical wilt symptoms are not usually produced.

Two types of control measures, that is, insecticide treatment to control the beetles and early removal and burning of dead and dying pine trees to eliminate the breeding habitat of the nematode and of the beetle, are only moderately effective and practical only in restricted localities. Neither of these controls is possible in large forests. Affected susceptible pine species planted as shade trees should be replaced with more resistant pine species or with other types of trees.

Stubby-root nematodes occur all over the world. They attack a wide variety of plants, including oats, cabbage, tomato, clover, corn, bean, grape, and peach. They affect plants by devitalizing root tips and stopping their growth, resulting in reduction of the root system of plants. This results in severe stunting and chlorosis of the whole plant, reduced yields, and poor quality of produce. Infected plants, however, are seldom, if ever, killed by these nematodes.

Infected plants appear stunted within 2 - 3 weeks of inoculation. They have fewer and smaller leaves and branches than healthy plants, although at first their color appears normal. As the growing season progresses, the difference in size between healthy and stubby-root-infected plants increases, healthy plants being 3-4 times as large as infected ones. The latter also begin to show changes in color, appearing chlorotic instead of normal green.

The root symptoms of infected plants appear as an abnormal growth of lateral roots and proliferation of branch roots. Parasitized root tips show no necrosis or other injury although they are usually darker than normal in color. In such root tips meristematic activity and root growth stops, but cells already formed may enlarge abnormally and cause swelling of the root tip. Frequently, affected roots produce numerous lateral roots, which are in turn attacked by nematodes. Repeated infections of lateral roots and their branches produce a smaller root system, devoid of feeder roots and characterized instead by short, stubby, swollen root branches, the growth of which was stopped by the nematode infections.

The Pathogen: Trichodorus christiei. Trichodorus christiei is a small nematode about 0.65 mm long by 40 μm wide. It lives in the upper 30 cm of the soil. It is an ectoparasite, feeding on the epidermal cells at or near the root-tip region, never entering the root tissue. It lays eggs in the soil, which hatch to produce larvae and then adults. The life cycle of this nematode is completed within about 20 days. Populations of *T. christiei* build up quickly around susceptible hosts but decline when host plants become old and do not produce new root tips or when good host plants are absent. Eggs, larvae, and adults are usually found in the soil throughout the year, although preadults and eggs seem to be the stages found mostly during winter.

Several species of Trichodorus, T christiei included, are capable of transmitting plant viruses from one plant to another. Tobacco-rattle virus and pea early browning virus, both rod-shaped viruses, are the only ones known to be transmitted by Trichodorus nematodes. Several other plant viruses, all polyhedral shaped, are transmitted by the only other nematode vectors: Longidorus and Xiphinema.

Development of disease. When susceptible host plants are growing in soil infested with Trichodorus, as soon as the nematode comes in contact with young roots or root tips, it bends its head at approximately a right angle to the root surface, places its lip region against the cell wall, and punctures the wall with direct thrusts of the stylet. Once the stylet is inside the cell, a viscous substance is released through it into the cell, causing the cytoplasm of the plant cell to aggregate around the stylet tip. Part of the cytoplasm is then ingested by the nematode, after which it moves on to another cell within seconds or perhaps a few minutes from the beginning of feeding. Although a small opening up to 0.5 μm in diameter can be seen on the cell-wall for many hours after the nematode has left the cell, no cell contents appear to be lost through the hole, and gradually the aggregated cytoplasm is dispersed and the cell returns to normal.

All free larval stages and the adults can attack plants and feed on them. Feeding is restricted to the epidermal cells at or near the root tip on older roots, and the whole length of young succulent roots. Although one root tip may be attacked by many nematodes simultaneously or over a period of time, the mechanical damage caused by *Trichodorus* in feeding is slight and does not account for the gross changes on roots nor for the symptoms of the aboveground part of the plant. Parasitized roots show loss of meristematic activity at the root tip, have no definite root cap or region of elongation, and their region of mitosis is much smaller than that of healthy roots. Branch roots are more abundant and closer together in infected than in healthy roots. These effects seem to be the result of inhibitory or stimulatory action of substances secreted by nematodes into cells rather than of direct mechanical injury.

Stubby-root nematodes can be controlled through application of nematodes over the entire field. Methyl bromide-chloropicrin mixtures. Telone or DD give good, but temporary, control of this nematode. Six to eight weeks after treatment, stubby-root nematodes begin to reappear in the field, and if susceptible hosts are present, nematode populations build up rapidly. Slow-acting nematicides, such as ethoprop, retard or prevent the rapid buildup of nematodes, thus increasing the effectiveness of the treatment.

Chapter 5

Genetics of Plant Diseases

The inheritance of pathogen infection type, however, that is, the degree of pathogen virulence or avirulence, has been studied intensively only in the last few decades. It has now become clear that pathogens consist of a multitude of races, each differing from others in its ability to attack certain varieties of a plant species but not other varieties.

When a variety is inoculated with two appropriately chosen races of a pathogen, the variety is susceptible to one race but resistant to the other. Conversely, when the same race of a pathogen is inoculated on two appropriately chosen varieties of a host plant, one variety is susceptible while the other is resistant to the same pathogen. This clearly indicates that, in the first case, one race possesses a genetic characteristic that enables it to attack the plant, while the other race does not, and in the second case, that the one variety possesses a genetic characteristic that enables it to defend itself against the pathogen, so that it remains resistant, while the other variety does not. When several varieties are inoculated separately with one of several races of the pathogen, it is again noted that one pathogen race can infect a certain group of varieties, another race can infect another group of varieties, including some that can and some that cannot be infected by the previous race, and so on.

Thus, varieties possessing certain genes of resistance or susceptibility react differently against the various pathogen races and their genes of virulence or avirulence. The progeny of these varieties react to the same pathogens in exactly the same manner as did the parent plants, indicating that the property of resistance or susceptibility against a pathogen is genetically controlled (inherited). Similarly, the progeny of each pathogen causes on each variety the same effect that was caused by the parent pathogens, indicating that the property of virulence or avirulence of the pathogen on a particular variety is genetically controlled (inherited).

Under favorable environmental conditions, the outcome—infection (susceptibility) or noninfection (resistance)—in each host-pathogen combination is predetermined by the genetic material of the host and of the pathogen. The number of genes determining resistance or susceptibility varies from plant to plant, as the number of genes determining virulence or avirulence varies from pathogen to pathogen.

In most host-pathogen combinations the number of genes involved and what they control are not yet known. In some diseases, however, particularly those caused by fungi, such as potato late blight, apple scab, powdery mildews, tomato leaf mold, the cereal smuts and rusts, and also in several viral and bacterial diseases of plants, considerable information regarding the genetics of host-pathogen interactions is available.

A plant is either immune to a pathogen—that is, it is not attacked by the pathogen even under the most favorable conditions—or it may show various degrees of resistance, ranging from almost immunity to complete susceptibility. Resistance may be conditioned by a number of internal and external factors that operate to reduce the chance and degree of infection. The first step in any compatible host-pathogen interaction, in other words, in any infection, is recognition of the host by the pathogen and perhaps the opposite, recognition of the pathogen by the host. Therefore, the absence of recognition factor(s) in the host would make it resistant to the particular pathogen. In addition, any heritable characteristic of the plant that contributes to localization and isolation of the pathogen at the points of entry, to reduction of the harmful effects of toxic substances produced by the pathogen, or to inhibition of the reproduction and, thereby, of the further spread of the pathogen contributes to the resistance of the plant to disease.

Furthermore, any heritable characteristic that enables a particular variety to complete Its development and maturation under conditions that do not favor the development of the pathogen, also contributes to resistance.

The contribution of the genes conditioning resistance in the host seems to consist, primarily, of providing the genetic potential in the plant for development of one or more of the morphological or physiological characters—including those described in the chapters on structural and biochemical defense—that contribute to disease resistance. With the exception of virus and viroid diseases of plants, in which the genes of the host could conceivably come into "face-to-face" confrontation with the "genes" of the viral nucleic acid, the genes of plants infected by other types of pathogens seem never to come in contact with the genes of the pathogen. In general, in all host-pathogen combinations, viruses and viroids included, the interactions between genes of the host and genes of the pathogen are believed to be brought about indirectly through the chemical molecules and physiological processes controlled by the respective genes. The mechanisms by which genes control the physiological processes that lead to disease resistance or susceptibility are not yet clear, but they are, presumably, no different from the mechanisms controlling any other pilysiological process in living organisms. Thus, it is known that the genes are each carried by the genetic material (DNA) as successive groups of nucleotide triplets (triplet code), which are first read and transcribed on messenger RNA as the latter is synthesized. The messenger RNA then becomes associated with clusters of ribosomes (polyribosomes) and leads to the production of a specific protein, which is either an enzyme or a structural protein.

The produced enzyme participates or initiates biochemical reactions related to one or another of the cellular processes, and may result in the production of a certain morphological characteristic or accumulation of a certain chemical substance. The genes responsible for determining the kind and properties of a protein are called structural genes. The timing of activation of the structural genes, the rate of their activity-protein synthesis-and the timing of their inactivity are controlled by other genes called regulatory genes. Furthermore, messenger-RNA formation seems to be initiated only at certain points of the DNA strand, and these points are called operators.

A single operator may control the transcription into a messenger-RNA of only one structural gene or of a series of structural genes concerned with the different steps of one particular metabolic function, for example the biosynthesis of a fungitoxic phenolic compound or a compound that reacts with and detoxifies a pathogen toxin. The group of genes controlled by such an operator is called an operon. Thus, it is possible that for the production of an inducible enzyme or a ftingitoxic substance, a stimulant (inducer) secreted by the pathogen inactivates a repressor molecule, which is the product of a regulatory gene. The function of the repressor was to combine with a specific operator locus and prevent the transcription of that operon, thereby blocking the synthesis and action of the relevant proteins in the absence of infection. After infection, however, and after inactivation of the repressor by the pathogenic stimulant, transcription of the operon can take place, the particular substance is produced and, if this substance is toxic enough to the pathogen, the infection stops and the variety is resistant. On the other hand, if a pathogen mutant appears that does not secrete the particular stimulant (inducer) that inactivates the repressor molecule, the defense reaction does not take place, the pathogen infects the host without opposition and so it causes disease. In that case, the resistance of the host is said to have broken down, but it is actually bypassed by the pathogen rather than broken down.

Today's cultivated crop plants are the result of selection, or selection and breeding, of plant lines that evolved naturally in one or many geographic areas over millions of years. The evolution of plants from their ancient ancestors to present day crop plants has occurred slowly and has produced countless genetically diverse forms of these plants. Many such plants still exist as wild types at the point or points of origin or in the areas of natural spread of the plant. Although these plants may appear as useless remnants of evolution that are not likely to play a role in any future advances in agriculture, their diversity and survival in the face of the various pathogens that affect the crop in question indicates that they carry numerous genes for resistance against these pathogens. Since the beginning of agriculture, some of the wild plants in each locality have been selected and cultivated and thus produced numerous cultivated lines or varieties. The most productive of these varieties were perpetuated in each locality from year to year, and those that survived the local climate and the pathogens continued to be cultivated. Nature and pathogens eliminated the weak and susceptible ones, while the farmers selected the best yielders among the survivors.

Surviving varieties had different sets of major and minor genes for resistance. In this fashion, selection of crop plants continued wherever they were grown, each locality independently selecting varieties adapted to its own environment and resistant to its own pathogens. Thus, numerous varieties of each crop plant were cultivated throughout the world and, by their own genetic diversity, contributed to making the crop locally adapted but overall genetically nonuniform and, thereby, safe from any sudden outbreak of a single pathogen over a large area.

During the present century, widespread, intensive, and systematic efforts have been made and continue to be made by plant breeders throughout the world to breed plants that combine the most useful genes for higher yields, better quality, uniform size of plants and fruit, uniform ripening, cold hardiness, and disease resistance. In searching for new useful genes, plant breeders cross existing, local, cultivated varieties with each other and with those of other localities, both here and abroad, and with wild species of crop plants from wherever they can be obtained. Furthermore, plant breeders often attempt to generate additional genetic variation by treating their plant material with mutagenic agents. More recently, plant breeders have been generating greater genetic variability, and modifying or accelerating plant evolution in certain directions, by various genetic engineering techniques. Using such techniques, plant breeders can introduce genetic material (DNA) into plant cells directly, via vectors, or via protoplast fusion. Breeders can also obtain plants with different characteristics through culture and regeneration of somatic plant cells, by diploidization of haploid plants, and so on. The initial steps in plant breeding generally increase the variability of genetic characteristics of plants in a certain locality by combining in such plants genes that were more or less widely separated before. As breeding programs advance, however, and as several of the most useful genes are identified, subsequent steps in breeding tend to eliminate variability by combining the best genes in a few cultivated varieties and leaving behind or discarding plant lines that seem to have no usefulness at the time. In a short time a few "improved" varieties replace most or all others over large expanses of land.

The most successful improved varieties are also adopted abroad, and before too long, some of them replace the numerous but commercially inferior—local varieties. Occasionally, even the wild types themselves may be replaced by such a variety.

Thus, Red Delicious apples, Elberta peaches, certain dwarf wheat and rice varieties, certain genetic lines of corn and potatoes, one or two types of bananas, and sugarcane are grown in huge acreages throughout the world. In almost every crop, relatively few varieties make up the great bulk of the cultivated acreage of the crop throughout a country or throughout the world. The genetic base of these varieties is often narrow, especially since many of them have been derived from crosses of the same or related ancestors. These few varieties are used so widely because they are the best available, they are stable and uniform, and therefore everybody wants to grow them, At the same time, however, because they are so widely cultivated, they carry with them not only the blessings but also the dangers of uniformity. The most serious of these dangers is the vulnerability of large uniform plantings to sudden outbreaks of catastrophic plant disease epidemics.

The source of genes for resistance is the same gene pool of the crop that provides genes for every other inherited characteristic; that is, other native or foreign commercial varieties, older varieties abandoned earlier or discarded breeders' stock, wild plant relatives, and occasionally, induced mutations. Often genes of resistance are present in the varieties or species normally grown in the area where the disease is severe and in which the need for resistant varieties is most pressing. With most diseases, a few plants remain virtually unaffected by the pathogen, although most or all other plants in the area may be severely diseased.

If no resistant plants can be found within the local population of the species, plants of the same species from other areas and plants of other species are checked for resistance. If resistant plants are found, they are crossed with the cultivated varieties In an effort to incorporate the resistance genes of the other species into the cultivated varieties.

The same methods used to breed for any heritable characteristic are also used for breeding for disease resistance and depend upon the mating system of the plant (self- or cross-pollinated). Breeding for disease resistance, however. Is considerably more complicated, first because it can be assayed only by making the plants diseased, that is by employing another living and variable organism that must interact with the plants; and second because resistance may not be stable and may break down under certain conditions. For these reasons, several more or less sophisticated systems of screening for resistance have been developed. These screening systems include (1) precise conditions for inoculating the plants with the pathogen, (2) accurate monitoring and control of the environmental conditions in which the inoculated plants are kept, and (3) accurate assessment of disease incidence (percentage of plants, leaves, or fruits infected) and disease seventy (proportion of the total area of plant tissue affected by disease).

The following techniques are the main ones used for breeding disease resistance.

Mass selection of seed from the most highly resistant plants surviving in a field where natural infection occurs regularly. It is a simple method but improves plants only slowly, and in cross-pollinated plants there is no control of pollen source.

Pure line or pedigree selection, in which individual highly resistant plants and their progenies are propagated separately and are inoculated repeatedly to test for resistance. This method is easy and most effective with self-pollinated crops but quite difficult with cross-pollinated ones.

Recurrent selection or back crossing, in which a desirable but susceptible variety of a crop is crossed with another cultivated or wild relative that carries resistance to a particular pathogen. The progeny is then tested for resistance, and the resistant individuals are back crossed to the desirable variety. This is repeated several times until the resistance is stabilized in the genetic background of the desirable variety. This method is time consuming, and its effectiveness varies considerably with each particular case. It can be applied somewhat more easily in cross-pollinated than in self-pollinated crops.

Other classical breeding techniques for disease resistance include: the use of F_1 hybrids of two different but homozygous lines carrying different genes for resistance, which allows us to take advantage of the phenomenon of heterosis: the use of natural or artificially induced (UV-light, X-rays) mutants that show increased resistance; and the change of the number of chromosomes in a plant and production of euploids (4n, 6n) or aneuploids (2n ± 1 or 2 chromosomes), by the use of chemicals such as colchicine, and by radiation.

Tissue culture of disease-resistant plants Tissue culture of disease-resistant plants is particularly useful with clonally propagated plants such as strawberries, apples, bananas, sugarcane, cassava, and potatoes. Prolific plantlet production from meristem and other tissue cultures facilitate the rapid propagation of plants with exceptional (resistant) genotypes, especially in those crops not easily propagated by seed. An even greater use of tissue culture is for production of pathogen-free stocks of clonally propagated susceptible plants.

Isolation of disease resistant mutants from plant cell cultures Plants regenerated from culture (callus, single cells, or protoplasts) often show considerable variability (somaclonal variation), much of it useless or deleterious. However, plants with useful characteristics may also emerge. For example, when plants were regenerated from leaf protoplasts of a potato variety susceptible to both Phytophthora infestans and Alternaria solani, some of them (5 of 500) were resistant to Alternaria solani and some (20 of 800) were resistant to Phytophthora infestans. Similarly, plants exhibiting increased resistance to diseases caused by Helminthosporium and Ustilago were obtained from tissue cultures of sugarcane.

Production of resistant dihaploids from haploid plants Immature pollen cells (microspores)-and less often megaspores-of many plants can be induced to develop into haploid (1n) plants in which single copies (alleles) of each gene are present in all sorts of combinations. By vegetative propagation and proper screening for disease resistance, the most highly resistant haploids can be selected. These haploids can be subsequently treated with colchicine, which results in diploitization of the nuclei, that is, doubling of the number of chromosomes and production of dihaploid plants homozygous for all genes, including genes for resistance.

Increasing, disease resistance by protoplast fusion Protoplasts from closely related and even from unrelated plants, under proper conditions, can be made to fuse. The fusion produces hybrid cells containing the nuclei (chromosomes) and the cytoplasm of both protoplasts, or perhaps result in cybrid cells containing the nucleus of one cell and the cytoplasm of the other cell. Generally, hybrids of unrelated cells sooner or later abort, or may produce callus, but do not regenerate plants.

In combinations of more or less related cells, however, while many or most of the chromosomes of one of the cells are eliminated during cell division, one or a few chromosomes of that cell survive and may be incorporated in the genome of the other cell. In this way, plants with more chromosomes and thereby new characteristics can be regenerated from the products of protoplast fusion. Protoplast fusion is particularly useful between protoplasts of different, highly resistant haploid lines of the same variety or species. Protoplast fusion of such lines results in diploid plants that combine the resistance genes of two highly resistant haploid lines.

Genetic transformation of plant cells for disease resistance Genetic material (DNA) can be introduced into plant cells or protoplasts by several methods. Such methods include direct DNA uptake, microinjection of DNA, liposome (lipid vesicle) mediated delivery of DNA, delivery by means of centromere plasmids (minichromosomes), by use of plant viral vectors, and most-importantly by use of the natural gene vector system of Agrobacterium tumefaciens, the cause of crown gall disease of many plants. In all of these methods, small or large pieces of DNA are introduced into plant cells or, protoplasts and the DMA may or may not be integrated in the plant chromosomal DNA.

When the introduced DNA carries appropriate regulatery genes recognized by the plant cell, or is integrated near appropriate regulatory genes along plant chromosomes, the DNA is "expressed," that is, it is transcribed into mRNA, which is then translated into protein. So far, only the Agrobacterium system has been used successfully to introduce into plants specific new genes that were then expressed by the plant. This was accomplished by isolating the seed protein gene from beans and splicing it into the appropriate area of the Ti-plasmid (tumor-inducing plasmid) of Agrobacterium; the bacteria were then allowed to infect other plants, for example, the sunflower. Upon infection, about one-tenth of the DNA of the plasmid, containing the new gene, is transferred to the plant cell and is incorporated into the plant's genome. There the new gene replicates during plant cell division and is expressed along with the other plant genes.

To date, no gene for disease resistance has been isolated, and therefore no genetic transformation for disease resistance has been accomplished in any host-pathogen combination. It is considered likely, however, that genes for resistance, particularly single genes involved in vertical resistance, will be among the first to be successfully used for genetic transformation of plants, and that breeding for disease resistance will be among the first areas of plant breeding to profit greatly from the application of techniques in genetic engineering.

Resistance may be obtained by incorporating into a variety one, a few, or many resistance genes. Some' of these genes may control important steps in disease development and may therefore play a major role in disease resistance. Other genes may control peripheral events of lesser importance in disease development and, therefore, play a relatively minor role in disease resistance.

Obviously, one or a few major-role genes could be sufficient to make a plant resistant to a pathogen (monogenic, oligogenic, or vertical resistance). However, it would take many minor-effect genes to make a plant resistant. More importantly, while a plant with vertical resistance may be completely resistant to a pathogen, a plant with horizontal resistance is never completely resistant or completely susceptible. Furthermore, vertical resistance is easy to manipulate in a breeding program, and therefore it is often preferred to horizontal resistance, but both vertical and horizontal have their advantages and limitations. Vertical resistance is aimed against specific pathogens or pathogen races. Vertical resistance is most effective when (1) it is incorporated in annual crops that are easy to breed, such as small grains; (2) it is directed against pathogens that do not reproduce and spread rapidly, such as Fusarium; or pathogens that do not mutate very frequently, such as Puccinia graminis; (3) it consists of "strong" genes that confer complete protection to the plant that carries it; and (4) the host population does not consist of a single genetically uniform variety grown over large acreages. If one or more of these, and of several other, conditions are not met, vertical resistance becomes short lived, that is, it breaks down as a result of appearance of new pathogen races that can bypass it or overcome it.

On the other hand, horizontal resistance confers incomplete but durable protection—it does not break down. Horizontal resistance involves host physiological processes that act as mechanisms of defense and that are beyond the limits of the capacity of the pathogen to change, that is, beyond the probable limits of its variability. Horizontal resistance is universally present in wild and domesticated plants but is at its highest in wild plants and at its lowest in greatly "improved" varieties.

Horizontal resistance operates against all races of a pathogen including the most pathogenic ones. Actually, the more pathogenic the races present, the greater the selection for general resistance in the host. Horizontal resistance is eroded in the absence of the pathogen because there is no selection pressure for resistance. In many cases, horizontal (polygenic) resistance is an important part of the resistance exhibited by plants possessing vertical (specific) resistance, but it is overshadowed by the latter.

Considerable horizontal resistance can be incorporated into cultivated crops by cross-breeding of existing, genetically different varieties. The wider the genetic base of a crop, the greater its horizontal resistance and the smaller the need for the usually temporary vertical resistance. Varieties with horizontal (polygenic, general, or nonspecific) resistance remain resistant much longer than do varieties with vertical (oligogenic or specific) resistance, but the level of resistance of the second group is much higher while it lasts than that of the first group. Also, varieties with vertical resistance are often attacked suddenly and rapidly by a new virulent race and lead to severe epidemics. These disadvantages can be avoided in some crops by the use of multilines.

Multilines are either mixtures of individual varieties (lines or cultivars) that are agronomically similar but differ in their resistance genes or varieties that are derived from crossing several to many varieties that contain different resistance genes and then selecting from those that contain the mixtures of genes. Multilines have been developed mostly in small grains against the rust fungi, but their use is likely to increase in these and in other crops as the control of plant diseases with specific resistance and with chemicals becomes more risky or less acceptable.

Varieties with even complete vertical resistance do not remain resistant forever. The continuous production of mutants and hybrids in pathogens sooner or later leads to the appearance of races that can infect previously resistant varieties. Sometimes, races may exist in an area in small populations and avoid detection until after the introduction of a new variety, or virulent races of the pathogen existing elsewhere may be brought in after introduction of the resistant variety.

In all cases, widespread cultivation of a single, previously resistant variety provides an excellent substrate for rapid development and spread of the new race of the pathogen, and usually leads to an epidemic. Thus, genetic uniformity in crops, although very desirable when it concerns horticultural characteristics, is undesirable and often catastrophic when it occurs in the genes of resistance to diseases. The cultivation of varieties with genetically uniform disease resistance is possible and quite safe if other means of plant disease control, such as chemical, are possible. Thus, a few fruit tree varieties, such as Delicious apples, Bartlett pears, Elberta peaches, and Navel oranges, are cultivated throughout the world in the face of numerous virulent fungal and bacterial pathogens that would destroy them in a short time were it not for the fact that the trees are protected from the pathogens by numerous chemical sprays annually. Even such varieties, however, suffer tremendous losses when affected by pathogens that cannot be controlled with chemicals, as is the case of fire blight of pears and pear decline and of tristeza disease of citrus. Another case in which varieties with genetically uniform disease resistance are not likely to suffer from severe disease epidemics is when the resistance is aimed against slow-moving soil pathogens such as Fusarium and Verticillium. Aside from the fact that some pathogens normally produce fewer races than others, even if new races are produced at the same rate, soilborne pathogens lack the dispersal potential of airborne ones.

As a result, a new race of a soilborne pathogen would be limited to a relatively small area for a long time, and although it could cause a locally severe disease, it would not spread rapidly and widely to cause an epidemic. The slow spread of such virulent new races of soilborne pathogens allows time for the control of the disease by other means or the replacement of the variety with another one resistant to the new race. Genetic uniformity in plant varieties becomes a serious disadvantage in the production of major crops because of the potential danger of sudden and widespread disease epidemics caused by airborne or insect-borne pathogens In the vast acreages in which each of these varieties is often grown.

Several examples of epidemics that resulted from genetic uniformity are known and some of them have already been mentioned. Southern corn leaf blight was the result of the widespread use of corn hybrids containing the Texas male-sterile cytoplasm; the destruction of the "Ceres" spring wheat by race 56 of Puccinia *graminis* and of the "Hope" and its relative bread wheats by race 15B of P. *graminis* was the result of replacement of numerous genetically diverse varieties by a few uniform ones. The Helminthosporium blight of Victoria oats was the result of replacing many varieties with the rust-resistant Victoria oats-, coffee rust destroyed all coffee trees in Ceylon because all of them originated from uniform susceptible stock of Coffea arabica; tristeza destroyed millions of orange trees in

South and North America because they were all propagated on hypersensitive resistant sour orange rootstocks; and pear decline destroyed millions of pear trees in the Pacific coast states because they were propagated on hypersensitive resistant oriental rootstocks. In spite of these and many other well-known examples of plant disease epidemics that occurred because of the concentrated cultivation of genetically uniform crops over large areas, crop production continues to depend on genetic uniformity.

A few varieties of each crop used to and for some crops still make up the bulk of the cultivated crop over as vast an area as the United States (Table 4). As can be seen in Table 4, although a relatively large number of varieties are available for each crop, only a few, often 2 or 3, varieties are grown in more than half the acreage of each crop, and in some they make up more than three-fourths of the crop. It is easy to see that two pea varieties make up almost the entire (96 percent) pea crop of, the country, that is, about 400,000 acres, that two varieties account for 42 percent of the sugarbeet crop, that is, about 600,000 acres.

It is apparent that several hundreds of thousands or several million acres planted to one variety present a huge opportunity for the development of an epidemic. The variety, of course, is planted so widely because it is resistant to existing pathogens. But this resistance puts extreme survival pressure on the pathogens over that area. It takes one "right" change in one of the zillions of pathogen individuals in the area to produce a new virulent race that can attack the variety. When that happens it is a matter of time -and, usually, of favorable weather-before the race breaks loose, the epidemic develops, and the variety is wiped out! In some cases the appearance of the new race is detected early, and the variety is replaced with another one, resistant to the new race, before a widespread epidemic occurs; this of course requires that varieties of a crop with different genetic base are available at all times. For this reason, most varieties must usually be replaced within about 3-5 years from the time of their widespread distribution.

In addition to the genetic uniformity within one variety, plant breeding often introduces genetic uniformity to several or all cultivated varieties of a crop by introducing one or several genes in all of these varieties or by replacing the cytoplasm of the varieties with a single type of cytoplasm. Uniformity through replacement of the cytoplasm occurred, of course, in most corn hybrids in the later 1960s when the Texas male-sterile cytoplasm replaced the normal cytoplasm; and cytoplasmic uniformity is commercially employed in several varieties of sorghum, sugar beet, and onions, it is studied in wheat, and is also present in cotton and cantaloupe.

Neither the introduced genes nor the replacement cytoplasm of course, make the plant less resistant to diseases, but if a pathogen appears that is favored by or can take advantage of the characters controlled by that gene or that cytoplasm, then the stage is set for a major epidemic. That this can happen was proved by the southern corn leaf blight epidemic of 1970, the susceptibility of dwarf wheats to new races of Septoria and Puccinia, of tomatoes with the determinate gene to Alternaria, and others.

Genetic information in DNA is encoded in a linear fashion, in the order of the four bases (A = ademine, C = cytosine, G = guanine, and T = thymine). Each triplet of adjacent bases codes for a particular amino acid. A gene is a stretch of a DNA molecule, usually of about one hundred to five hundred or more adjacent triplets, that codes for one protein molecule or, in a few cases, one RNA molecule. Actually, in eukaryotes, the coding region of a gene is often interrupted by noncoding stretches of DNA called introns. When a gene is active, that is, it is expressed, one of its DNA strands is copied (transcribed) into RNA. If the gene codes for an RNA and the RNA is a transfer RNA (tRNA) or ribosomal RNA (rRNA), expression of the gene is more or less completed upon transcription. However, if the gene, like the vast majority of them, codes for a protein molecule, then the transcription product is a messenger RNA (mRNA). The mRNA then becomes attached to ribosomes, which with the help of tRNAs, translate the base sequence of the mRNA into a specific sequence of amino acids and eventually construct a particular protein. Each gene codes for a different protein. It is the proteins, which are either part of the structure of cell membranes or act as enzymes, that give cells and organisms their characteristic properties such as shape, size, and color and determine what kinds of chemical substances are produced by the cell. Of course, not all genes in a cell are expressed at all times, since different kinds of cells and at different times have different functions and needs.

In many cases of host-pathogen interaction, genes in the one component are triggered to be expressed by a substance produced by the other component. For example, genes for cell-wall-degrading enzymes in the pathogen are apparently induced by the presence in the host of cell wall macromolecules that are substrates for these enzymes. Also, genes for defense reactions in the host, for example, production of phytoalexins, apparently are triggered to expression by certain inducer molecules (elicitors) produced by the pathogen.

When different plants, such as tomato, apple, or wheat, become diseased as a result of infection by a pathogen, the pathogen is generally different for each kind of host plant, and it is often specific for that particular host plant. Thus, the fungus Fusarium oxysporum f. sp. lycopersici that causes tomato wilt attacks only tomato and has absolutely no effect on apple, wheat, or any other plant. Similarly, the fungus Venturia inaequalis that causes apple scab affects only apple, while the fungus Puccinia graminis f, sp. tritici that causes stem rust of wheat attacks only wheat. What makes possible the- development of disease in a host is the presence in the pathogen of one or more genes for specificity and for virulence against the particular host, which in turn is thought to have certain genes for specificity and for susceptibility to the particular pathogen.

The gene or genes for virulence In the pathogen are usually specific for one or a few related kinds of host plants. Also, the genes that make a host plant susceptible to a particular pathogen are present only in that one host and possibly a few related kinds of host plants. It is, therefore, the concurrent occurrence and interaction of specific genes for virulence in the pathogen and of specific genes for susceptibility in the host that determine the initiation and development of disease. A pathogen, then, has a set of genes for virulence that is specifically found in that pathogen and is aimed specifically against its own host or hosts. On the other hand, each host has a set of genes for susceptibility to a particular pathogen, such genes are found only in that particular host plant and apparently accommodate only the specific pathogen. The specificity of genes for virulence and of genes for susceptibility explains why a pathogen that is virulent on one host Is not virulent on all other kinds of host plants and why a host plant that is susceptible to one pathogen is not susceptible to all other pathogens of other host plants. Of course, a few pathogens are able to attack many kinds, sometimes hundreds, of host plants. Such pathogens can attack so many hosts apparently because they either have many diverse genes for virulence or because their genes of virulence somehow have a much wider spectrum of host specificity than those of the commonly more specialized pathogens. Each species of plant, however, seems to be susceptible to a fairly small number of different pathogens, usually less than a hundred for most plants, although some plants seem to be attacked by close to two hundred different pathogens. This means that a single plant species has genes for susceptibility that would allow it to become infected by any of its one to two hundred pathogens.

In spite of the genes for susceptibility that plants have to so many pathogens, countless numbers of individuals of a single plant species, such as corn, wheat, or soybean, survive in huge land expanses year after year. These plants survive either free of disease or with only minor symptoms, even though most of their pathogens are often widespread among the plants. Why aren't all the plants attacked by their pathogens, and why are those that are attacked not usually killed by the pathogens? The answer is complex, but basically it happens because plants, through evolution or through systematic breeding, have acquired in addition to their genes for susceptibility one or more genes for resistance, which protect them from infection or from severe disease. Such pathogens contain one and usually more than one gene for virulence, but if they do not contain the additional new gene for virulence that is required to overcome the effect of the new resistance gene in the plant, they cannot infect the plant and the plant remains resistant. Thus, even one new gene for resistance to a pathogen can protect plants that have the gene from the disease caused by many races of the pathogen-at least for several months and possibly for a few to several years.

It has been the experience of researchers with numerous host-pathogen combinations, however, that after a new gene for resistance to a pathogen is introduced into a crop variety and that variety is planted in the fields, a new population of the pathogen appears that contains a new gene for virulence that enables the pathogen to attack the crop plants containing the new gene for resistance.

After such plants were introduced, however, the new resistance gene excluded all other pathogen individuals except the few containing the new gene for virulence, which could attack these plants. Exclusion of the pathogens that lacked the new gene allowed the few that carried the gene to multiply and take over. Or the new gene may have appeared suddenly *de novo,* that is, through a mutation or by rearrangement of the genetic material of the pathogens through the ever ongoing events of genetic variability in organisms.

One of the most dynamic and significant aspects of biology is that characteristics of individuals within a species are not "fixed" in their morphology and physiology but vary from one individual to another.

As a matter of fact, all individuals produced as a result of a sexual process are expected to be different from each other and from their parents in a number of characteristics, although they retain most similarities with them and belong to the same species. This is true of fungi produced from sexual spores such as oospores, ascospores, and basidiospores, of parasitic higher plants produced from seeds, and of nematodes produced from fertilized eggs, as well as of cultivated plants produced from seeds.

When individuals are produced asexually, the frequency and degree of variability among the progeny are reduced greatly but even then certain individuals among the progeny will show different characteristics. This is the case in the overwhelmingly asexual reproduction of fungi by means of conidia, zoospores, sclerotia, and uredospores, and in bacteria, mycoplasmas and viruses, as well as in the asexual propagation of plants by means of buds, cuttings, tubers, and so on.

In host plants and in pathogens, such as most fungi, parasitic higher plants, and nematodes, which can, and usually do, reproduce by means of a sexual process, variation in the progeny is introduced primarily through segregation and recombination of genes during the meiotic division of the zygote. Bacteria too, however, and even viruses, exhibit variation that seems to be the result of a sexual like process. In many fungi, heteroploidy and certain parasexual processes lead to variation. On the other hand, all plants and all pathogens, especially bacteria, viruses, and fungi, and probably mycoplasmas, can and do produce variants in the absence of any sexual process by means of mutations and, perhaps, by means of cytoplasmic adaptation.

Two mechanisms of variability—mutation and recombination—occur in both plants and pathogens.

Mutation

A mutation is a more or less abrupt change in the genetic material of an organism, which is then transmitted in a hereditary fashion to the progeny. Mutations represent changes in the sequence of bases in the DNA, either through substitution of one base for another, or through addition or deletion of one or many base pairs. Additional changes may be brought about by amplification of particular segments of DNA to multiple copies, by insertion of a movable DNA segment into a coding or regulatory sequence of a gene, and by inversion of a DNA segment. Mutations occur spontaneously in nature in all living organisms, those that produce only sexually or only asexually and those that reproduce both sexually and asexually. Mutations in single-celled organisms, such as bacteria, in fungi with haploid mycelium, and in viruses are expressed immediately after their occurrence. Most mutant factors, however, are usually recessive; therefore, in diploid or dikaryotic organisms mutations can remain unexpressed until they are brought together in a hybrid.

Mutations for virulence probably occur no more frequently than for any other inherited characteristics, but given the great number of progeny produced by pathogens, it is probable that large numbers of mutants differing in virulence from their parent are produced in nature every year.

Besides, considering that only a few genetically homogeneous varieties of each crop plant are planted continuously over enormous land expanses for a number of years, and considering the difficulties involved in shifting from one variety to another on short notice, the threat of new, more virulent, mutants appearing and attacking a previously resistant variety is a real one. Moreover, once a new factor for virulence appears in a mutant, this factor will take part in the sexual or parasexual processes of the pathogen and may produce recombinants possessing virulence quite different in degree or nature from that existing in the parental strains.

Since plants and pathogens contain genetic material (DNA) outside the cell nucleus, mutations in the extranuclear DNA are just as common as in the nuclear DNA and affect- whatever characteristics are controlled by the extranuclear DNA. Because the inheritance of characteristics controlled by extranuclear DNA (cytoplasmic inheritance) does not follow the Mendelian laws of genetics, however, mutations on that DNA are more difficult to detect and characterize. Through mutations in extrachromosonal DNA, many pathogens acquire the ability to carry out a physiological process that they could not before. Cytoplasmic inheritance presumably occurs in all organisms except viruses and viroids, which lack cytoplasm. Three types of adaptations brought about by changes in the genetic material of the cytoplasm have been shown in pathogens. Pathogens may acquire the ability to tolerate previously toxic substances, to utilize new substances for growth, and to change their virulence toward host plants. Several characteristics of plants are also inherited through the cytoplasm, including the resistance to infection by certain pathogens.

Recombination

Recombination occurs during the sexual reproduction of plants, fungi, and nematodes whenever two haploid (1N) nuclei, containing slightly different genetic material, unite to form a diploid (2N) nucleus, called a zygote. Recombination of genetic factors occurs during the meiotic division of the zygote as a result of genetic crossovers in which parts of chromatids (and the genes they carry) of the one chromosome of the pair are exchanged with parts of chromatids of the other chromosome of the pair. In this way a recombination of the genes of the two parental nuclei takes place in the zygote, and the haploid nuclei or gametes resulting after meiosis are different both from gametes that produced the zygote and from each other. In the fungi, the haploid nuclei or gametes often divide mitotically to produce haploid mycelium and spores, which results in genetically different groups of relatively homogeneous individuals that may produce large populations asexually until the next sexual cycle.

Certain mechanisms of variability appear to be operating only in certain kinds of organisms or to be operating in a rather different manner than those described as general mechanisms of variability. These specialized mechanisms of variability are sexuallike or parasexual processes and include heterokaryosis, heteroploidy, and parasexualism in fungi; conjugation, transformation and transduction in bacteria; and genetic recombination in viruses.

Heterokaryosis Heterokaryosis is the condition in which as a result of fertilization or anastomosis, cells of fungus hyphae or parts of hyphae contain two or more nuclei that are genetically different. For example, in the Basidiomycetes, the dikaryotic state may differ drastically from the haploid mycelium and spores of the fungus. Thus in Puccinia graminis tritici, the fungus causing stem rust of wheat, the haploid basidiospores can infect barberry but not wheat, and the haploid mycelium can grow only in barberry, while the dikaryotic aeciospores and uredospores can infect wheat but not barberry and the dikaryotic mycelium can grow in both barberry and wheat. Heterokaryosis also occurs in other fungi, but its importance in plant disease development in nature is not known.

Parasexualism Parasexualism is the process by which genetic recombinations can occur within fungal heterokaryons. This comes about by the occasional fusion of the two nuclei and the formation of a diploid nucleus. During multiplication, crossing over occurs in a few mitotic divisions and results in the appearance of genetic recombinants by the occasional separation of the diploid nucleus into its haploid components.

Heteroploidy heteroploidy is the existence of cells, tissues, or whole organisms with numbers of chromosomes per nucleus that are different from the normal 1N or 2N for the particular organism. Heteroploids may be haploids, diploids, triploids, or tetraploids, or they may be aneuploids, that is, they have 1, 2, 3, or more extra chromosomes or are missing one or more chromosomes from the normal euploid number. Heteroploidy is often associated with cellular differentiation and represents a normal situation in the development of most eukaryotes. In several studies, spores of the same fungus were found to contain nuclei with chromosome numbers ranging from 2 to 12 per nucleus and also diploids and polyploids.

Since it has been shown that the expression of different genes is proportional to, inversely proportional to, or unaffected by dosage, obviously the existence of heteroploid cells or heteroploid whole individuals of some pathogens increases the degree of variability that can be exhibited by these pathogens.

Heteroploidy has been repeatedly observed in fungi and has been shown to affect the growth rate, spore size and rate of spore production, hyphal color, enzyme activities, and pathogenicity. It has been shown, for example, that some heteroploids, such as diploids of the normally haploid fungus Verticillium albo-atrum, the cause of wilt in cotton, lose the ability to infect cotton plants even when derived from highly virulent haploids. How much of the variability in pathogenicity in nature is due to heteroploidy is still unknown. Sectoring, that is, the appearance of morphologically distinct sectors in fungus colonies, is a common occurrence when most fungi are cultured on nutrient media. In addition to morphological differences, sectors sometimes also show differences in pathogenicity. Sectoring has yet to be explained genetically, but it appears that a large proportion of the sectors may be the result of heteroploidy, although mutations, heterokaryosis, and parasexualism are also probably involved.

New biotypes of bacteria seem to arise with varying frequency by means of at least three sexuallike processes. It is probable that similar processes occur in mycoplasmas. (i) Conjugation, in which two compatible bacteria come in contact with each other and a small portion of the chromosomal or nonchromosomal (plasmid) genetic material of the one bacterium is transferred to the genetic material of the other. (2) Transformation, in which bacterial cells are transformed genetically by absorbing and incorporating in their own cells genetic material secreted by, or released during rupture of, other compatible bacteria. (3) Transduction, in which a bacterial virus (phage) transfers genetic material from the bacterium in which the phage was produced to the bacterium it infects next.

When two strains of the same virus are inoculated into the same host plant, one or more new virus strains are recovered with properties (virulence, symptomatology, and so on) different from those of either of the original strains introduced into the host.

The new strains probably are recombinants, although their appearance through mutation, not hybridization, cannot always be ruled out. In multipartite viruses consisting of 2, 3, or more nucleic acid components, new virus strains may also arise in host plants or vectors from recombination of the appropriate components of two or more strains of such viruses.

The virulence of pathogenic microorganisms toward one or all of their hosts often decreases when the pathogens are kept in culture for relatively long periods of time or when they are passed one or more times through different hosts.

If the culturing of the pathogen is prolonged sufficiently, the pathogen may lose virulence completely. Such partial or complete loss of virulence in pathogens is sometimes called attenuation, and it has been shown to occur in bacteria, fungi, and viruses.

Pathogens that have experienced partial or complete loss of virulence in culture or in other hosts are often capable of regaining part or all of their virulence if they are returned to their hosts under the proper conditions. Sometimes, however, the loss of virulence may be irreversible. "Loss" of virulence in culture, or in other hosts, seems to be the result of selection of individuals of less virulent or avirulent pathogen strains that happen to be capable of growing and multiplying in culture, or in the other host, much more rapidly than the virulent ones. After several transfers in culture or the other hosts, such attenuated individuals largely, or totally, overtake and replace the virulent ones in the total population so that the pathogen is less virulent or totally avirulent. Upon reinoculation of the proper host, isolates, in which the virulent individuals have been totally replaced by avirulent ones, continue to be avirulent, and therefore loss of pathogenicity is irreversible.

On the other hand, upon reinoculation of the proper host with isolates in which at least some virulent individuals survived through the transfers in culture or the other host, the few surviving virulent individuals infect the host and multiply, often in proportion to their virulence. The virulent individuals increase in numbers with each subsequent inoculation, while at the same time nonvirulent individuals are reduced or eliminated with each reinoculation.

The entire population of a particular organism on earth, for example, a fungal pathogen, has certain morphological characteristics in common and makes up the species of pathogen, such as Puccinia graminis, the cause of stem rust of cereals. Some individuals of this species, however, attack only wheat or only barley, or oats, and these individuals make up groups that are called varieties or special forms (formae specialis) such as P. graminis tritici, P. g. hordei, and P. g. avenae. But even within each special form, some individuals attack some of the varieties of the host plant but not the others, some attack another set of host plant varieties, and so on, each group of such individuals making up a race. Thus, there are more than 200 races of Puccinia graminis tritici (race 1, race 15, race 59, and so on). Occasionally, one of the offspring of a race can suddenly attack a new variety or can cause severe symptoms on a variety that it could barely infect before. This individual is called a variant. The identical individuals produced asexually by the variant make up a biotype. The appearance of new pathogen biotypes may be very dramatic when the change involves the host range of the pathogen.

If the variant has lost the ability to infect a plant variety that is widely cultivated, this pathogen simply loses its ability to procure a livelihood for itself and will die without even making its existence known to us. If, on the other hand, the change in the variant pathogen enables it to infect a plant variety cultivated because of its resistance to the parental strain, the variant individual, being the only one that can survive on this plant variety, grows and multiplies on the new variety without any competition and soon produces large populations that spread and destroy the heretofore resistant variety.

Plants are resistant to certain pathogens either because they belong to taxonomic groups that are immune to these pathogens (nonhost resistance), or because they possess genes for resistance directed against the genes of virulence of the pathogen (true resistance), or because for various reasons, the plants escape or tolerate infection by these pathogens (apparent resistance). Each kind of plant, for example, potato, corn, orange, is a host to a small and different set of pathogens that make up a small proportion of the total number of known plant pathogens. In other words, each kind of plant is a non-host to the vast majority of known plant pathogens. Non-hosts are immune, that is, completely resistant, to all pathogens of all other plants, even under the most favorable conditions for disease development (nonhost resistance). The same plants, however, are susceptible, to a lesser or greater extent, to their own pathogens. Moreover, each plant exhibits specific susceptibility toward each of its own pathogens while it exhibits unspecific immunity to all the other pathogens. Even within a species of plant that is susceptible to a particular species of pathogen, however, there is considerable variation in both the susceptibility of the various plant cultivars (varieties) towards the pathogen and in the virulence of the various pathogen races towards the plant variety. It is the genetics of such host - pathogen interactions that are of considerable biological interest and of the utmost importance in developing disease control strategies through breeding for resistance,

The variation in susceptibility to the pathogen among plant varieties is due to different kinds and, perhaps, different numbers of genes for resistance that may be present in each variety. The effects of individual resistance genes vary from large to minute, depending on the importance of the functions they control. A variety that is very susceptible to a pathogen isolate obviously has no effective genes for resistance against that isolate.

Lack of susceptibility to the second isolate would indicate that the plant variety, which had no genes for resistance against the first pathogen isolate, has one or more genes for resistance against the second isolate. If the same plant variety is inoculated with more pathogen isolates, obtained from still different plant varieties, it is possible that the variety would be susceptible to some of them but not susceptible (it would be resistant) to the other isolates. The latter case would again show that the variety has one or more genes for resistance against each of the isolates to which it is resistant. Although the resistance against some of the isolates might be the result of the same genes for resistance in the variety, it is likely that the variety also contains several genes for resistance, each specific against a particular pathogen isolate.

Disease resistance that is genetically controlled by the presence of one, a few, or many genes for resistance in the plant is known as true resistance. In true resistance, the host and the pathogen are more or less incompatible with each other, either because of lack of chemical recognition between the host and the pathogen or because the host plant can defend itself against the pathogen by the various defense mechanisms already present, or activated, in response to infection by the pathogen. There are two kinds of true resistance: horizontal and vertical.

Horizontal resistance

All plants have a certain, but not always the same, level of unspecific resistance that is effective against each of their pathogens. Such resistance is sometimes called nonspecific, general, quantitative, adult-plant, field, or durable resistance, but is most commonly referred to as horizontal resistance. Horizontal resistance is controlled by many (probably dozens, perhaps hundreds of) genes, thereby the name polygenic or multi-gene resistance. Each of these genes alone may be rather ineffective against the pathogen and may play a minor role in the total horizontal resistance (minor gene resistance). The many genes involved in horizontal resistance seem to exert their influence by controlling the numerous steps of the physiological processes in the plant that provide the materials and structures that make up the defense mechanisms of the plant.

The horizontal resistance of a plant variety toward all races of a pathogen may be somewhat greater, or smaller, than those of other varieties toward the same pathogen, but the differences are usually small and insufficient to routinely distinguish varieties by horizontal resistance (nondifferential resistance). In addition, horizontal resistance is affected by, and may vary under, different environmental conditions.

Generally, horizontal resistance does not protect plants from becoming infected, but it slows down the development of individual infection loci on a plant and thereby slows down the spread of the disease and the development of epidemics in the field. Some degree of horizontal resistance is present in plants regardless of whether or not vertical resistance is present.

Vertical resistance

Many plant varieties are quite resistant to some races of a pathogen while they are susceptible to other races of the same pathogen. In other words, depending on the race of the pathogen used to infect a variety, the variety may appear resistant to one pathogen race and susceptible to another race. This type of plant resistance differentiates clearly between races of a pathogen since it is effective against specific races of the pathogen and ineffective against others. Such resistance is sometimes called specific, qualitative, or differential resistance, but is most commonly referred to as vertical resistance. Vertical resistance is usually controlled by one or a few genes (thereby the name monogenic or oligogenic resistance). These genes apparently control a major step in the interaction of the pathogen with the host plant and therefore play a major role in the expression of vertical resistance (major gene resistance).

In the presence of vertical resistance, the host and pathogen appear incompatible, the host usually responds with a hypersensitive reaction, and so the pathogen fails to become established and multiply in the host. Generally, vertical resistance inhibits the initial establishment of pathogens that arrive at a field from host plants that lack or have different major genes for resistance. Vertical resistance inhibits the development of epidemics by limiting the initial inoculum. Complete resistance may be provided by a single resistance gene, for example, R1, R2, or R3, but more than one resistance gene may be combined (R1R2, R1R3, R1R2R3) in the same plant, which then is resistant to all the pathogen races to which each of the genes provides resistance.

A plant species may have as many as 20-40 resistance genes against a particular pathogen, although each variety may have only one or a few of these genes. For example, wheat has 20-40 genes for resistance against the leaf rust fungus Puccinia recondita; barley has a similar number of genes against the powdery mildew fungus Erysiphe graminis tritici, and cotton has almost as many against the bacterium Xanthomonas malvacearum.

Each gene for resistance, such as R2, is in reality unspecific for resistance; that is, it makes the plant resistant to all the races of the pathogen except to the race (such as P2) that contains the corresponding gene for virulence. This pathogen race (P2) and its virulence gene (V2), however, are detected because the pathogen specifically attacks plants that carry this particular gene for resistance (R2). Whether horizontal or vertical, true resistance is generally controlled by genes located in the plant chromosomes in the cell nucleus. There are, however, several plant diseases in which either type of resistance is controlled by genetic material contained in the cytoplasm of the cell in which genes do not normally follow the Mendelian laws of genetics. Such resistance is some times referred to as cytoplasmic resistance. The two best known cases of cytoplasmic resistance occur in corn in which resistance to two leaf blights, the southern corn leaf blight caused by Bipolaris (*Helmindthosporium*) *maydis* and the yellow leaf blight caused by Phyllosticta maydis, is conferred by characteristics present in normal cytoplasm of various types of corn but absent or suppressed in Texas male-sterile cytoplasm. Varieties with specific (monogenic or oligogenic) resistance generally show complete resistance to a specific pathogen under most environmental conditions, but a single or a few mutations in the pathogen may produce a new race that may infect the previously resistant variety. On the contrary, varieties with general (polygenic) resistance are less stable and may vary in their reaction to the pathogen under different environmental conditions, but a pathogen will have to undergo many more mutations to completely break down the resistance of the host. As a rule, a combination of major and minor genes for resistance against a pathogen is the most desirable makeup for any plant variety.

In any area and almost every year, limited or widespread plant disease epidemics occur on various crop plants. Under certain conditions or circumstances, however, some very susceptible plants or varieties of these crops may remain free from infection or symptoms and thus appear resistant. Apparent resistance to disease of plants known to be susceptible is generally a result of disease escape or tolerance to disease:

Disease escape

occurs whenever genetically susceptible plants do not become infected because the three factors necessary for disease (susceptible host, virulent pathogen, and favorable environment) do not coincide and interact at the proper time or for sufficient duration. Plants may escape disease because their seeds germinate faster, or their seedlings harden earlier than others, and before the temperature becomes favorable for the pathogen to attack them. Some plants escape disease because they are susceptible to a pathogen only at a particular growth stage (young leaves, stems, or fruits; at blossoming or fruiting; at maturity and early senescence) and therefore, if the pathogen is absent or inactive at that particular time, such plants avoid becoming infected. For example, young tissues and plants are infected and affected much more severely by Pythium, powdery mildews, and most bacteria and viruses than older ones. However, full), grown, mature, and senescent plant parts are much more susceptible to certain pathogens, such as Allernaria and Botrytis, than are their younger counterparts. Plants may also escape disease because of the distance between fields, the number and position of plants in the field, the spacing of plants in a field, and so on. In many cases, plants escape disease because they are interspersed with other types of plants that are insusceptible to the pathogen, and the amount of inoculum that reaches them is much less than if they were in monocultural plantations; because their surface hairs and wax repel water and pathogens suspended in it; because their growth habit is too erect or otherwise unfavorable for pathogen attachment and germination; or because their natural openings, such as stomata, are at a higher level than the rest of the leaf surface, or open too late in the day by which time the leaves, ared dry and the germ tubes of spores, such as of Puccinia graminis, have desiccated. In plant diseases in which pathogens penetrate primarily through wounds caused by heavy winds and rain, dust storms, and insects, lack of such wounds allows disease escape.

Factors that affect the survival, infectivity, multiplication, and dissemination of the pathogen are also likely to allow some plants to escape disease. Such factors include: absence or poor growth of the pathogen at the time the susceptible plant stage is available; destruction or weakening of the pathogen by hyperparasites or by antagonistic microflora at the place of production or at the infection court; misdirection to or trapping of the pathogen by other plants; and lack of pathogen disemination because winds, rain, or vectors are absent. Several environmental factors play crucial roles in plant disease escape in almost every location. Temperature, for example, determines the geographical distribution of most pathogens, and plants growing outside the range of that temperature escape disease from such pathogens. Most commonly, however, temperature increases plant disease escape in ranges that favor plant growth much more than they do the growth of the pathogen.

For example, many plants escape disease from Pythium and Phytophthora if the temperature is high and the soil moisture low, while some low temperature crops, such as wheat, escape similar diseases from Fusarium and Rhizoctonia if the temperature is low. Temperatures outside certain ranges inhibit sporulation of fungi as well as spore germination and infection, thereby increasing the chances for disease escape.

Low temperatures also reduce the mobility of many insect vectors or pathogens, allowing more plants to escape disease. Lack of moisture caused by low rainfall or dew or low relative humidity is probably the most common cause of disease escape in plants. Plants in most dry areas or during dry years remain generally free of apple scab, late blight, most downy mildews, and anthracnoses because these diseases require a film of water on the plant or high relative humidity in almost every stage of their life cycle. Similarly, in dry soils such diseases as clubroot of crucifers and damping off induced by Pythium and Phytophthora are quite rare because such soils inhibit the production and activity of the motile spores of these pathogens. On the other hand, with some diseases, such as common scab of potato caused by Streptomyces scabies, plants escape disease in irrigated or wet soils because the plants can defend themselves better in the absence of water stress and because these pathogens are lysed or otherwise inhibited by microorganisms favored by high moisture.

Many trees are also in a better position to defend themselves and to escape damage by the canker-causing fungus Cytospora sp. in years in which sufficient rainfall or irrigation provides adequate soil moisture in later summer and early fall. Some other environmental factors also allow plants to escape disease.

For example, wind may increase disease escape by blowing from the wrong direction at the right time, thus carrying spores and vectors away from the crop plants, and by drying up plant surfaces quickly, before the pathogen has time to germinate and infect.

Also, soil pH increases disease escape in a few diseases, for example, in crucifers from Plasmodiophora brassicae at high pH, and in potatoes from Streptomyces scabies At low pH; in both cases because the particular pH inhibits survival and growth of the pathogen. In general, many plant diseases are present some years in some areas and absent on the same kinds of plants in other years or in nearby areas. This suggests that in these areas or years the plants remain free of disease not because they are resistant, but because they escape disease. Earliness is often bred into many wheat and potato varieties to help them escape disease from the rusts and the late blight, respectively. Lateness, rapid growth, resistance to bruising, unattractiveness to vectors, and tolerance to low temperatures are also often bred into crop varieties to help them escape specific diseases.

Escape from disease depends on environmental conditions as well as on heritable characteristics in the host and the pathogen and is often entirely controlled by the environment. Escape from disease, moreover, is a manageable quality, and farmers, through many of the most common cultural practices actually aim at helping plants escape disease.

Such practices include using disease-free, vigorous seed, choosing the proper soil, planting date, depth of sowing, distance between plants and between fields, proper crop rotation, sanitation (roguing, pruning, and so on), interplantings and multilines, insect and vector control, and several others.

Tolerance to disease

It is the ability of plants to produce a good crop even when they are infected with a pathogen. Tolerance results from specific, heritable characteristics of the host plant that allow the pathogen to develop and multiply in the host while the host, either by lacking receptor sites for, or by inactivating or compensating for the irritant excretions of the pathogen, still manages to produce a good crop. Tolerant plants are, obviously, susceptible to the pathogen but they are not killed by it and generally show little damage from the pathogen.

The genetics of tolerance to disease are not understood; neither is its relationship, if any, to horizontal resistance. Tolerant plants, whether because of exceptional vigor or a hardy structure, probably exist in most host -parasite combinations. Tolerance to disease is most commonly observed in many plant-virus infections in which mild viruses, or mild strains of virulent viruses, infect plants such as potato and apple systemically and yet cause few or no symptoms and have little discernible effect on yield. Generally, however, although tolerant plants produce a good crop even when they are infected, they produce an even better crop when they are not infected.

Infectious plant diseases are the result of the interaction of at least two organisms, the host plant and the pathogen. The properties of each of these two organisms are governed by their genetic material, the DNA, which is organized in numerous segments making up the genes. The inheritance of host reaction, that is, the degree of susceptibility or resistance to various pathogens, has been known for a long time and has been used quite effectively in breeding and distributing varieties resistant to pathogens causing particular diseases.

The inheritance of pathogen infection type, however, that is, the degree of pathogen virulence or avirulence, has been studied intensively only in the last few decades. It has now become clear that pathogens consist of a multitude of races, each differing from others in its ability to attack certain varieties of a plant species but not other varieties.

When a variety is inoculated with two appropriately chosen races of a pathogen, the variety is susceptible to one race but resistant to the other. Conversely, when the same race of a pathogen is inoculated on two appropriately chosen varieties of a host plant, one variety is susceptible while the other is resistant to the same pathogen. This clearly indicates that, in the first case, one race possesses a genetic characteristic that enables it to attack the plant, while the other race does not, and in the second case, that the one variety possesses a genetic characteristic that enables it to defend itself against the pathogen, so that it remains resistant, while the other variety does not. When several varieties are inoculated separately with one of several races of the pathogen, it is again noted that one pathogen race can infect a certain group of varieties, another race can infect another group of varieties, including some that can and some that cannot be infected by the previous race, and so on. Thus, varieties possessing certain genes of resistance or susceptibility react differently against the various pathogen races and their genes of virulence or avirulence.

The progeny of these varieties react to the same pathogens in exactly the same manner as did the parent plants, indicating that the property of resistance or susceptibility against a pathogen is genetically controlled (inherited). Similarly, the progeny of each pathogen causes on each variety the same effect that was caused by the parent pathogens, indicating that the property of virulence or avirulence of the pathogen on a particular variety is genetically controlled (inherited).

It appears from the above that, under favorable environmental conditions, the outcome -infection (susceptibility) or noninfection (resistance)-in each host - pathogen combination is predetermined by the genetic material of the host and of the pathogen.

The number of genes determining resistance or susceptibility varies from plant to plant, as the number of genes determining virulence or avirulence varies from pathogen to pathogen.

In most host-pathogen combinations the number of genes involved and what they control are not yet known. In some diseases, however, particularly those caused by fungi, such as potato late blight, apple scab, powdery mildews, tomato leaf mold, the cereal smuts and rusts, and also in several viral and bacterial diseases of plants, considerable information regarding the genetics of host-pathogen interactions is available.

Of the four possible gene combinations only AR is resistant, that is, when the host has a certain gene for resistance (R) against which the pathogen lacks the specific gene for virulence (A), although it may have other genes for virulence. In the Ar combination, infection results because the host lacks genes for resistance (r) and so the pathogen can attack it with its other genes for virulence (after all, it is a pathogen), even though it too lacks a specific virulence gene for the resistance gene the host does not have. In aR, infection results because, although the host has a gene for resistance, the pathogen has the gene for virulence that can attack specifically this particular gene for resistance. Finally, in ar, infection results because the plant is susceptible (r) and, in addition, the pathogen is virulent (a). Genes for reistance appear first in hosts through evolution and may later be used in breeding programs. Genes for virulence appear in pathogens after the appearance of particular genes for resistance in the host, and each is specific for attack of a particular gene for resistance. Whenever a new gene for virulence that attacks the existing gene for resistance appears, the resistance of the host breaks down.

This produces a resistant variety until another gene for virulence appears in the pathogen. When a variety has two or more genes for resistance (R_1, R_2, . . .) against a particular pathogen, the pathogen must also have two or more genes for virulence (a_1, a_2, . . .) each aimed specifically against one of the genes for resistance in the host, for infection to take place.

The nature of resistance to disease

A plant is either immune to a pathogen-that is, it is not attacked by the pathogen even under the most favorable conditions -or it may show various degrees of resistance, ranging from almost immunity to complete susceptibility. Resistance may be conditioned by a number of internal and external factors that operate to reduce the chance and degree of infection.

Therefore, the absence of recognition factor(s) in the host would make it resistant to the particular pathogen. In addition, any heritable characteristic of the plant that contributes to localization and isolation of the pathogen at the points of entry, to reduction of the harmful effects of toxic substances produced by the pathogen, or to inhibition of the reproduction and, thereby, of the further spread of the pathogen contributes to the resistance of the plant to disease.

Furthermore, any heritable characteristic that enables a particular variety to complete Its development and maturation under conditions that do not favor the development of the pathogen, also contributes to resistance (disease escape).

The contribution of the genes conditioning resistance in the host seems to consist, primarily, of providing the genetic potential in the plant for development of one or more of the morphological or physiological characters—including those described in the chapters on structural and biochemical defense-that contribute to disease resistance. With the exception of virus and viroid diseases of plants, in which the genes of the host could conceivably come into "face-to-face" confrontation with the "genes" of the viral nucleic acid, the genes of plants infected by other types of pathogens seem never to come in contact with the genes of the pathogen.

In general, in all host-pathogen combinations, viruses and viroids included, the interactions between genes of the host and genes of the pathogen are believed to be brought about indirectly through the chemical molecules and physiological processes controlled by the respective genes. The mechanisms by which genes control the physiological processes that lead to disease resistance or susceptibility are not yet clear, but they are, presumably, no different from the mechanisms controlling any other pilysiological process in living organisms. Thus, it is known that the genes are each carried by the genetic material (DNA) as successive groups of nucleotide triplets (triplet code), which are first read and transcribed on messenger RNA as the latter is synthesized.

The messenger RNA then becomes associated with clusters of ribosomes (polyribosomes) and leads to the production of a specific protein, which is either an enzyme or a structural protein.

The produced enzyme participates or initiates biochemical reactions related to one or another of the cellular processes, and may result in the production of a certain morphological characteristic or accumulation of a certain chemical substance.

The timing of activation of the structural genes, the rate of their activity-protein synthesis-and the timing of their inactivity are controlled by other genes called regulatory genes. Furthermore, messenger-RNA formation seems to be initiated only at certain points of the DNA strand, and these points are called operators.

A single operator may control the transcription into a messenger-RNA of only one structural gene or of a series of structural genes concerned with the different steps of one particular metabolic function, for example the biosynthesis of a fungitoxic phenolic compound or a compound that reacts with and detoxifies a pathogen toxin.

The group of genes controlled by such an operator is called an operon. Thus, it is possible that for the production of an inducible enzyme or a ftingitoxic substance, a stimulant (inducer) secreted by the pathogen inactivates a repressor molecule, which is the product of a regulatory gene. The function of the repressor was to combine with a specific operator locus and prevent the transcription of that operon, thereby blocking the synthesis and action of the relevant proteins in the absence of infection.

After infection, however, and after inactivation of the repressor by the pathogenic stimulant, transcription of the operon can take place, the particular substance is produced and, if this substance is toxic enough to the pathogen, the infection stops and the variety is resistant. On the other hand, if a pathogen mutant appears that does not secrete the particular stimulant that inactivates the repressor molecule, the defense reaction does not take place, the pathogen infects the host without opposition and so it causes disease. In that case, the resistance of the host is said to have broken down, but it is actually bypassed by the pathogen rather than broken down. Other possible ways by which a pathogen could "break down" the resistance of a host are through a mutation in the pathogen, which enables it to produce a substance that can react with and neutralize the defensive toxic substance of the host that is directed against the pathogen, and through a mutation in the pathogen that would eliminate or block its receptor site on which the host defensive substance becomes attached.

Today's cultivated crop plants are the result of selection, or selection and breeding, of plant lines that evolved naturally in one or many geographic areas over millions of years.

The evolution of plants from their ancient ancestors to present day crop plants has occurred slowly and has produced countless genetically diverse forms of these plants. Many such plants still exist as wild types at the point or points of origin or in the areas of natural spread of the plant. Although these plants may appear as useless remnants of evolution that are not likely to play a role in any future advances in agriculture, their diversity and survival in the face of the various pathogens that affect the crop in question indicates that they carry numerous genes for resistance against these pathogens. Since the beginning of agriculture, some of the wild plants in each locality have been selected and cultivated and thus produced numerous cultivated lines or varieties. The most productive of these varieties were perpetuated in each locality from year to- year, and those that survived the local climate and the pathogens continued to be cultivated. Nature and pathogens eliminated the weak and susceptible ones, while the farmers selected the best yielders among the survivors. Surviving varieties had different sets of major and minor genes for resistance. In this fashion, selection of crop plants continued wherever they were grown, each locality independently selecting varieties adapted to its own environment and resistant to its own pathogens.

During the present century, widespread, intensive, and systematic efforts have been made and continue to be made by plant breeders throughout the world to breed plants that combine the most useful genes for higher yields, better quality, uniform size of plants and fruit, uniform ripening, cold hardiness, and disease resistance. In searching for new useful genes, plant breeders cross existing, local, cultivated varieties with each other and with those of other localities, both here and abroad, and with wild species of crop plants from wherever they can be obtained. Furthermore, plant breeders often attempt to generate additional genetic variation by treating their plant material with mutagenic agents. More recently, plant breeders have been generating greater genetic variability, and modifying or accelerating plant evolution in certain directions, by various genetic engineering techniques.

As breeding programs advance, however, and as several of the most useful genes are identified, subsequent steps in breeding tend to eliminate variability by combining the best genes in a few cultivated varieties and leaving behind or discarding plant lines that seem to have no usefulness at the time.

In a short time a few "improved" varieties replace most or all others over large expanses of land. The most successful improved varieties are also adopted abroad, and before too long, some of them replace the numerous but commercially inferior- local varieties. Occasionally, even the wild types themselves may be replaced by such a variety. Thus, Red Delicious apples, Elberta peaches, certain dwarf wheat and rice varieties, certain genetic lines of corn and potatoes, one or two types of bananas, and sugarcane are grown in huge acreages throughout the world. In almost every crop, relatively few varieties make up the great bulk of the cultivated acreage of the crop throughout a country or throughout the world. The genetic base of these varieties is often narrow, especially since many of them have been derived from crosses of the same or related ancestors.

The source of genes for resistance is the same gene pool of the crop that provides genes for every other inherited characteristic; that is, other native or foreign commercial varieties, older varieties abandoned earlier or discarded breeders' stock, wild plant relatives, and occasionally, induced mutations.

Often genes of resistance are present in the varieties or species normally grown in the area where the disease is severe and in which the need for resistant varieties is most pressing. With most diseases, a few plants remain virtually unaffected by the pathogen, although most or all other plants in the area may be severely diseased. Such survivor plants are likely to have remained healthy because of resistant characteristics present in them. If no resistant plants can be found within the local population of the species, plants of the same species from other areas and plants of other species (cultivated or wild) are checked for resistance. If resistant plants are found, they are crossed with the cultivated varieties In an effort to incorporate the resistance genes of the other species into the cultivated varieties. With some diseases, such as late blight of potatoes, it has been necessary to look for resistance genes in species growing in the area where the disease originated. Presumably, plants existing in these areas managed to survive the long, continuous presence of the pathogen because of their resistance to it.

The same methods used to breed for any heritable characteristic are also used for breeding for disease resistance and depend upon the mating system of the plant (self- or cross-pollinated). Breeding for disease resistance, however. Is considerably more complicated, first because it can be assayed only by making the plants diseased, that is by employing another living and variable organism that must interact with the plants; and second because resistance may not be stable and may break down under certain conditions. For these reasons, several more or less sophisticated systems of screening for resistance have been developed.

These screening systems include (1) precise conditions for inoculating the plants with the pathogen, (2) accurate monitoring and control of the environmental conditions in which the inoculated plants are kept, and (3) accurate assessment of disease incidence (percentage of plants, leaves, or fruits infected) and disease seventy (proportion of the total area of plant tissue affected by disease). The following techniques are the main ones used for breeding disease resistance.

Mass selection of seed from the most highly resistant plants surviving in a field where natural infection occurs regularly. It is a simple method but improves plants only slowly, and in cross-pollinated plants there is no control of pollen source.

Pure line or pedigree selection, in which individual highly resistant plants and their progenies are propagated separately and are inoculated repeatedly to test for resistance. This method is easy and most effective with self-pollinated crops but quite difficult with cross-pollinated ones.

Recurrent selection or back crossing, in which a desirable but susceptible variety of a crop is crossed with another cultivated or wild relative that carries resistance to a particular pathogen. The progeny is then tested for resistance, and the resistant individuals are back crossed to the desirable variety. This is repeated several times until the resistance is stabilized in the genetic background of the desirable variety. This method is time consuming, and its effectiveness varies considerably with each particular case. It can be applied somewhat more easily in cross-pollinated than in self-pollinated crops.

Other classical breeding techniques for disease resistance include: the use of F_1 hybrids of two different but homozygous lines carrying different genes for resistance, which allows us to take advantage of the phenomenon of heterosis: the use of natural or artificially induced (UV-light, X-rays) mutants that show increased resistance; and the change of the number of chromosomes in a plant and production of euploids (4n, 6n) or aneuploids (2n ± 1 or 2 chromosomes), by the use of chemicals such as colchicine, and by radiation.

Tissue culture of disease-resistant plants

Tissue culture of disease-resistant plants is particularly useful with clonally propagated plants such as strawberries, apples, bananas, sugarcane, cassava, and potatoes. Prolific plantlet production from meristem and other tissue cultures facilitate the rapid propagation of plants with exceptional (resistant) genotypes, especially in those crops not easily propagated by seed. An even greater use of tissue culture is for production of pathogen-free stocks of clonally propagated susceptible plants.

Isolation of disease resistant mutants from plant cell cultures

Plants regenerated from culture (callus, single cells, or protoplasts) often show considerable variability (somaclonal variation), much of it useless or deleterious. However, plants with useful characteristics may also emerge. For example, when plants were regenerated from leaf protoplasts of a potato variety susceptible to both Phytophthora infestans and Alternaria solani, some of them (5 of 500) were resistant to Alternaria solani and some (20 of 800) were resistant to Phytophthora infestans. Similarly, plants exhibiting increased resistance to diseases caused by Helminthosporium and Ustilago were obtained from tissue cultures of sugarcane.

Production of resistant dihaploids from haploid plants

Immature pollen cells (microspores)-and less often megaspores-of many plants can be induced to develop into haploid (1n) plants in which single copies (alleles) of each gene are present in all sorts of combinations. By vegetative propagation and proper screening for disease resistance, the most highly resistant haploids can be selected. These haploids can be subsequently treated with colchicine, which results in diploitization of the nuclei, that is, doubling of the number of chromosomes and production of dihaploid plants homozygous for all genes, including genes for resistance.

Increasing, disease resistance by protoplast fusion

Protoplasts from closely related and even from unrelated plants, under proper conditions, can be made to fuse. The fusion produces hybrid cells containing the nuclei (chromosomes) and the cytoplasm of both protoplasts, or perhaps result in cybrid cells containing the nucleus of one cell and the cytoplasm of the other cell. Generally, hybrids of unrelated cells sooner or later abort, or may produce callus, but do not regenerate plants.

In combinations of more or less related cells, however, while many or most of the chromosomes of one of the cells are eliminated during cell division, one or a few chromosomes of that cell survive and may be incorporated in the genome of the other cell. In this way, plants with more chromosomes and thereby new characteristics can be regenerated from the products of protoplast fusion. Protoplast fusion is particularly useful between protoplasts of different, highly resistant haploid lines of the same variety or species. Protoplast fusion of such lines results in diploid plants that combine the resistance genes of two highly resistant haploid lines.

Genetic transformation of plant cells for disease resistance

Genetic material (DNA) can be introduced into plant cells or protoplasts by several methods. Such methods include direct DNA uptake, microinjection of DNA, liposome (lipid vesicle)-mediated delivery of DNA, delivery by means of centromere plasmids (minichromosomes), by use of plant viral vectors, and most-importantly by use of the natural gene vector system of Agrobacterium tumefaciens, the cause of crown gall disease of many plants. In all of these methods, small or large pieces of DNA are introduced into plant cells or, protoplasts and the DMA may or may not be integrated in the plant chromosomal DNA. When the introduced DNA carries appropriate regulatery genes recognized by the plant cell, or is integrated near appropriate regulatory genes along plant chromosomes, the DNA is "expressed," that is, it is transcribed into mRNA, which is then translated into protein. So far, only the Agrobacterium system has been used successfully to introduce into plants specific new genes that were then expressed by the plant. This was accomplished by isolating the seed protein gene from beans and splicing it into the appropriate area of the Ti-plasmid (tumor-inducing plasmid) of Agrobacterium; the bacteria were then allowed to infect other plants, for example, the sunflower. Upon infection, about one-tenth of the DNA of the plasmid, containing the new gene, is transferred to the plant cell and is incorporated into the plant's genome. There the new gene replicates during plant cell division and is expressed along with the other plant genes.

To date, no gene for disease resistance has been isolated, and therefore no genetic transformation for disease resistance has been accomplished in any host-pathogen combination. It is considered likely, however, that genes for resistance, particularly single genes involved in vertical resistance, will be among the first to be successfully used for genetic transformation of plants, and that breeding for disease resistance will be among the first areas of plant breeding to profit greatly from the application of techniques in genetic engineering.

Resistance may be obtained by incorporating into a variety one, a few, or many resistance genes. Some' of these genes may control important steps in disease development and may therefore play a major role in disease resistance. Other genes may control peripheral events of lesser importance in disease development and, therefore, play a relatively minor role in disease resistance.

Obviously, one or a few major-role genes could be sufficient to make a plant resistant to a pathogen (monogenic, oligogenic, or vertical resistance). However, it would take many minor-effect genes to make a plant resistant (polygenic or horizontal resistance).

More importantly, while a plant with vertical resistance may be completely resistant to a pathogen, a plant with horizontal resistance is never completely resistant or completely susceptible. Furthermore, vertical resistance is easy to manipulate in a breeding program, and therefore it is often preferred to horizontal resistance, but both vertical and horizontal have their advantages and limitations. Vertical resistance is aimed against specific pathogens or pathogen races. Vertical resistance is most effective when (1) it is incorporated in annual crops that are easy to breed, such as small grains; (2) it is directed against pathogens that do not reproduce and spread rapidly, such as Fusarium; or pathogens that do not mutate very frequently, such as Puccinia graminis; (3) it consists of "strong" genes that confer complete protection to the plant that carries it; and (4) the host population does not consist of a single genetically uniform variety grown over large acreages.

On the other hand, horizontal resistance confers incomplete but durable protection-it does not break down. Horizontal resistance involves host physiological processes that act as mechanisms of defense and that are beyond the limits of the capacity of the pathogen to change, that is, beyond the probable limits of its variability.

Horizontal resistance is universally present in wild and domesticated plants but is at its highest in wild plants and at its lowest in greatly "improved" varieties. Horizontal resistance operates against all races of a pathogen including the most pathogenic ones.

Actually, the more pathogenic the races present, the greater the selection for general resistance in the host. Horizontal resistance is eroded in the absence of the pathogen because there is no selection pressure for resistance. In many cases, horizontal (polygenic) resistance is an important part of the resistance exhibited by plants possessing vertical (specific) resistance, but it is overshadowed by the latter.

Considerable horizontal resistance can be incorporated into cultivated crops by cross-breeding of existing, genetically different varieties. The wider the genetic base of a crop, the greater its horizontal resistance and the smaller the need for the usually temporary vertical resistance. Varieties with horizontal (polygenic, general, or nonspecific) resistance remain resistant much longer than do varieties with vertical (oligogenic or specific) resistance, but the level of resistance of the second group is much higher while it lasts than that of the first group. Also, varieties with vertical resistance are often attacked suddenly and rapidly by a new virulent race and lead to severe epidemics. These disadvantages can be avoided in some crops by the use of multilines. Multilines are either mixtures of individual varieties that are agronomically similar but differ in their resistance genes or varieties that are derived from crossing several to many varieties that contain different resistance genes and then selecting from those that contain the mixtures of genes. Multilines have been developed mostly in small grains against the rust fungi, but their use is likely to increase in these and in other crops as the control of plant diseases with specific resistance and with chemicals becomes more risky or less acceptable.

Incorporating genes for resistance from wild or unsatisfactory plants into susceptible but agronomically desirable varieties is a difficult and painstaking process involving repeated crossings, testings, and backcrossings to the desirable varieties.

The feasibility of the method in most cases, however, has been proved repeatedly. Through breeding, varieties of some crops, such as tobacco, have been developed in which genes for resistance against several different diseases have been incorporated.

Varieties with even complete vertical resistance do not remain resistant forever. The continuous production of mutants and hybrids in pathogens sooner or later leads to the appearance of races that can infect previously resistant varieties.

Sometimes, races may exist in an area in small populations and avoid detection until after the introduction of a new variety, or virulent races of the pathogen existing elsewhere may be brought in after introduction of the resistant variety. In all cases, widespread cultivation of a single, previously resistant variety provides an excellent substrate for rapid development and spread of the new race of the pathogen, and usually leads to an epidemic.

Thus, genetic uniformity in crops, although very desirable when it concerns horticultural characteristics, is undesirable and often catastrophic when it occurs in the genes of resistance to diseases. The cultivation of varieties with genetically uniform disease resistance is possible and quite safe if other means of plant disease control, such as chemical, are possible. Thus, a few fruit tree varieties, such as Delicious apples, Bartlett pears, Elberta peaches, and Navel oranges, are cultivated throughout the world in the face of numerous virulent fungal and bacterial pathogens that would destroy them in a short time were it not for the fact that the trees are protected from the pathogens by numerous chemical sprays annually.

Even such varieties, however, suffer tremendous losses when affected by pathogens that cannot be controlled with chemicals, as is the case of fire blight of pears and pear decline and of tristeza disease of citrus. Another case in which varieties with genetically uniform disease resistance are not likely to suffer from severe disease epidemics is when the resistance is aimed against slow-moving soil pathogens such as Fusarium and Verticillium. Aside from the fact that some pathogens normally produce fewer races than others, even if new races are produced at the same rate, soilborne pathogens lack the dispersal potential of airborne ones.

As a result, a new race of a soilborne pathogen would be limited to a relatively small area for a long time, and although it could cause a locally severe disease, it would not spread rapidly and widely to cause an epidemic.

The slow spread of such virulent new races of soilborne pathogens allows time for the control of the disease by other means or the replacement of the variety with another one resistant to the new race. Genetic uniformity in plant varieties becomes a serious disadvantage in the production of major crops because of the potential danger of sudden and widespread disease epidemics caused by airborne or insect-borne pathogens In the vast acreages in which each of these varieties is often grown.

Several examples of epidemics that resulted from genetic uniformity are known and some of them have already been mentioned. Southern corn leaf blight was the result of the widespread use of corn hybrids containing the Texas male-sterile cytoplasm; the destruction of the "Ceres" spring wheat by race 56 of Puccinia *graminis* and of the "Hope" and its relative bread wheats by race 15B of P. *graminis* was the result of replacement of numerous genetically diverse varieties by a few uniform ones. The Helminthosporium blight of Victoria oats was the result of replacing many varieties with the rust-resistant Victoria oats-, coffee rust destroyed all coffee trees in Ceylon because all of them originated from uniform susceptible stock of Coffea arabica; tristeza destroyed millions of orange trees in South and North America because they were all propagated on hypersensitive resistant sour orange rootstocks; and pear decline destroyed millions of pear trees in the Pacific coast states because they were propagated on hypersensitive resistant oriental rootstocks.

In spite of these and many other well-known examples of plant disease epidemics that occurred because of the concentrated cultivation of genetically uniform crops over large areas, crop production continues to depend on genetic uniformity. A few varieties of each crop used to and for some crops still make up the bulk of the cultivated crop over as vast an area as the United States (Table 4). Although a relatively large number of varieties are available for each crop, only a few, often 2 or 3, varieties are grown in more than half the acreage of each crop, and in some they make up more than three-fourths of the crop. It is easy to see that two pea varieties make up almost the entire (96 percent) pea crop of, the country, that is, about 400,000 acres, that two varieties account for 42 percent of the sugarbeet crop, that is, about 600,000 acres. Thus, although six corn varieties account for 71 percent, or 47 million acres, one of them alone accounts for 26 percent, or 17 million acres. Furthermore, most of the varieties shared the same male-sterile cytoplasm. Similarly, six varieties of soybean account for about 24 million acres of that crop, and most of these varieties share common ancestors.

It is apparent that several hundreds of thousands or several million acres planted to one variety present a huge opportunity for the development of an epidemic. The variety, of course, is planted so widely because it is resistant to existing pathogens. But this resistance puts extreme survival pressure on the pathogens over that area. It takes one "right" change in one of the zillions of pathogen individuals in the area to produce a new virulent race that can attack the variety. When that happens it is a matter of time -and, usually, of favorable weather-before the race breaks loose, the epidemic develops, and the variety is wiped out! In some cases the appearance of the new race is detected early, and the variety is replaced with another one, resistant to the new race, before a widespread epidemic occurs; this of course requires that varieties of a crop with different genetic base are available at all times. For this reason, most varieties must usually be replaced within about 3 - 5 years from the time of their widespread distribution. In addition to the genetic uniformity within one variety, plant breeding often introduces genetic uniformity to several or all cultivated varieties of a crop by introducing one or several genes in all of these varieties or by replacing the cytoplasm of the varieties with a single type of cytoplasm. Induced uniformity through introduced genes includes, for example, the dwarfism gene in the dwarf wheats and rice varieties, the monogerm gene in sugar beet varieties, the determinate gene in tomato varieties, and the stringless gene in bean varieties.

Chapter 6

Control of Plant Diseases

Noninfectious diseases occur in the absence of pathogens, and cannot, therefore, be transmitted from diseased to healthy plants. Noninfectious diseases may affect plants in all stages of their lives, such as seed, seedling, mature plant, or fruit, and they may cause damage in the field, in storage, or at the market. The symptoms caused by noninfectious diseases vary in kind and severity with the particular environmental factor involved and with the degree of deviation of this factor from its normal. Symptoms may range from slight to severe, and affected plants may even die.

Control

Noninfectious plant diseases can be controlled by ensuring that plants are not exposed to the extreme environmental conditions responsible for such diseases or by supplying the plants with protection or substances that would bring these conditions to levels favorable for plant growth.

Temperature effects

Plants normally grow at a temperature range from 1 to 40°C, most kinds of plants growing best between 15 and 30°C. Perennial plants and dormant organs, such as seeds and corms, of annual plants may survive temperatures considerably below or above the normal temperature range of 1 to 40°C. The young, growing tissues of most plants, however, and the entire growth of many annual plants are usually quite sensitive to temperatures near or beyond the extremes of this range. The minimum and maximum temperatures at which plants can still produce normal growth vary greatly with the plant species and with the stage of growth the plant is in during the low or high temperatures. Thus, plants such as tomato, citrus, and other tropical plants grow best at high temperatures and are injured severely when the temperature drops to near or below freezing.

On the other hand, plants such as cabbage, winter wheat, alfalfa, and most perennials of the temperate zone can withstand temperatures considerably below freezing without any apparent ill effects. Even the latter plants, however, are injured and finally killed if the temperature drops too low. A plant may also differ in its ability to withstand extremes in temperature at different stages of its growth. Thus, older, hardened plants are more resistant to low temperatures than are young seedlings. Also, different tissues or organs on the same plant may vary greatly in their sensitivity to the same low temperature. Buds are more sensitive than twigs, flowers and newly formed fruit are more sensitive than leaves, and so on.

High-temperature effects

Plants are generally injured faster and to a greater extent when temperatures become higher than the maximum for growth than when they are lower than the minimum. However, too high a temperature rarely occurs in nature. High temperature seems to cause its effects on the plant in conjunction with the effects of other environmental factors, particularly excessive light, drought, lack of oxygen, or high winds accompanied by low relative humidity. High temperatures are usually responsible for sunscald injuries appearing on the sun-exposed sides of fleshy fruits and vegetables, such as peppers, apples, tomatoes, onion bulbs, and potato tubers. On hot, sunny days the temperature of the fruit tissues beneath the surface facing the sun may be much higher than that of those on the shaded side and of the surrounding air. This results in discoloration, a water-soaked appearance, blistering, and a desiccation of the tissues beneath the skin, which leads to sunken areas on the fruit surface. Succulent leaves of plants may also develop sunscald symptoms, especially when hot sunny days follow periods of cloudy, rainy weather.

Irregular areas on the leaves become pale green at first but soon collapse and form brown, dry spots. This is a rather common symptom of fleshy leaved house plants kept next to windows with a southern exposure in early spring and summer when the sun's rays heat the fleshy leaves excessively. Too high a soil temperature at the soil line sometimes kills young seedlings or causes cankers at the crown on the stems of older plants. High temperatures also seem to be involved in the water core disorder of apples and, in combination with reduced oxygen, in the blackheart of potatoes.

Low-temperature effects

Far greater damage to crops is caused by low than by high temperatures. Low temperatures, even if above freezing, may damage warm-weather plants such as corn and beans. They may also cause excessive sweetening and, upon frying, undesirable caramelization of potatoes due to hydrolysis of starch to sugars at the low temperatures. Temperatures below freezing cause a variety of injuries to plants. Such injuries include the damage caused by late frosts to young meristematic tips or entire herbaceous plants, the frost-killing of buds of peach, cherry, and other trees, and the killing of flowers, young fruit, and sometimes, succulent twigs of most trees.

Frost bands, consisting of discolored, corky tissue in a band or large area of the fruit surface, are often produced on apples, pears, and so on, after a late frost. Low winter temperatures may kill the young roots of trees, such as apple, and may also cause bark-splitting and canker development on trunks and large branches, especially on the sun-exposed side, of several kinds of fruit trees. Cross sections of limbs may show a black ring or a "blackheart" condition in the wood. Fleshy tissues, such as potato tubers, may be injured at subfreezing temperatures.

The injury varies depending on the degree of temperature drop and the duration of the low temperature. Early injury affects only the main vascular tissues and appears as a ringlike necrosis; injury of the finer vascular elements that are interspersed in the tuber gives the appearance of netlike necrosis. With more general injury, large chunks of the tuber are damaged, creating the so-called "blotch-type" necrosis.

Low temperature effects on indoor plants

Indoor plants, whether grown in a home or a greenhouse, are particularly sensitive to low temperatures, both where they are growing and during transportation from a greenhouse or florist's shop to a home or from one home to another. Often, indoor plants are tropical plants grown far away from their normal climate. Exposure of such plants to low, not necessarily freezing, temperatures may cause stunting, yellowing, leaf or bud drop, and so -on. Similarly, when grown indoors, even local plants remain in a succulent vegetative state and are completely unprepared for the stresses of low, particularly subfreezing, temperatures.

Plants near windows or doors during cold winter days and, especially, nights are subject to temperatures that are much lower than those away from the window. Also, cracks or breaks in windows or the holes of electrical outlets on outside walls let in cold air that may injure the plants. A drop of night temperatures below 12°C may cause leaves and particularly flower buds of many plants to turn yellow and drop. Exposure of indoor plants to subfreezing temperatures for a few minutes or a few hours, for example, while they are carried in the trunk of a car from the greenhouse to the house, may result in the death of many shoots and flowers, or in a sudden shock to the plants from which they may take weeks or months to recover completely.

Such a shock is often observed on plants that had been kept indoors and are then transplanted in the field in the spring when temperatures outdoors, although not freezing, are nevertheless much lower than those in the greenhouse. Even without the shock effect, plants growing at temperatures that are generally near the lower- or near the upper - limit of their normal range grow poorly and produce fewer and smaller blossoms and fruits.

Mechanisms of low and high temperature injury to plants

The mechanisms by which high and low temperatures injure plants are quite different. High temperatures apparently inactivate certain enzyme systems and accelerate others, thus leading to abnormal biochemical reactions and cell death. High temperature may also cause coagulation and denaturation of proteins, disruption of cytoplasmic membranes, suffocation, and possibly release of toxic products into the cell. Low temperatures, on the other hand, injure plants primarily by inducing ice formation between or within the cells.

The rather pure water of the intercellular spaces freezes first and normally at about 0°C, while the water within the cell contains dissolved substances that, depending on their nature and concentration, depress the freezing point of water several degrees. Furthermore, when the intercellular water becomes ice, more vapor (water) moves out of the cells and into the intercellular spaces, where it also becomes ice. The reduced water content of the cells depresses further the freezing point of the intracellular water. This could continue, up to a point, without damaging the cell, but below a certain point, ice crystals form within the cell, disrupt the plasma membrane, and cause injury and death to the cell. Ice formation in supercooled water within leaves is greatly influenced by the kinds and numbers of epiphytic bacteria that may be present on the surface of the leaves.

Certain strains of some pathogenic (for example, Pseudomonas syringae) bacteria and of some saprophytic bacteria, when present on or in the substomatal cavities of leaves, act as catalysts for ice nucleation. By their presence alone, such ice-nucleation-active bacteria induce the supercooled water around them and in the leaf cells to form crystals, thereby causing frost injury to the leaves, blossoms, and so on at temperatures considerably higher (–1°C) than would have happened in the absence of such bacteria (≈ –5 to –10°C). The freezing point of water in cells varies with the tissues and species of the plant; in some tissues of the winter-hardy species of the north, ice probably never forms within the cells regardless of how low the temperatures become. Even when ice forms only in the intercellular spaces, cells and tissues may be damaged either by the inward pressure exerted by the ice crystals, or by loss of water from their protoplasm to the intercellular spaces.

This loss causes plasmolysis and dehydration of the protoplasm, which may cause coagulation. The rapidity of the temperature drop in a tissue is also important, since this affects the amount of water remaining in a cell and, therefore, the freezing point of the cell contents. Thus, a rapid drop in temperature may result in intracellular ice formation where a slow drop to the same low temperature would not. The rate of thawing may have similarly variable effects, since rapid thawing may flood the area between cell wall and protoplast and may cause tearing and disruption of the protoplast if the latter is incapable of absorbing the water as fast as it becomes available from the melting of ice in the intercellular spaces.

Low relative humidity effects

Lack of moisture in the atmosphere, that is, low relative humidity, is usually temporary and seldom causes damage. When combined with high wind velocity and high temperature, however, it may lead to excessive loss of water from the foliage and may result in leaf scorching or burning, shrivelled fruit, and temporary or permanent wilting of plants. Conditions of low relative humidity are particularly common and injurious to house plants during the winter. In modern homes and apartments, heating provides comfortable temperatures for plant growth, but it often dries the air to relative humidities of 15 to 25 percent, which are equivalent to that of desert environments.

The air is particularly dry over or near the sources of dry heat, such as radiators. Potted plants kept under these conditions not only use up the water much faster, grow poorly, and may begin to wilt sooner, but the leaves, especially the lower ones, of many kinds of plants become spotted or scorched and fall prematurely, while their flowers suddenly wither and drop off. These effects are particularly noticeable when plants are brought into such a hot, dry house directly from a cool, moist greenhouse or florist's shop. Generally, all house plants prefer high humidity, and certain ones require high humidity if they are to grow properly and produce flowers.

Therefore, house plants should never be placed over radiators, and humidity should be increased with a commercial humidifier, by occasionally dampening the leaves with water by placing the pot on a brick or pebbles in a large pan of water, in a plastic case, or some other container.

High soil moisture effects

Excessive soil moisture occurs much less often than drought where plants are grown, but poor drainage or flooding of planted fields, gardens, or potted plants may result in more serious and quicker damage, or death, to plants than that from lack of moisture. Poor drainage results in plants that lack vigor, wilt frequently, and have leaves that are pale green or yellowish green. Flooding during the growth season may cause permanent wilting and death of succulent annuals within 2 to 3 -days.

Trees, too, are killed by waterlogging, but the damage usually appears more slowly and after their roots have been continually flooded for several weeks. As a result of excessive soil moisture caused by flooding or by poor drainage, the fibrous roots of plants decay, probably because of the reduced supply of oxygen to the roots.

Oxygen deprivation causes stress, asphyxiation, and collapse of many root cells. Wet, anaerobic conditions favor the growth of anaerobic microorganisms that, during their life processes, form substances ' such as nitrites, that are toxic to plants. Besides, the root cells damaged directly by the lack of oxygen lose their selective permeability and may allow toxic metals or other poisons to be taken up by the plant. Also, once parts of roots are killed, more damage is done by faculative parasites that may be greatly favored by the new environment.

Thus, the wilting of the plants, which soon follows flooding, is probably the result of lack of water in the aboveground parts of plants caused by the death of the roots, although it appears that translocated toxic substances may also be involved. In addition, many plants, particularly potted house plants, show several symptoms that are the result of incorrect watering: Either the soil is allowed to dry out too much before it is then repeatedly flooded with water or the plant is almost constantly overwatered. In either case, overwatered plants may suddenly drop their lower leaves, or their leaves may turn yellow. Sometimes they develop brown or black wet patches on the leaves or stems, or the roots and lower stem may turn black and rot as a result of infection by pathogenic microorganisms encouraged by the excessive watering. Such symptoms can be avoided or corrected by watering only when the topsoil feels dry and then applying enough water to saturate thoroughly the whole mass of soil.

Plants should never be watered when the soil is still wet, especially during the winter. When watering, any excess water should be drained through the drainage hole, which should always be present in the bottom of the pot. A period of dryness should not be followed with repeated heavy watering but by a gradual return to normal watering. Generally, the supply of water should be maintained as uniform as possible. Another common symptom of house plants, and sometimes of outdoor plants, that is caused by excessive moisture is the so-called edema (swelling). Edema appears as numerous small bumps on the lower side of leaves or on stems.

The "bumps" are small masses of cells that divide, expand, and break out of the normal leaf surface and at first form greenish-white swellings or galls. Later, the exposed surface of the swelling becomes rusty colored and has a corky texture. Edema is caused by overwatering, especially during cloudy, humid weather, and can be avoided by reduced watering and providing better lighting and air circulation to the plant.

Many other disorders are caused by excessive or irregular watering. It is known, for example, that tomatoes grown under rather low moisture conditions at the time they are ripening often crack if they are suddenly supplied with abundant moisture by overwatering or by a heavy rainfall. Also, bitter pit of apples, consisting of small, sunken, black spots on the fruit, is the result of irregular supply of moisture, although excessive nitrogen and low calcium fertilization seem also to be involved in bitter pit development.

Light

Lack of sufficient light retards chlorophyll formation and promotes slender growth with long internodes, thus leading to pale green leaves, spindly growth, and premature drop of leaves and flowers. This condition is known as etiolation. Etiolated plants are found outdoors only when plants are spaced too close together or when they are growing under trees or other objects. Etiolation of various degrees, however, is rather common in house plants, and also in greenhouses, seedbeds, and cold frames, where plants often receive inadequate light. Etiolated plants are usually thin and tall and are susceptible to lodging. Excess light is rather rare in nature and seldom injures plants.

Many injuries attributed to light are probably the result of high temperatures accompanying high light intensities. Excessive light, however, seems to cause sunscald of pods of beans grown at high altitudes where, due to the absence of dust, more light of short wavelengths reaches the earth. The pods develop small water-soaked spots, which quickly become brown or reddish brown and shrink.

The amount of light is considerably more important in relation to house plants. Some of them prefer shade or semishade during the growth season but full sunlight during the winter. Others prefer shade throughout the year, while still others must have sunlight all year long. As a rule, house plants with deep green leaves prefer or tolerate shade much better than do plants with colored leaves, the latter generally doing better when they receive considerable sunlight. Most flowering house plants grow and flower best with full exposure to sunlight at all seasons. Lack of sufficient light for any of these kinds of plants has the same effects as on the outdoor plants, that is, pale green leaves, spindly growth, leaf drop, few or no flowers, and flower drop. On the other hand, excessive sunlight on plants that prefer less light often results in the appearance of yellowish-brown or silvery spots on their leaves. Plants suddenly moved to an area with strikingly different light intensity than the previous one often respond with general defoliation.

Air pollution

The air at the earth's surface consists primarily of nitrogen and oxygen (78 and 21 percent, respectively). Much of the remaining i percent is water vapor and carbon dioxide. The activities of humans in generating energy, manufacturing goods, and disposing of wastes result in the release into the atmosphere of a number of pollutants that may alter plant metabolism and induce disease. Air pollution damage to plants, especially around certain types of factories, has been recognized for about a century. Its extent and importance, however, increased with the industrial revolution and will, apparently, continue to increase with the world's increasing population, industrialization, and urbanization.

Air pollutants and kinds of injury to plants

Almost all air pollutants causing plant injury are gases, but some particulate matter or dusts may also affect vegetation. Some gas contaminants, such as ethylene, ammonia, chlorine, and sometimes mercury vapors, exert their injurious effects over limited areas. Most frequently they affect plants or plant products stored in poorly ventilated warehouses in which the pollutants are produced by the plants themselves (ethylene), or from leaks in the cooling system (ammonia).

More serious and widespread damage is caused to plants in the field by chemicals such as ozone, sulfur dioxide, hydrogen fluoride, nitrogen dioxide, peroxyacyl nitrates, and particulates. In many localities, for example, the Los Angeles basin, air pollutants spread into the area surrounding the source(s) of pollution, become trapped, and cause serious plant damage. More frequently, most air pollutants are transported downwind from the urban or industrial centers in which they are produced and may be carried by the wind to areas that are several miles, often hundreds of miles and some times thousands of miles, from the source. High concentrations of or long exposure to these chemicals cause visible and sometimes characteristic symptoms (such as necrosis) on the affected plants.

More important economically, however, is the fact that even when plants are exposed to dosages less than those that cause acute damage, their growth and productivity may still be suppressed because of interference by the pollutants with the metabolism of the plant. Moreover, prolonged exposure to air pollutants seems to weaken plants and to predispose them to attack by insects and by some pathogens.

Sources of air pollutants

Some air pollutants, such as sulfur dioxide and hydrogen flouride, are produced as such directly from a source, such as refineries, combustion of fuel, and ore and fertilizer processing. Others, such as ozone and peroxyacyl nitrates, are produced in the atmosphere as secondary products of photochemical reactions involving NO_2, O_2, hydrocarbons, and sunlight. Automobile exhaust in the streets and highways and exhausts of other internal combustion engines in factories are probably the most important sources of ozone and other phytotoxic pollutants. Thousands of tons of incompletely burned hydrocarbons and NO_2 are released into the atmosphere daily by automobile exhausts. In the presence of ultraviolent light from the sun, this nitrogen dioxide reacts with air oxygen and forms ozone and nitric oxide. The ozone may react with nitric oxide to form the original compounds:

$$NO_2 + O_2 \xrightarrow{\text{sunlight}} O_3 + NO$$

In the presence of unburned hydrocarbon radicals, however, the nitric oxide reacts with these instead of ozone, and therefore the ozone concentration builds up.

$$O_3 + [NO + \text{Unburned hydrocarbons from automobiles, etc.}] \rightarrow O_3 + \text{Peroxyacyl nitrates}$$

Ozone, too, can react with vapors of certain unsaturated hydrocarbons, but the products of such reactions (various organic peroxides) are also toxic to plants. Normally, the noxious fumes produced by automobiles and other engines are swept up by the warm air currents from the earth's surface rising into the cooler air above, where the fumes are dissipated.

During periods of calm, stagnant weather, however, an inversion layer of warm air is formed above the cooler air, and this prevents the upward dispersion of atmospheric pollutants. The pollutants then are trapped near the ground, where after sufficient buildup, they may seriously damage living organisms. Peroxyacyl nitrate (PAN) injury has been observed primarily around metropolitan areas where large amounts of hydrocarbons are released into the air from automobiles.

The problem is especially serious in areas like Los Angeles and New Jersey, where the atmospheric conditions are conducive to the formation of inversion layers. Many different kinds of plants are affected by PAN over large geographical areas surrounding the locus of PAN formation, due to diffusion or to dispersal of the pollutant by light air currents.

How air pollutants affect plants

The concentration at which each pollutant causes injury to a plant varies with the plant and even with the age of the plant or the plant part. As the duration that the plant is exposed to the pollutant is increased, damage can be caused by increasingly smaller concentrations of the pollutant until a minimum dose—injury threshold is reached.

Plant injury by air pollutants generally increases with increased light intensity, increased soil moisture and air relative humidity, increased temperature, and with the presence of other air pollutants. Ozone injures the leaves of plants exposed for even a few hours at concentrations of 0.1 to 0.5 parts per million (ppm). Ozone is taken into leaves through stomata and injures primarily pallisade but also other cells by disrupting the cell membrane. Affected cells near stomata collapse and die, and white (bleached) necrotic flecks appear, first on the upper side and later on either leaf surface.

Many crop plants, such as alfalfa, bean, citrus, grape, potato, soybean, tobacco, and wheat, and many ornamentals and trees, such as ash, lilac, several pines, and poplar, are quite sensitive to ozone, while some other crops, such as cabbage, peas, peanuts, and pepper, are of intermediate sensitivity, and some, such as beets, cotton, lettuce, strawberry, and apricot, are tolerant. Sulfur dioxide may injure plants in concentrations as low as 1 to 5 ppm. Since sulfur dioxide is absorbed through the leaf stomata, conditions that favor or inhibit the opening of stomata similarly affect the amount of sulfur dioxide absorbed. After absorption by the leaf, sulfur dioxide reacts with water and forms phytotoxic sulfite ions.

The latter, however, are slowly oxidized in the cell to produce harmless sulfate ions. Thus, if the rate of sulfur dioxide absorption is slow enough, the plant may be able to protect itself from the buildup of phytotoxic sulfites. PAN is also taken into leaves through stomata and causes injury at concentrations as low as 0.01 to 0.02 ppm. In large urban areas, concentrations of 0.02 to 0.03 are not uncommon, and in the downtown areas of some cities PAN concentrations of 0.05 to 0.21 have been measured. Once inside leaves, PAN attacks preferentially the spongy parenchyma cells, which collapse and are replaced by air pockets that give the leaf a glazed or silvery appearance.

The symptoms on broad-leaved plants appear on the lower leaf surface, while monocot leaves show symptoms on both sides. Young leaves and tissues are more sensitive to PAN, and periodic exposures of leaves to PAN often cause "banding" and in some plants even margin "pinching" of leaves because of discoloration and death of the most sensitive affected cells, respectively.

Acid rain

Normal, unpolluted rain would contain almost pure water (H_2O) in which there would be dissolved some carbon dioxide (CO_2), some ammonia (NH_3) originating from organic matter and existing in water as NH_4^+, and varying but small amounts of cations (Ca^{++}, Mg^{++}, K^+, and Na^+) and anions (Cl^-, SO_4^-). Although the pH of pure water is a neutral 7.0, the pH of normal, "unpolluted" rain is usually 5.6; in other words, it is already acidic. Such rain, however, is considered "normal," and only when the pH of rain or snow is below 5.6 is it considered acidic ("acid rain").

Acid rain is the result of human activities, primarily the combustion of fossil fuels (oil, coal, natural gas) and the smelting of sulfide ores. These activities release in the atmosphere large quantities of sulfur and nitrogen oxides, which when in contact with atmospheric moisture are converted into two of the strongest acids known (sulfuric and nitric) and fall to the ground in rain and snow. The pH of rain and snow over large regions of the world ranges from 4.0 to 4.5, which is from 5 to 30 times more acid than the lowest pH (5.6) expected for unpolluted areas. The lowest rain pH's reported so far (2-4 in Scotland, 1.5 in West Virginia and 1.7 in Los Angeles) are more acidic than vinegar (pH 3.0) and of lemon juice (pH 2.2). It is estimated that about 70 percent of the acid in acid rain is sulfuric acid, with nitric acid contributing about 30 percent.

In addition to sulfur contained in the acids carried in the rain, it is believed that an approximately equal amount of sulfur reaches all surfaces through dry deposition of particulate sulfur. In humid or wet weather; this sulfur too is oxidized to sulfuric acid. Acid rain exerts a variety of influences by greatly increasing the solubility of all kinds of molecules and by directly (through the low pH and the toxicity of the —SO_4^- and —NO_3^- ions) or indirectly (through the dissolved molecules) affecting many forms of life. The adverse effects of acid rain on the microorganisms, plants, and fishes of rivers and lakes have been well documented. The effects of acid rain on crop plants have been more difficult to document.

Experiments in which acidic rain (pH 3-0) was applied to plants showed that, under some conditions, treated leaves developed pits, spots, and curling and that treated plants, with or without symptoms, sometimes showed reductions in dry weight. Also, more seeds of some plant species germinated when the soil in which they were planted received acid rain than when it did not, while the opposite was observed for other species. Experiments conducted to determine the effect of acid rain on the initiation and development of plant diseases have shown that in some diseases, such as Cronartium fusiforme rust of oak, only 14 percent as many telia formed under acidic (pH 3.0) rain treatment than under a pH 6.0 rain treatment and that beans treated with acidic rain (pH 3.2) had only 34 percent as many nematode egg masses than they did under a pH 6.0 rain treatment. On the other hand, a bacterial disease (halo blight) and the rust disease of bean were sometimes more severe and others milder with the acidic rain than with the pH 6.0 rain. In general, although some evidence exists that acid rain causes variable amounts of damage to at least some plants, consistent quantitative data are still insufficient to determine the extent of such damage on various crops in the areas where they occur.

Soil minerals toxic to plants

Soils often contain excessive amounts of certain essential or nonessential elements, both of which at high concentration may be injurious to the plants. Of the essential elements, those required by plants in large amounts, such as nitrogen and potassium, are usually much less toxic when present in excess than are the elements required only in trace amounts, such as manganese, zinc, and boron. Even among the latter, however, some trace elements such as manganese and magnesium have a much wider range of safety than do others, such as boron or zinc. Besides, not only do the elements differ in their ranges of toxicity, but various kinds of plants also differ in their susceptibility to the toxicity to a certain level of a particular element.

Concentrations at which nonessential elements are toxic also vary among elements, and plants in turn vary in their sensitivity to them. For example, some plants are injured by very small amounts of nickel but can tolerate considerable concentrations of aluminum. The injury occurring from the excess of an element may be slight or severe and is usually the result of direct injury by the element to the cell.

On the other hand, the element may interfere with the absorption or function of another element and thereby lead to the symptoms of a deficiency of the element being interfered with. Thus, excessive sodium induces a deficiency of calcium in the plant, while the toxicity of copper, manganese, or zinc is both direct on the plant and induces a deficiency of iron in the plant. Excessive amounts of sodium salts, especially sodium chloride, sodium sulfate, and sodium carbonate, raise the pH of the soil and cause what is known as alkali injury. This injury varies in the different plants and may range from chlorosis to stunting, leaf burn, wilting, to outright killing of seedlings and young plants.

Some plants, such as wheat and apple, are very sensitive to alkali injury, while others, such as sugar beets, alfalfa, and several grasses, are quite tolerant. On the other hand, when the soil is too acidic, the growth of some kinds of plants is impaired and various symptoms may appear. Plants usually grow well in a soil pH range from 4 to 8, but some plants grow better in the lower pH than others, and vice versa.

Thus, blueberries grow well in acid soils, while alfalfa grows best in alkaline soils. The injury caused by low pH is, in most cases, brought about by the greater solubility of mineral salts in acid solutions. These salts then become available in concentrations that, as was pointed out above, either are toxic to the plants or interfere with the absorption of other necessary elements and so cause symptoms of mineral deficiency. Boron, manganese, and copper have been most frequently implicated in mineral toxicity diseases, although other minerals, such as aluminum and iron, also damage plants in acid soils.

Excess boron is toxic to many vegetables and trees. Excess manganese is known to cause a crinkle-leaf disease in cotton and has been implicated in the internal bark-necrosis of Red Delicious apple and in many other diseases of several crop plants. Sodium and chlorine ions also have been shown to cause symptoms of poor growth and decline, like those shown by some of the trees along roads in northern areas where heavy salting is carried out in the winter to remove ice from roads.

Herbicide Injury

Some of the most frequent plant disorders seem to be the result of the extensive use of herbicides (weed killers), The constantly increasing number of herbicides in use by more and more people for general or specific weed control is creating numerous problems among those who use them, their neighbors, and those who use soil that has been treated with herbicides. Herbicides are either specific against broad-leaved weeds [atrazine, simazine, 2,4-D, dicamba, (Banvel-D)] and are applied in corn and other small grain fields and on lawns, or they are specific against grasses and some broad-leaved weeds [DCPA (Dacthal), trifluralin (Treflan)] and are applied in pastures, orchards, and in vegetable and truck crop fields. In addition, some herbicides are general weed or shrub killers [glyphosate (Roundup], paraquat, terbacil (Sinbar), picloram].

Most herbicides are safe as long as they are used to control weeds among the right crop plants, at the right time, at the correct dosage, and when the correct environmental conditions prevail. When any one of the above conditions is not met, abnormalities develop on the cultivated plants with which the herbicides come in contact. Affected plants show various degrees of distortion or yellowing of leaves, browning, drying and shedding of leaves, stunting and even death of the plant. Much of this damage is caused by too high doses of herbicides, or when applied too early in the season or on too cold or too hot a day, or when dust or spray droplets of an herbicide are carried by the wind to nearby sensitive plants or to gardens or fields on which plants sensitive to the herbicide are grown. Of course, direct application of the wrong pesticide in a field with a particular crop plant will kill the crop just as if it were a weed. Use of preplant or preemergence herbicides through application to the soil before or at planting time often affects seed germination and growth of the young seedlings if too much or the wrong herbicide has been applied.

Most herbicides are used up or are inactivated within a few days to a few months from the time of application; some, however, persist in the soil for more than a year. Sensitive plants planted in fields previously treated with such a persistent herbicide may grow poorly and may produce various symptoms. Also, home owners, home gardeners, and greenhouse operators often obtain what looks like good, weed-free soil from fields that, unbeknown to them, had been treated with herbicides. Such soil when used to grow potted, bench, or garden plants results in smaller, distorted, yellowish plants, which sometimes shed some or all of their leaves and either die or finally recover.

Other improper agricultural practices

As with herbicides, a variety of other agricultural practices improperly carried out may cause considerable damage to plants and significant financial losses. Almost every agricultural practice can cause damage when applied the wrong way, at the wrong time, or with the wrong materials. Most commonly, however, losses result from the application of chemicals, such as fungicides, insecticides, nematicides, and fertilizer, at too high concentrations or on plants sensitive to them.

Spray injury resulting in leaf bum or spotting or russeting of fruit is common on many crop plants. Excessive or too deep cultivation between rows of growing plants may be more harmful than useful because it cuts or pulls many of the plants' roots. Road or other construction often cuts a large portion of the roots of nearby trees and results in their dieback and decline. Inadequate or excessive watering may cause wilting or any of the symptoms described earlier. In the case of African violets, droplets of cold water on the leaves cause the appearance of rings and ringlike patterns reminiscent of virus ringspot diseases.

Potatoes stored next to hot water pipes under the kitchen sink often develop black heart. Trees frequently grow poorly and their leaves are chlorotic, curled, or reddened because their trunk is girdled by the fence wire. The roots of plants potted in pots that are too small for their size are often badly distorted and twisted and the whole plant grows poorly.

The often confused etiology of stress diseases

Diagnosis of an abiotic disease is often every bit as difficult as the diagnosis of a biotic disease. When combinations of single or multiple abiotic and biotic diseases occur on the same plant or in an entire area, however, the diagnosis of the diseases and the determination of the relative importance of each become extremely difficult and often impossible. When plants are adversely affected by an environmental factor, such as low moisture, nutrient deficiency, air pollution, or freezing, they are generally and concurrently weakened and predisposed to infection by one or more weakly parasitic pathogens. For example, all three conditions mentioned above predispose annual plants to infection by the fungus Alternaria and many perennial plants to infection by canker-causing fungi such as Cytospora and Botryosphaeria. A late blossom frost is often followed by infection with Botrytis, Alternaria, or Pseudomonas. Herbicide injury is likely to be followed by root rots caused by Fusarium and Rhizoctonia. Flooding injury is often followed by Pythium root infections.

Obviously, many of the stresses discussed in this chapter are often complicated by biotic diseases that follow. As a matter of fact, many epidemic disease problems, such as stalk rot of corn, tree declines, and stand depletions in forage legumes, although thought of as being caused by one or more biotic agents, they are in reality set off by one or another of the environmental factors discussed in this book.

Thus, stalk rot of corn, although caused by one of several common fungi (Fusarium, Diplodia, Gibberella), actually occurs or becomes important only under conditions of low potassium and low moisture stress in early season. Similarly, the additional stress caused by some herbicides on soybean, sugar beet, and cotton seedlings increases the susceptibility of these crops to the Thielaviopsis basicola and Rhizoctonia root rots and damping off.

A striking example of the often confused etiology of stress diseases has been developing in recent years in Europe, where many different forest tree species, shurbs, and herbs have been exhibiting various degrees of yellowing, reduced growth, defoliation, abnormal growth, decline, and eventually death. Such decline seems to be triggered by the stress caused by atmospheric depositions of toxic or growth-altering air pollutants but is subsequently aggravated by additional abiotic and biotic predisposing or stress-inducing factors. The air pollutants themselves, such as ozone, cause some direct injury and reduction in photosynthesis, but the mixture of deposited acidic pollutants may also cause acidification of soils. This may result in leaching out and therefore deficiency in certain elements such as magnesium, or in increases in solubility of certain toxic elements, such as aluminum, thereby causing aluminum toxicity in plants.

The latter then causes necrosis of fine roots, which

leads to increased moisture or nutrient stress and eventually drying out and death of trees, particularly during dry periods. Methods of control vary considerably from one disease to another, depending on the kind of pathogen, the host, and the interaction of the two. In controlling diseases, plants are generally treated as populations rather than as individuals, although certain hosts (especially trees, ornamentals, and sometimes, virus-infected plants) may be treated individually. With the exception of trees, however, the damage or loss of one or a few plants is usually considered insignificant, and control measures are generally aimed at saving the populations rather than a few individual plants.

Considering the regularity with which most serious diseases of crop plants appear in an area year after year, the rapid spread of most plant diseases, and the difficulty of curing a disease after it has begun to develop, it is easy to understand why almost all control methods are aimed at protecting plants from becoming diseased rather than at curing them after they have become diseased. As a matter of fact, few infectious plant diseases can be satisfactorily controlled in the field by therapeutic means, although certain diseases can be cured under experimental conditions. The various control methods can be classified as regulatory, cultural, biological, physical, and chemical, depending on the nature of the agents employed. Regulatory control measures aim at excluding a pathogen from a host or from a certain geographic area.

Most cultural control methods aim at helping plants avoid contact with a pathogen and at eradicating or reducing the amount of a pathogen in a plant, a field, or an area. Biological and some cultural control methods aim at improving the resistance of the host or at favoring microorganisms antagonistic to the pathogen. Finally, physical and chemical methods aim at protecting the plants from pathogen inoculum that is likely to arrive and at curing an infection that is already in progress. Epidemiological studies can help determine how effective various controls might be for a particular disease. In general, reducing or excluding the initial inoculum is most effective for the management of monocyclic pathogens.

Controls such as crop rotation, removal of alternate hosts, and soil fumigation reduce the initial inoculum. Because polycyclic pathogens increase many times the amount of initial inoculum during the growing season, reducing the initial inoculum must usually be accompanied by a control (such as chemical protection or horizontal resistance) that also reduces the infection rate. Many controls, for example totally excluding a pathogen from an area, are useful for both monocyclic and polycyclic pathogens.

Control methods that exclude the pathogen from the host

As long as plants and pathogens can be kept away from each other, no disease will develop. Many plants are grown in areas of the world where certain pathogens are still absent. They are, therefore, free of the diseases caused by such pathogens. To prevent the import and spread of plant pathogens into areas where they are absent, national and state laws regulate the conditions under which certain crops may be grown and distributed between states and countries.

Such regulatory control is applied by means of quarantines, inspections of plants in the field or warehouse, and occasionally by voluntary or compulsory eradication of certain host plants. Furthermore, plants are sometimes intentionally grown in areas from which a pathogen is largely or entirely excluded by unfavorable climatic conditions such as low rainfall and low relative humidity or by lack of vectors. This type of exclusion is called evasion.

Quarantines and inspections

When plant pathogens are introduced into an area in which they did not previously exist, they are likely to cause much more catastrophic epidemics than do the' existing pathogens. Plants that develop in the absence of a pathogen have no opportunity to select resistance factors specific against the pathogen and are, therefore, extremely vulnerable to attack. Some of the worst plant disease epidemics that have occurred throughout the world, for example the downy mildew of grapes in Europe and the bacterial canker of citrus, the chestnut blight, the Dutch elm disease, and the soybean cyst nematode in the United States, are all diseases caused by pathogens that were introduced from abroad.

It has been estimated, for example, that if soybean rust were introduced into the United States, it would result in total losses to consumers and other sectors of the U.S. economy of more than seven billion dollars per year. In order to keep out foreign plant pathogens and to protect the nation's farms, gardens, and forests, the Plant Quarantine Act of 1912 was passed by Congress. This act prohibits or restricts entry into or passage through the United States from foreign countries of plants, plant products, soil, and other materials carrying or likely to carry plant pathogens not known to be widely established in this country. Similar quarantine regulations exist in most other countries. Experienced inspectors stationed at all points of entry into the country enforce quarantines of produce likely to introduce new pathogens.

Plant quarantines are already credited for the interception of numerous foreign plant pathogens and, thereby, with saving the country's plant world from potentially catastrophic diseases. Plant quarantines are considerably less than foolproof, however, because pathogens may be introduced in the form of spores or eggs on unsuspected carriers, and latent infections of seeds and other plant propagative organs may exist even after treatment. Various steps taken by plant quarantine stations, such as growing plants under observation for certain periods of time before they are released to the importer and repeated inspection of imported nursery stock in the grower's premises, tend to reduce the chances of introduction of harmful pathogens. With the annual imports of flower bulbs from Holland, U.S. quarantine inspectors may visit the flower fields in Holland and inspect them for diseases.

If they find the fields to be disease free, they issue inspection certificates allowing the import of such bulbs into the United States without further tests. Similar quarantine regulations govern the interstate, and even the intrastate, sale of nursery stock, tubers, bulbs, seeds, and other propagative organs, especially of certain crops, such as potatoes and fruit trees. The movement and sale of such materials within and between states is controlled by the regulatory agencies of each state.

Several voluntary inspection systems are also in effect in various states in which appreciable amounts of nursery stock and potato seed tubers are produced. Growers interested in producing and selling disease-free plants submit to a voluntary inspection or indexing of their crop in the field and in storage by the state regulatory agency, by experiment station personnel, or others. If, after certain procedures recommended by the inspecting agency are carried out, the plant material is found to be free of certain, usually virus, diseases, the inspecting agency issues a certificate indicating that the plants are free from these specific diseases, and the grower may then advertise the produce as disease free.

Evasion of pathogen

In several plant diseases, control depends largely on

attempts to evade pathogens. For example, bean anthracnose, caused by the fungus *Colletotrichum lindemuthianum*, and the bacterial blights of bean, caused by the bacteria *Xanthomonas phaseoli* and *Pseudomonas phaseolicola*, are transmitted through the seed. In most areas where beans are grown, at least a portion of the plants and the seeds become infected with these pathogens.

In the dry, irrigated regions of the western United States, however, the conditions of low humidity are unsuitable for these pathogens, and therefore the plants and the seeds are free of them. Using western-grown seeds free of these pathogens is the main recommendation for control of these diseases. Similarly, in order to produce potato seed tubers free of viruses, potatoes are grown in remote locations in the cooler, northern states (Maine, Wisconsin, and Idaho) and at higher elevations, where aphids, the vectors of these viruses, are absent or their populations are small and can be controlled. In many cases, a susceptible crop is planted at a great enough distance from other fields containing possibly diseased plants that the pathogen would not likely infect the crop. This type of crop isolation is practiced mostly with perennial plants, such as peach orchards isolated from x-disease mycoplasma-infected chokecherry shrubs or trees.

During much of this century, banana production in Central America depended on evading the fungus *Fusarium oxysporum* f. *cubense*, the cause of Fusarium wilt (Panama disease) of banana, by moving on to new, previously uncultivated fields as soon as older banana fields became infested with *Fusarium* and yields became unprofitable. Growers carry out numerous activities aimed at helping the host evade the pathogen. Such activities include using vigorous seed, selecting proper (early or late) planting dates and proper sites, maintaining proper distances between fields and between rows and plants, and using proper insect and weed control. All these practices increase the chances that the host will remain free of the pathogen or go through its susceptible stage before the pathogen reaches the host.

Use of pathogen-free propagating material

When a pathogen is excluded from the propagating material (seed, tubers, bulbs, nursery stock) of a host, it is often possible to grow the host free of that pathogen for the rest of its life. Examples are woody plants affected by nonvectored viruses. In most crops, if the host can be grown free of the pathogen for a considerable period of its early life, during which the plant can attain normal growth, it can then produce a fairly good yield in spite of a potential later infection. Examples are crops affected by vectored viruses and mycoplasmas, fungal, bacterial, and nematode pathogens.

There is absolutely no question that every host plant and every crop grows better and produces a greater yield if the starting propagating material is free of pathogens, or at least free of the most important pathogens. For this reason, every effort should be made to obtain and use pathogen-free seed or nursery stock, even if the cost is considerably greater than for propagating material of unknown pathogen content. All types of pathogens can be carried in or on propagating material. True seed, however, is invaded by relatively few pathogens, although several may contaminate its surface.

Seed may carry internally one of a few fungi (such as those causing anthracnoses and smuts), certain bacteria (bacterial wilts, spots, and blights), and one of several viruses (tobacco ringspot in soybean, bean common mosaic, lettuce mosaic, barley stripe mosaic, squash mosaic, and prunus necrotic ringspot). On the other hand, vegetatively propagating material such as buds, grafts, rootstocks, tubers, bulbs, corms, cuttings, and rhizomes are expected to carry internally almost every virus, viroid, mycoplasma, protozoan, and vascular fungus or bacterium present systemically in the mother plant, in addition to any fungi, bacteria, and nematodes that may be carried on these organs externally. Some nematodes may also be carried internally in some below-ground propagating organs (tubers, bulbs, corms, and rhizomes) and in or on the roots of nursery stock.

Pathogen-free seed

Seed that is free of fungal, bacterial, and some viral pathogens is usually obtained by growing the crop and producing the seed in (i) an area free of or isolated from the pathogen, (2) an area not suitable for the pathogen (such as the and western regions where bean seed is produced free of anthracnose and bacterial blights), or (3) an area not suitable for the vector of the pathogen (such as the northern or high altitude fields where aphids, the vectors of many viruses, are absent or rare). It is very important, and with seed-transmitted and aphid-borne viruses it is indispensable, that seed be essentially free of the pathogen, especially virus.

Because the pathogen will be present in the field at the beginning of the growth season, even a small proportion of infected seeds is sufficient to provide enough inoculum to spread and infect many plants early, thus causing severe losses. It has been shown, for example, that to control lettuce mosaic virus, only seed lots that contain less than i infected seed per 30,000 lettuce seeds must be used. For this purpose seed companies have their lettuce seed tested for lettuce mosaic virus every year. In past years, seeds were tested (indexed) by growing out hundreds of thousands of lettuce seedlings in insect-proof greenhouses, observing them over several weeks for lettuce mosaic symptoms, and attempting to transmit the virus from suspect plants to healthy plants.

Later, indexing was done by inoculating a local lesion indicator plant (in, this case *Chenopodium quinoa*) with sap from ground samples of groups of seeds and observing it for virus symptoms. At present, testing for lettuce mosaic virus in seed is done with serological techniques, particularly via ELISA, which is faster, more sensitive, and less expensive than the other methods.

Testing seed for fungal and bacterial pathogens if done by symptomatology, microscopically, and by culturing the pathogen on general or selective nutrient media. To detect and identify bacteria, serological tests are now being used with increasing frequency and accuracy. If seed free of fungal and bacterial pathogens cannot be obtained by other means, hot water (50°C) treatment of the seed can free it from the pathogen.

Examples are cabbage seed freed from *Xanthomonas campestris*, the cause of black rot of cabbage, and from *Phoma lingam*, the cause of black leg of cabbage, and seed of wheat and other cereals freed from *Ustilago* sp., the cause of loose smuts of cereals. With some crops, such as carnation and chrysanthemum, greenhouse growers need cuttings free of the vascular wilt-causing fungi Fusarium and Verticillium each time, but it is almost impossible to keep these two fungi from the production beds. It was noted early, however, that short cuttings taken from the tips of rapidly growing shoots were usually free of either of these fungi, and this became a common practice to control these diseases.

Sometimes, it is impossible to find even a single plant of a variety that is free of a particular pathogen, especially viruses. In that case, one or a few healthy plants are initially obtained by tissue culture of the upper millimeter or so of the growing meristematic tip of the plant, which most viruses do not invade. In some cases, healthy plants can be obtained from virus-infected plants by eliminating the virus through heat treatment. Dormant plant material, such as budwood, dormant trees, and tubers, is usually treated with hot water at temperatures ranging from 35 to 54°C, with treatment times lasting from a few minutes to several hours. Actively growing plants are sometimes treated with hot air, which allows better survival of the plant and better elimination of the pathogen than does hot water.

Temperatures of 35 to 40°C seem to be optimal for air treatment of growing plants. For hot-air treatment, the infected plants are usually grown in growth chambers for varying periods, generally lasting 2-4 weeks. Some viruses, however, require treatment for 2 - 8 months, while others may be eliminated in just one week. All mycoplasmas, all fastidious bacteria, and many viruses can be eliminated from their hosts by heat treatment, but for some viruses such treatment has not always been dependable.

In recent years, with some crops such as strawberries and orchids, once one or a few pathogen-free plants have been obtained by any of the above methods, they are subsequently used as foundation material from which thousands, hundreds of thousands, and even millions of pathogen-free plants are produced through tissue culture techniques in the laboratory. These plants are later set out in the greenhouse or the field before they are sold to growers or retailers as pathogen-free plants at a premium price.

Reduce the pathogen inoculum

Many different types of control methods aim at eradicating or reducing the amount of pathogen present in an area, a plant, or plant parts (such as seeds). Many such methods are cultural, that is, they depend primarily on certain actions of the grower, such as host eradication, crop rotation, sanitation, improving plant growing conditions, creating conditions unfavorable to pathogens, polyethylene mulching, trickle irrigation, ecofallow, and reduced tillage farming. Some methods are physical, that is, they depend on a physical factor, such as heat, or cold. Examples are soil sterilization, heat treatment of plant organs, refrigeration, and radiations. Several methods are chemical, that is, they depend on the use and action of a chemical substance to reduce the pathogen. Examples are soil treatment, soil fumigation, and seed treatment. Some methods are biological, that is, they use living organisms to reduce the pathogen inoculum. Examples are use of trap crops and antagonistic plants against nematodes and use of amendments that favor microflora antagonistic to the pathogen.

Cultural methods

When a pathogen has been introduced into a new area in spite of quarantine, a plant disease epidemic frequently follows. To prevent such an epidemic, all the host plants infected by or suspected of harboring the pathogen may have to be removed and burned. This eliminates the pathogen and prevents greater losses from the spread of the pathogen to additional plants.

In the last quarter century, a campaign to contain and eradicate witchweed (*Striga asiatica*) in the eastern Carolinas in the United States has been successful. On the other hand, attempts by several European countries to eradicate fire blight of apple and pear (caused by the bacterium *Erwinia amylovora*) and plum pox virus of stone fruits and attempts by several South American countries to eradicate coffee rust (caused by the fungus *Hemileia vastatrix*) have not been successful, and the pathogens continue to spread.

Host eradication (roguing) is also carried out routinely in many nurseries, greenhouses, and fields to prevent the spread of numerous diseases by eliminating infected plants that provide a ready source of inoculum within the crop. Certain pathogens of annual crops, for example cucumber mosaic virus, overwinter only or mainly in other perennials, usually wild plants, Eradication of the host in which the pathogen overwinters- is sometimes enough to eliminate completely or to reduce drastically the amount of inoculum that can cause infections the following season. In some crops, such as potatoes, pathogens of all types may overwinter in infected tubers that are left in the field.

Many such tubers produce plants in the spring that allow the pathogen to come above ground from where it can be spread further by insects, rain, and wind, Eradication of such volunteer plants helps greatly to reduce the inoculum of these pathogens. Some pathogens require two alternate hosts to complete their life cycles. For example, *Puccinia graminis tritici* requires wheat and barberry, *Cronartium ribicola* requires pine and currant (*Ribes*), and *Gymnosporangium juniperi-virginianae* requires cedar and apple.

In these cases, eradication of the wild or economically less important alternate host interrupts the life cycle of the pathogen and leads to control of the disease. This has been carried out somewhat successfully with stem rust of wheat and white pine blister rust through eradication of barberry and currant, respectively, although, owing to other factors, both diseases are still widespread and catastrophic. In cases like the cedar-apple rust, however, in which both hosts may be important, control through eradication of the alternate host is impractical.

Crop rotation

Soil-borne pathogens which attack plants of one or a few species or even families of plants, can sometimes be eliminated from the soil by planting, for 3 or 4 years, crops belonging to species or families not attacked by the particular pathogen. Complete control through crop rotation is possible with pathogens that are soil invaders, that is, survive only on living plants or only as long as the host residue persists as a substrate for their saprophytic existence. When the pathogen is a soil inhabitor, however, that is, it produces long-lived spores or can live as saprophytes, for more than 5 or 6 years - crop rotation becomes -ineffective or impractical. In the latter cases, crop rotation can still reduce although not eliminate the pathogen (for example, *Verticillium*) populations in the soil. In such cases appreciable yields from the susceptible crop can be obtained every third or fourth year of the rotation. In some cropping systems the field is tilled and left fallow for a year or part of the year.

During fallow, debris and inoculum are destroyed by microorganisms with little or no replacement. In areas with hot summers, fallow allows greater heating and drying of the soil and marked reduction of nematodes and some other pathogens. Other cropping systems utilize herbicides and reduced tillage or reduced tillage and fallow (ecofallow). In some such systems, certain diseases (for example, stalk rot of grain sorghum, caused by *Fusarium moniliforme*) have been dramatically reduced, but other diseases (for example, Septoria leaf blotch of wheat) have been increased.

Sanitation

Sanitation consists of all activities aimed at eliminating or reducing the amount of inoculum present in a plant, a field, or a warehouse and- at preventing the spread of the pathogen to other healthy plants and plant products. Thus, plowing under or removing and properly disposing of infected leaves, pruning infected or dead branches, and removing or destroying any other plant debris that may harbor the pathogen reduce the amount of disease that will develop later. In the Pacific Northwest and in parts of California, infected crop debris of grass seed and rice crops was destroyed by burning, Which reduced or eliminated the surface inoculum of several pathogens. By washing their hands before handling certain kinds of plants, such as tomato, workers who smoke may reduce the spread of tobacco mosaic virus. Washing the soil off farm equipment before moving it from one field to another may also help to prevent the spread of any pathogens present in the soil. Similarly, by washing the produce, its containers, and the walls of storage houses, the amount of inoculum and subsequent infections may be reduced considerably.

Creating conditions unfavorable to the pathogen

Stored products should be properly aerated to hasten the drying of their surfaces and inhibit germination and infection by any fungal or bacterial pathogens present on them. Similarly, spacing plants properly in the field or greenhouse prevents the creation of high humidity conditions on plant surfaces and inhibits infection by certain pathogens, such as *Botrytis*. Good soil drainage also reduces the number and activity of certain fungal pathogens (for example, Pythium) and nematodes and may result in significant disease control. Appropriate choice of fertilizers or soil amendments may also lead to changes in the soil pH, which may unfavorably influence the development of the pathogen.

Flooding fields for long periods of time or dry fallowing may also reduce the number of certain pathogens in the soil (for example, Fusarium and nematodes) by starvation, lack of oxygen, or desiccation. In the production of many crops, particularly containerized nursery stock, using composted tree bark in the planting medium has resulted in the successful control of diseases caused by several soil-borne pathogens, for example, *Phytophthora, Pythium* and *Thielaviopsis* root rots, and Rhizoctonia damping-off and crown rot, *Fasarium* wilt, and some nematode diseases of several crops, especially of Easter lily, poinsettia, and rhododendron. The suppressive effect is apparently a result of the release from the bark of substances with fungicidal activity.

Polyethylene traps and mulches

Many plant viruses, such as cucumber mosaic, are brought into crops, such as peppers, by airborne aphid vectors. When vertical, sticky, yellow polyethylene sheets are erected along the edges of susceptible crops, a considerable number of aphids are attracted to and stick to the plastic, thereby reducing the amount of virus inoculum reaching the crop.

On the other hand, if reflectant aluminum or whitish-gray polyethylene sheets are used as mulches between the plants or rows in the field, incoming aphid vectors are repelled and misled away from the field. Reflectant mulches, however, cease to function as soon as the crop canopy covers them. When clear polyethylene is placed over moist soil, during sunny summer days the temperature at the top 5 cm of soil may reach as high as 52°C compared to a maximum of 37°C in unmulched soil. If sunny weather continues for several days or weeks, the increased soil temperature from solar heat, known as solarization, inactivates many soil-borne pathogens, for example, Verticillium, and thereby reduces the inoculum and the potential for disease.

Biological methods

Biological control of pathogens, that is, the total or partial destruction of pathogen populations by other organisms, occurs routinely in nature. There are, for example, several diseases in which the pathogen cannot develop in certain areas either because the soil, called suppressive soils contains microorganisms antagonistic to the pathogen, or because the plant that is attacked by a pathogen has also been naturally inoculated, before or after the pathogen attack, with antagonistic microorganisms. Sometimes, the antagonistic microorganisms may consist of avirulent strains of the same pathogen that destroy or inhibit the development of the pathogen, as happens in hypovirulence and cross protection. In some cases, even higher plants reduce the amount of inoculum either by trapping available pathogens (trap plants) or by releasing into the soil substances toxic to the pathogen.

In recent years, humans have been trying to take advantage of such natural biological antagonisms and have been developing strategies by which biological control can now be used effectively against several plant diseases. Biological antagonisms, although subject to numerous ecological limitations, can be expected to become an important part of the control measures employed against many more diseases.

Examples of antagonistic microorganisms reducing the amount of pathogen inoculum

The mycelium and resting spores (oospores, sclerotia) of several phytopathogenic soil fungi such as *Pythium, Phytophthora, Rhizoctonia, Sclerotinia,* and *Sclerotium,* are invaded and parasitized (mycoparasitism) or are lysed (mycolysis) by several fungi, which as a rule are not pathogenic to plants. Several fungi, including some oomycetes, chytridiomycetes, and hyphomycetes and some pseudomonad and actinomycetous bacteria, infect the resting spores of several fungi. Among the most common mycoparasitic fungi are *Trichoderma* sp., mainly *T. harzianum,* which has been shown to parasitize mycelium of *Rhizoctonia* and *Sclerolium,* to inhibit the growth of many others, for example, *Pythium, Fusarium,* and *Fomes,* and to reduce the diseases caused by most of these pathogens. Other common mycoparasitic fungi are *Laetisaria arvalis* (*Corticium* sp.), a mycoparasite and antagonist of *Rhizoctonia* and *Pythium;* also, *Sporidesmium sclerotivorum, Gliocladium virens,* and *Coniothyrium minitants,* all destructive parasites and antagonists of *Sclerotinia sclerotiorum* and all effectively controlling several of the *Sclerotinia* diseases. Many other fungi have been shown to antagonize and inhibit numerous fungal pathogens of aerial plant parts.

For example, *Chaetomium* sp. suppressed *Venturia inaequalis* ascospore and conidia production in fallen and growing leaves, respectively. *Tuberculina maxima* parasitizes the white pine blister rust fungus *Cronartium ribicola; Darluca filum* and *Verticillium lecanii* parasitize several rusts; Ampelomyces quisqualis parasitizes several powdery mildews; Tilletiopsis sp. parasitizes the cucumber powdery mildew fungus Spaerotheca fuligena; and *Nectria* inventa and Gonatobotrys simplex parasitize two pathogenic species of Alternaria.

In addition to fungi, bacteria of the genus Streptomyces and Pseudomonas have been shown to parasitize and/or inhibit the pathogenic fungi Pythium sp. and Gaeumannomyces tritici, the mycophagous nematode Aphelenchus avenae parasitizes Rhizoctonia and Fusarium, and the amoeba Vampyrella parasitizes the pathogenic fungi Cochliobolus sativus and Gaeumannomyces graminis.

Plant pathogenic nematodes are also parasitized by other microorganisms. For example, the cyst nematodes Heterodera and Globodera are parasitized by the nematophagous fungi Catenaria auxiliaris, Nematophthora gynophila, and Verticillium chlamydosporium, while the root knot nematode Meloidogyne sp. is parasitized by the fungus Dactylella oviparasitica. Meloidogyne javanica is also parasitized by the bacterium Bacillus (Pasteuria) penetrans.

The mechanisms by which antagonistic microorganisms affect pathogen populations are not always clear, but they are generally attributed to one of four effects: (i) direct parasitism and death of the pathogen, (2) competition with the pathogen for food, (3) direct toxic effects on the pathogen by antibiotic substances released by the antagonist, and (4) indirect toxic effects on the pathogen by volatile substances, such as ethylene, released by the metabolic activities of the antagonist.

Many of the above antagonistic microorganisms are naturally present in crop soils and exert a certain degree of biological control over one or many plant pathogens, regardless of human activities. Humans, however, have been attempting to increase the effectiveness of antagonists either by introducing new and larger populations of antagonists, for example, Trichoderma harzianum and Bacillus penetrans, in fields where they are lacking, and/ or by adding soil amendments that serve as nutrients for, or otherwise stimulate growth of, the antgonistic microorganisms and increase their inhibitory activity against the pathogen. Unfortunately, while both approaches are effective in the laboratory and in the greenhouse, neither has been successful in the field.

New microorganisms added to the soil of a field cannot compete with the existing microflora and cannot maintain themselves for very long. Also, soil amendments, so far, have not been selective enough to support and build up only the populations of the introduced or existing antagonists; so the eventual diseases control is quite limited. There are several cases of successful biological control of plant pathogens when the antagonistic microorganism is used for direct protection of the plant from infection by the pathogen.